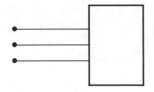

HUMAN RIGHTS

LAW AND POLITICAL CHANGE

Series Editors: Cosmo Graham and Professor Norman Lewis, Centre for Socio-legal Studies, University of Sheffield

Titles in the series:

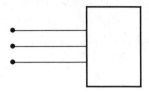

HUMAN RIGHTS

Scott Davidson

OPEN UNIVERSITY PRESS
Buckingham • Philadelphia

Open University Press
Celtic Court
22 Ballmoor
Buckingham
MK18 1XW

and
1900 Frost Road, Suite 101
Bristol, PA 19007, USA

First Published 1993

A catalogue record of this book is available from the British Library

ISBN 0 335 15768 8 (pb)   0 335 15769 6 (hb)

Library of Congress Cataloging-in-Publication Data
Davidson, Scott, 1954–
    Human rights / Scott Davidson.
      p.   cm. — (Law and political change)
    Includes bibliographical references and index.
    ISBN 0–335–15769–6 (hb). — ISBN 0–335–15768–8 (pbk.)
    1. Human rights. I. Title. II. Series.
K3240.4.D39   1993
342′.085 – dc20
[342.285]   92–40622
                                                       CIP

Typeset by Colset Private Limited, Singapore
Printed in Great Britain by Biddles Ltd, Guildford and King's Lynn

To my son Paul

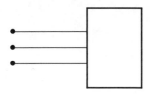

CONTENTS

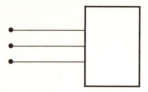

PREFACE

When I was approached by Norman Lewis to write a book on human rights for this series, I was immediately confronted by two major problems. First, which method of exposition should I use to guide readers through the labyrinth of theories, instruments and institutions with which the area is replete? Second, whichever method of exposition I used, how could I fit it all within the bounds of the 70 000 word limit imposed by the publisher? While the second problem remained a regrettable but irresistible constant, the first compelled me to address some fundamental questions about the notion of human rights and how best to communicate these to a readership which did not necessarily include people with any knowledge of law.

As I considered this latter problem, it became apparent to me that there were certain aspects of the subject which were indispensable for an understanding of the international law of human rights which could be dealt with in a relatively discrete way. These were the historical, political and philosophical components of human rights. It is impossible to give meaning to the institutional aspects of human rights without appreciating the various forces that shaped them. History and politics provide the contextual dimension of human rights, philosophy gives them meaning, and law deals with the mechanics of their application. Since human rights law is also a specialized branch of public international law, it was apparent that some explanation of the major facets of this system was necessary in order to provide non-lawyers with an adequate frame of reference.

Having identified those issues which appeared to me to be the indispensable prerequisites to an understanding of the subject, it then became necessary to consider the method by which the present institutional framework of international human rights law should be explained. Two broad possible solutions presented themselves. First, the various instruments, institutions and supervision and enforcement mechanisms could be considered as an integrated whole with points of convergence and divergence highlighted as they arose. Second, the various systems could be dealt with as separate and discrete entities having their own forms and peculiarities but with points of similarity to, and dissimilarity from, other cognate systems. While the first approach possessed a certain intellectual consistency, it seemed that the second approach would be more 'user-friendly' to readers approaching the subject for the first time. Having assimilated the distinctive features of one system, readers will be able to make appropriate comparisons with, perhaps, a little help from the final chapter of the book which seeks to raise some issues of general concern in the human rights field.

Some further explanation should also be offered about the layout and content of the book. As this is primarily an introductory text, footnotes have been kept to a minimum and, where possible, they refer only to primary sources and materials. At the end of each chapter, however, I have included a list of further reading which, I hope, will allow readers to develop their interests in the appropriate areas. While I cannot pretend that the lists of further reading are exhaustive, they nevertheless include material which I have found to be of particular use in writing this book. As regards the content of this work, it may be a matter of criticism that I have not included a chapter on humanitarian law. There are, however, two good reasons for this. First, it is by no means universally agreed that humanitarian law – or the law concerning the treatment of individuals in time of armed conflict – is part of the *corpus* of international human rights law or a separate subject in its own right. Second, to have included a chapter on this subject would have been impossible given the constraints of space. While the latter is not a good intellectual defence, it is, nevertheless, compelling. A rather more telling point of criticism about the content of this book might be that it focuses too heavily on institutions and mechanisms of human rights protection rather than on the substantive law of human rights. The emphasis on institutions and mechanisms is, however, a conscious policy on my part, for I believe that it is these aspects of the law which reveal more about its place and role in international society. In a sense, this is a book about how the law works in the international system rather than a book about the specifics of substantive rights.

I have received considerable assistance from a number of people in producing this work and I must record my thanks to them here. In particular, I should like to thank Margaret Greville, Law Librarian at the University of Canterbury, and the members of her staff for assistance above and beyond the call of duty. I must also thank my colleague David Rowe whose expert knowledge of word-processing and immense patience made preparation of the typescript less traumatic than it would otherwise have been. And, finally, to my wife Olivia and son Paul I owe a very special debt of gratitude, for without their happy and unstinting support this book would have been considerably more difficult to write.

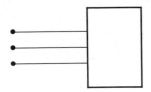

ABBREVIATIONS

AC	Appeal Cases
ACHPR	African Convention on Human and Peoples' Rights
ACHR	American Convention on Human Rights
AJIL	American Journal of International Law
All ER	All England Law Reports
BYIL	British Yearbook of International Law
CHR	United Nations Commission on Human Rights
ECOSOC	United Nations Economic and Social Council
EHRR	European Human Rights Reports
ETS	European Treaty Series
Eur. Ct. H.R.	Reports of the European Court of Human Rights
HRC	United Nations Human Rights Committee
HRLJ	Human Rights Law Journal
HRQ	Human Rights Quarterly
ICCPR	International Covenant on Civil and Political Rights
ICESCR	International Covenant on Economic, Social and Cultural Rights
ICJ Rep.	Reports of the International Court of Justice
ICLQ	International and Comparative Law Quarterly
ILM	International Legal Materials
ILO	International Labour Organization
ILR	International Law Reports

LNTS   League of Nations Treaty Series
LQR   Law Quarterly Review
Meron   *Human Rights in International Law* (1985)
NGO   Non-Governmental Organization
OAS   Organization of American States
PL   Public Law
UKTS   United Kingdom Treaty Series
UN   United Nations Organization
UNTS   United Nations Treaty Series
Vasak   *The International Dimensions of Human Rights* (1982)
WLR   Weekly Law Reports
YB   Yearbook of the European Convention on Human Rights

HISTORICAL DEVELOPMENT OF HUMAN RIGHTS

INTRODUCTION

International concern with human rights is a phenomenon of comparatively recent origin. Although it is possible to point to a number of treaties or international agreements affecting humanitarian issues before the Second World War, it is only with the entry into force of the United Nations Charter in 1945,[1] that it is possible to speak of the advent of systematic human rights protection within the international system. None the less, it is clear that the international protection of human rights has its antecedents in domestic efforts to secure legal protection for individuals against the arbitrary excesses of state power. Such domestic attempts have a long and dignified history, and are intimately connected with revolutionary activity directed towards the establishment of constitutional systems based on democratic legitimacy and the rule of law. Even today, the protection of human rights at both the national and international level are intimately connected, if not symbiotic. All international instruments require states' domestic constitutional systems to provide adequate redress for those whose rights have been violated. It is only when those states' own internal protective systems falter or where, in extreme cases, they are non-existent, that international mechanisms for securing human rights come into play. In a sense, therefore, international mechanisms operate to reinforce domestic protection of human rights and to provide redress when the domestic system fails or is found wanting.

DOMESTIC ORIGINS OF HUMAN RIGHTS

Although some scholars claim to be able to trace a rudimentary concept of human rights back to the Stoic philosophy of classical times *via* the natural law jurisprudence of Grotius and the *ius naturale* of Roman law,[2] it seems evident that the origins of the modern concept are to be found in the English, American and French revolutions of the seventeenth and eighteenth centuries.

The English experience

While Magna Carta (1215)[3] is often erroneously seen as the origins of the liberties of English citizens (it was, in reality, simply a compromise on the distribution of powers between King John and his nobles, the language of which only later assumed the wider significance which is attributed to it today), it was not until the Bill of Rights (1689)[4] that rules directed towards the protection of individual rights or liberties emerged. But even this development must be seen in context. The Bill of Rights, which is described in its long title as 'An Act Declaring the Rights and Liberties of the Subject and Setting the Succession of the Crown', was the outcome of the seventeenth-century struggle of Parliament against the arbitrary rule of the Stuart monarchs. Passed after the enforced abdication of James II and the accession to the throne of William III and Mary II following the 'Glorious Revolution' of 1688, the Bill, which expressed itself to be declaratory of existing law and not creative of new law, subjected the monarchy to the power of Parliament by declaring illegal the claimed suspending and dispensing powers of the Crown. It also forbade the levying of taxes or the maintenance of a standing army in peacetime by the Crown without Parliamentary consent.

In Marxist analysis, the Glorious Revolution of 1688 and the Bill of Rights which institutionalized it, was a bourgeois revolution: it simply confirmed the ascendancy of the gentry and merchant class over the monarchy.[5] For the most part, therefore, the Bill represented a constitutional settlement which protected the sectional interests of one group. Whig historians, however, saw the Bill as the triumph of liberty over despotism and the protection of Englishmen (women had little say in the matter) from absolutist and arbitrary government.[6] There is merit in both these views, for the Bill of Rights not only secured the interests of the bourgeoisie, but it also dealt with certain matters having the characteristics of 'human rights', although they were not referred to as such at the time. In particular, the Bill provided that 'excessive bail ought not to be required, nor excessive fines imposed, nor cruel and unusual punishment inflicted'. It further provided that 'jurors ought to be duly impanelled and returned' and that 'all grants and promises of fines and forfeitures of particular persons before conviction are illegal and void'. While the 'human rights' element of the Bill of Rights might appear to be slight and biased in favour of a particular class of citizens, nevertheless the whole context of the instrument was of fundamental importance, since it sought to replace the vagaries and excesses of arbitrary monarchical absolutism with parliamentary constitutional legitimacy. The Glorious Revolution was also significant because it provided a precedent – that rulers could be removed by popular will if they failed to observe the requirements of constitutional legitimacy. In the view of the eighteenth-century English political philosopher John Locke, who sought to discover a theoretical basis for the constitutional revolutions of the seventeenth and eighteenth centuries, bad government violated the social contract which rulers enjoyed with the governed and empowered the latter to rid themselves of the former.

The American experience

The experience of the English Revolution and the various philosophical and theoretical attempts to justify it were not lost on the leaders of Britain's rebellious North American colonies in the latter part of the eighteenth century. Seeking to disengage the colonies from British rule following dis-satisfaction over the levels of taxation and lack of representation in the British Parliament, the American Founding Fathers sought justification in the social contract and natural rights theories of Locke and the French *philosophes*. In the American Declaration of Independence (1776), drafted by Thomas Jefferson, these ideas find particularly clear and felicitous expression:[7]

> We hold these truths to be self-evident, that all men are created equal, that they are endowed by their creator with certain unalienable rights, that among these are Life, Liberty and the pursuit of Happiness – That to secure these rights, Governments are instituted among Men, deriving their just powers from the consent of the governed. That whenever any Form of government becomes destructive of these ends, it is the right of the People to alter or abolish it.

While the high sounding ideals of the protection of life, liberty and the pursuit of happiness were sufficient for a declaration of independence, they were clearly inadequate as a catalogue of individual rights which the state was obliged to protect. The Virginia Declaration of Rights, which was drafted by George Mason and which pre-dated the Declaration of Inde-pendence by a month, included specific liberties that were to be protected from state interference. These included freedom of the press, the free exercise of religion and the obligation that no person should be deprived of their liberty except by the law of the land or the judgment of their peers. The drafters of the US Constitution, influenced by Mason's Virginia Declaration, included the protection of these minimum rights. It was not until 1791, however, that the US adopted a Bill of Rights containing a list of guaranteed individual rights. This was effected by a number of amendments to the constitution. Among the more well-known amendments are the First, which protects freedom of religion, freedom of the press, freedom of expression and the right of assembly; the Fourth, which protects individuals against unreasonable search and seizure; and the Fifth, establishing the rule against self-incrimination and the right to due process of law. Subsequent amendments to the US Constitution have extended the Bill of Rights (for example, the Thirteenth adopted after the Civil War forbade the practice of slavery), but no rights have ever been removed or abridged by Congress.

In many ways, the eighteenth-century post-independence constitutional settlement of the US established the model to be used in subsequent revolutionary struggles. Nowhere was this more apparent than France, where the US experience directly influenced the revolution against the *ancien regime*.

The French experience

Although the French Revolution and the American struggle for independence had many common features, they differed in one crucial aspect. Whereas the rebellious colonies had simply sought to establish themselves as an independent sovereign nation, the French revolutionaries were concerned with the demolition of an old, absolutist system of government and the establishment of a new democratic order. This, of course, posed the same question of legitimacy which had been raised by the English Revolution a century earlier when the English had rid themselves of their monarch by enforced abdication. The theoretical solution to this problem identified by the French, taking the lead from American notions of popular legitimacy, was that of self-determination. The central proposition of this concept was that the sovereignty of a nation lay with its people. Government was therefore to be by the people for the people, and any government which was not responsive to its citizens' demands could be changed by expression of the popular will.

The settlement following the French Revolution also reflects the social contract and natural rights theory of Locke and the French *philosophes*, Montesquieu and Rousseau. The Declaration of the Rights of Man and the

Citizen (1789) made it perfectly apparent that government is a necessary evil, and that as little of it as possible is desirable. According to the Declaration, true happiness is to be found in individual liberty which is the product of the 'natural, unalienable and sacred rights of man'. Thus, while the Declaration states that certain individual rights are protected – the right to due process, the presumption of innocence, the freedom to hold opinions and religious beliefs, and the freedom to communicate ideas and opinions – it prefaces these with a clear libertarian philosophy. Article 2 of the Declaration provides that 'the aim of every political association is the preservation of the natural and imprescriptible rights of man. These rights are Liberty, Property, Safety and Resistance to Oppression'. Article 4 goes on to say:

> Liberty consists in being able to do anything that does not harm others: thus the exercise of the natural rights of every man has no bounds other than those that ensure to the other members of society the enjoyment of these same rights. These bounds may be determined only by Law.

A number of recurring themes and concepts in human rights law originate from the American and French Revolutions. Foremost among these is that rights are by nature inherent, universal and inalienable: they belong to individuals simply because they are human beings and not because they are the subjects of a state's law. Second, that the protection of rights is best afforded within a democratic framework. The concept of political self-determination formulated by the drafters of the French Declaration made it clear that the effective protection of rights was to be found only within the bounds of democratic legitimacy. Third, that the limits to the exercise of rights could be determined or abrogated only by law. This might be seen as part of the concept of the rule of law which requires that rights should be protected by law, and that in abrogating or diminishing individual rights a government is obliged to conform to constitutional legal requirements. It also requires governments to act according to law, and that the law upon which the government seeks to act should be neither oppressive, arbitrary or discriminatory. Of course, one should not forget that the revolution which gave birth to these high sounding ideals and principles also gave birth to the Terror and the guillotine. Indeed, it was for these very reasons that the political philosophers Burke, Hume, Mill, Bentham and Austin rejected the notion of natural rights as being nothing more than unverifiable metaphysical phenomena.[8]

Whatever the theoretical or doctrinal debates over the bases for the English, American and French Revolutions, it is clear that each, in its own way, contributed towards the development of forms of liberal democracy in which certain rights were regarded as paramount in protecting individuals from the state's inbuilt tendency to authoritarianism. What was significant about the protected rights was that they were individualistic and libertarian in character: they were predominantly 'freedoms from' rather than 'rights to'.[9] In modern parlance, these would be called civil and political rights, since they dealt primarily with an individual's relationship to the organs of the state. Such was the power of these revolutionary ideas, that there are few modern written constitutions which do not claim to protect these individual rights.

The 'new' rights

Civil and political rights are not, however, the only rights which are protected by modern constitutions and contemporary international law. A variety of economic, social, cultural and other rights are also the subjects of various forms of protection. Karel Vasak has sought to classify the historical development of human rights according to the French revolutionary slogan 'Liberty, Equality and Fraternity'.[10] Each of these, he argues, corresponds, more or less, to the development of distinct categories or generations of rights. Liberty, or first-generation rights, are represented by civil and political rights: the right of individuals to be free from arbitrary interference by the state. Equality, or second-generation rights, correspond to the protection of economic, social and cultural rights: the right to the creation of conditions by the state which will allow every individual to develop their maximum potential. These second-generation 'rights to' require the state to put in place programmes for the full realization of the rights. Economic, social and cultural rights are sometimes seen as a socialist legacy or as derivative rights not worthy of the name, but such rights were protected in the domestic constitutions of the Soviet Union, Mexico and Germany in the early part of the twentieth century and since then have been included in a number of other domestic constitutions and explicitly recognized by international law. Fraternity, third-generation rights or rights of solidarity, are the newest and most controversial category of rights. These are asserted by developing states which wish to see the creation of an international legal and economic order that will guarantee the right to development, to disaster relief assistance, to peace and to a good environment. Clearly, the implementation of such rights – if rights they be – depends upon international cooperation and not simply internal constitutional measures.[11]

From this brief historical exposition, it will be apparent that the notion of human rights has made a transition from exclusive concern with the protection of the individual from state absolutism to the creation of social and economic conditions calculated to allow the individual to develop to the maximum of his or her potential. As Szabo puts it, the purpose of human rights is to 'defend by institutionalized means the rights of human beings against abuses of power committed by the organs of the State and, at the same time, to promote the multidimensional development of the human personality'.[12] It will also be apparent that the notion of human rights is not static but dynamic, and that there may well be considerable debate about whether certain interests are worthy to be classified as rights in the proper sense – whatever that might be. The dialectic process by which it is determined that some claims or interests are protectable and others are not, is of crucial importance if it is believed that rights have a quality that is fundamentally different to other rules of law. This is an issue which will be addressed in detail in the next chapter.

PRE-SECOND WORLD WAR INTERNATIONAL DEVELOPMENTS

The individual in the international system[13]

Although the origins of human rights law can be traced back to the revolutionary constitutionalism of the seventeenth and eighteenth centuries, it was not until the end of the Second World War that the international community began to manifest an interest in the promotion and protection of such rights through the medium of international law. In addition to the absence of the necessary political will to undertake the appropriate action, the structure of international law itself was one of the main impediments to progress in the field. At that time, international law was simply a law which regulated relations between states. States were the sole subjects of the international legal system; other entities, including individuals, were merely objects of the system. States might adopt rules for the *benefit* of individuals, but such rules conferred neither substantive rights on those individuals nor were they enforceable by any procedural mechanisms. Individuals, as citizens of the state, were subject to the complete authority of their government, and other states, in general, had no legal right to intervene to protect them should they be maltreated.

The position of aliens in a foreign state was, however, slightly different. The state of which an alien was a national might, under certain conditions, be entitled to bring a claim under international law against a delinquent host state. This would usually occur where an alien had suffered arbitrary treatment at the hands of state agents, such as the police, and had not been afforded an appropriate remedy in the state in question. Western states also argued that there should be an international minimum standard of treatment applicable to all aliens travelling abroad against which state conduct could be judged. Developing states, however, rejected this notion, claiming that an alien in a foreign country could not expect a better standard of treatment than that which a state meted out to its own nationals. It is arguable, however, that the minimum standards and equality of treatment dispute has been overtaken by developments in international human rights law. The main purpose of such state claims was not necessarily to seek redress for the injured citizen; rather, it was to vindicate the rights of the state which had been indirectly injured through the mistreatment of its own national.[14]

Humanitarian intervention

Notwithstanding the position of aliens in international law, the general proposition remains that before the entry into force of the UN Charter, individuals remained essentially at the disposal of their rulers. An alleged exception to this was the so-called right of humanitarian intervention. Under this 'right', states could intervene militarily in order to protect the population or a portion of the population in another state if the ruler of that state treated his or her people in such a way as to 'deny their fundamental human rights and to shock the conscience of mankind'.[15] It is doubtful whether such a right existed – although it has been asserted recently by the US and Vietnam as a justification for military incursions into foreign states – but even if it had, it was largely abused by powerful states seeking to expand their political influence.[16] None the less, a claimed right of humanitarian intervention was invoked by a number of the Great Powers during the nineteenth century to prevent the Ottoman Empire from persecuting minorities in the Middle East and the Balkans.

Abolition of slavery

There were, however, certain humanitarian developments which occurred in international law during the nineteenth and early twentieth centuries. Foremost among these was, perhaps, the abolition of the slave trade. Although the economics of slavery in the late eighteenth and early nineteenth centuries made the practice commercially less attractive to European states than it had been previously, its abolition was also motivated by humanitarian concerns. The practice of slavery was first condemned in the Paris Peace Treaty (1814) between Britain and France, but within the space of 50 years the General Act of the Berlin Conference providing for the European colonization of Africa declared that 'trading in slaves is forbidden in conformity with the principles of international law'. International action against slavery and the slave trade has continued throughout the twentieth century. The League of Nations adopted the Convention to Suppress the Slave Trade and Slavery in 1926[17] and prohibited the practice of slavery within the former German and Turkish colonies under the League's mandate system at the end of the First World War.[18] The 1926 Convention still remains the basic international document prohibiting the practice of slavery, although it was amended by a protocol (an addendum to the treaty) in 1953[19] and supplemented in 1956[20] to deal with problems of defining the acts which constitute slavery in the modern world.

The Red Cross

The other major achievement in international humanitarian law in the second half of the nineteenth century was the formation of the International Committee of the Red Cross (1863) and that organization's sponsorship of two international conventions to protect the victims of war and the treatment of prisoners of war. The work of the Red Cross has continued throughout two world wars and beyond, and it has sponsored a number of conventions dealing not simply with the status and treatment of combatants, but also with the treatment of civilian populations during times of war and limiting the methods by which wars may be waged. Although of considerable importance, consideration of humanitarian law in time of military conflict falls outside the scope of this work, which is concerned solely with human rights in time of peace.

The International Labour Organization (ILO)

Early twentieth-century efforts in the humanitarian field are largely associated with the post-First World War international settlement. The International Labour Organization, created by the Treaty of Versailles (1919),[21] was a response to the Allied Powers' concerns about social justice and standards of treatment of industrial workers which had largely been prompted by the Bolshevik Revolution of 1917. The ILO, which became a specialized agency of the UN in 1946,[22] may be seen as the precursor of systems for the protection of economic, social and cultural rights. The ILO has sponsored over 150 conventions dealing with, *inter alia*, conditions of work, remuneration, child and forced labour, the provision of holidays and social security, discrimination and trade union rights. Its work continues today and the organization ranks among the more important human rights institutions, although its work seldom attracts the attention it deserves.

The League of Nations

The League of Nations, an international organization established after the First World War to provide a system for ensuring peace and security, and facilitating international cooperation, made no provision for the protection of human rights. Nevertheless, the League's founding document, the Covenant,[23] committed the member states to work towards certain humanitarian objectives such as establishing humane working conditions for individuals, the prohibition of traffic in women and children, the prevention and control of disease and the just treatment of native and colonial peoples. The creation of the mandate system under the League, by which the former colonies of the defeated Axis Powers of Germany and Turkey were placed under the tutelage of the victorious powers, was, perhaps, one of the major humanitarian achievements of the organization. Under this system, 'a sacred trust of civilisation'[24] was placed upon the administering states to bring the mandated territories to self-government. While the paternalistic language of the Covenant might be viewed with distaste today, nevertheless the administering powers were required to ensure the absence of racial or religious discrimination in the territories under their guidance. In fact, few of the mandates achieved independence before the Second World War, and two of the territories – Palestine and Namibia – created international problems of considerable longevity. The mandates which had not achieved independence before the Second World War were subsequently transferred to the Trusteeship system under the UN Charter.[25]

Minorities treaties

Mention should also be made here of various treaties concluded after the First World War, since many of these contained provisions for the protection of minorities. While the post-war peace settlement attempted to respect the principle of self-determination based on the concept of national cohesion, it became clear that the re-establishment of Poland and the creation of successor states to the old Austro-Hungarian Empire meant that state boundaries would inevitably create divisions among certain peoples and consign them to live as ethnic, linguistic or religious minorities in the new states. A number of treaties were therefore concluded between the Allied Powers and these states in order to secure the protection of the civil and political rights of the minorities. Specific minority protection treaties were concluded with Poland, Czechoslovakia, Romania and Greece, while provisions on the protection of minorities were included in the peace treaties with Austria, Hungary and Turkey. In addition to these treaties, certain states made declarations concerning the protection of minorities within their states as a condition of becoming members of the League of Nations: these were Finland, Albania, Latvia, Lithuania, Estonia and Iraq. The League of Nations also exercised a supervisory function in respect of these 'obligations of international concern'.[26] A procedure was established whereby minority groups which considered that their rights were being violated could bring the matter to the attention of the Council of the League. The Council could then refer the matter to an *ad-hoc* Minorities Committee for conciliation and to an attempt a friendly settlement between the parties. If a settlement was not forthcoming, the full Council could determine the matter itself or remit it to the Permanent Court of International Justice for determination.

It is clear that the minorities protection treaties were not concerned with the question of individual rights but rather with the rights of groups. The main purpose of the treaties was to ensure the equal treatment of the ethnic, religious or linguistic minorities in the states in question and to allow the peoples constituting these group to preserve and develop their own distinct identities within the framework of the nation state. It will also be apparent from the states with which treaties were concluded that the existence of minorities within them has proved fertile ground for dispute throughout the twentieth century. While the minority protection treaties did not amount to human rights treaties in the classic individualistic and libertarian mould, none the less they were of substantial significance in that they provided a basis within the context of the League of Nations of a right of petition under international law by a group of private individuals. It is possible to discern here the germ of the right to individual petition to a supervisory and protective international institution under international law.

POST-SECOND WORLD WAR INTERNATIONAL DEVELOPMENTS

The United Nations

Despite the advances made in the sphere of humanitarian law and in the protection of economic, social and cultural rights during the nineteenth and early twentieth centuries, it was not until after the cataclysmic events of the Second World War that international human rights law began to develop in a coherent and recognizable way. The atrocities of the Nazis against their own people in Germany and against those in its conquered territories created such revulsion that, even before the conclusion of the war, the Allies determined that the post-war settlement should include a commitment to the protection of human rights. This they saw as a necessary prerequisite to the creation of a just and stable international order under the auspices of the planned United Nations Organization. No longer should a state be able to argue that the way in which it treated its own citizens was simply a matter of exclusive domestic concern, but the treatment of those individuals should, where appropriate national protection of rights was deficient, become the concern of the international community. The irony here was that while the Soviet Union denounced the Nazi genocide, Stalin himself had, before the war, systematically violated the rights of his own people, disposing of an estimated five million political opponents and enforcing collectivization on large numbers of peasants. The Soviet Union could also legitimately argue here that the matter was entirely within its domestic jurisdiction. None the less, the Charter of the International Military Tribunal at Nuremburg,[27] which had been created by the Allied Powers, including the Soviet Union, to try Nazi war criminals on the basis of international law existing at the outset of the Second World War, declared that crimes against humanity were crimes under international law. While the Tribunal's judgment may have been flawed in that assertion, it nevertheless established the basic principle that how a state treated its own citizens was now a legitimate matter of international concern.

The UN Charter and the Universal Declaration

Although Article 2(7) of the UN Charter reaffirmed the principle of non-intervention by the Organization in matters essentially within the domestic jurisdiction of the member states, thus appearing to preclude international intervention in the human rights field, it also contained several specific references to human rights. The Preamble to the Charter reaffirmed the faith of the 'peoples of the United Nations' in 'fundamental human rights, in the dignity and worth of the human person' and in 'the equal rights of men and women'. The language of reaffirmation is interesting, since it appears to presuppose the existence of human rights prior to the entry into force of the Charter which, at least in the sense of positive law, would have seemed at that time to be a dubious claim. The Charter also included as one of its purposes in Article 1 'promoting respect for human rights and fundamental freedoms for all'. The promotion of human rights by the UN was also reinforced by Article 55, and under Article 56 the member states pledged themselves to take joint and separate action in cooperation with the UN for the achievement of this and other objectives under Article 55. A number of other provisions in the Charter concerning various institutional competences also referred to human rights as a general category. Although the UN Charter therefore appeared to acknowledge the prior existence of phenomena known as human rights, it contained no list of such rights, nor did it refer to a source for discovering exactly what the rights were. There had been a proposal to incorporate a list of rights in the Charter during its drafting, but this had been defeated. The absence of a catalogue of human rights was nevertheless viewed as a defect and a move to draft, in the words of US President Truman, 'an international bill of rights' was undertaken within one year of the entry into force of the Charter.

The work of drafting the 'international bill of rights' was assigned to the Commission on Human Rights (CHR), a subsidiary organ of the UN's Economic and Social Council (ECOSOC).[28] The Commission, which was composed of government representatives, decided that the catalogue of human rights should take the form of a resolution of the UN General Assembly, since it was unlikely that any consensus could be achieved on incorporation of the rights into the Charter or that support for a legally binding human rights treaty would be forthcoming. The major advantage of a declaration in the form of a resolution was that it would not be legally binding but would, in the words of Eleanor Roosevelt, the chairman of the CHR, proclaim 'a common standard of achievement for all peoples and all nations'. The Universal Declaration in its final form contained a list of civil and political rights and economic, social and cultural rights to which all persons were entitled without discrimination. Significantly, however, the Declaration did not contain any institution or mechanism for ensuring that the rights were observed. Although the Declaration was originally adopted in a non-legally binding form, subsequent practice has transformed it into an instrument of considerable juridical potency, although its precise legal status is still the subject of some debate.[29]

The International Covenants

As it was recognized by the UN General Assembly at the outset that the Universal Declaration was not intended to create legally binding obligations on the member states, it mandated the CHR to complete the drafting of an internationally binding treaty which would not only transform the rights referred to in the Declaration into positive law, but would also provide institutions and mechanisms for supervision and enforcement. Unfortunately, this task proved to be more difficult than originally envisaged, since a dispute arose between members of the Commission about the relationship between civil and political rights on the one hand and economic and social rights on the other, and also over the appropriate means of implementation, supervision and protection. It was finally decided that instead of a single treaty or covenant being drafted to protect both categories of rights, two covenants would be prepared, each devoted to the different groups of rights. The two separate covenants, the International Covenant on Civil and Political Rights (ICCPR)[30] and the International Covenant on Economic and Social Rights (ICESCR),[31] were opened for signature in 1966, but did not enter into force – that is become effective – until a full decade later in 1976. The salient difference between the covenants is that while Article 2 of the ICCPR provides that the protected rights will be respected and ensured immediately, Article 2 of the ICESCR simply provides that states should 'recognize' the rights contained in the Covenant and should implement them progressively in accordance with specific programmes. It is also of particular significance that while the ICCPR establishes the Human Rights Committee (HRC) to supervise implementation of the Covenant and to provide by means of an optional protocol a mechanism by which individuals may petition the HRC, the ICESCR simply consigns the function of supervision to a political body of the UN, i.e. ECOSOC.[32]

The UN special conventions[33]

Notwithstanding the difficulties of establishing the 'universal' system for promoting and protecting human rights, the UN also undertook programmes to draft legally binding instruments to deal with specific aspects of human rights. These have included treaties on the prevention and punishment of genocide, the prohibition of sexual and religious discrimination, the suppression and punishment of apartheid, the prohibition of the practice of torture, international cooperation on matters relating to refugees and statelessness and, most recently, a specific convention on the rights of the child. Brief mention should also be made here of a number of institutional measures and initiatives taken by the UN in order to promote and protect human rights. ECOSOC in particular has established procedures under Resolutions 1235 and 1503 by which gross and consistent violations of human rights by particular states may be investigated.[34]

The UN and decolonization

Of fundamental importance in the overall development of the UN's concern with human rights has been its practice in the field of decolonization. As indicated earlier, a number of the mandates created by the League of Nations after the First World War had not proceeded to self-government before the outbreak of the Second World War. The UN Charter therefore provided for the transfer of the mandates to a trusteeship system under which the territories would be administered and prepared for independence. One of the basic objectives of the trusteeship system was stated in Article 76(1)(c) of the Charter to be encouragement of respect for human rights and fundamental freedoms for all. This is supervised by the UN through the medium of the Trusteeship Council. There is now only one trust territory left in the world – the Pacific Islands Territory – which is administered by the USA.

It was not only the former mandates which became subject to UN super-vision under Chapter XI of the Charter. States with colonies or non-self-governing territories (NSGTs) were placed under an obligation to have paramount regard for the well-being of the peoples within the territories and to facilitate their development. Administering states were placed under an obligation to report to the Secretary-General of the UN on the advances made in their colonies. While Chapter XI did not place an obligation on administering states to grant independence to their colonies, none the less subsequent developments in the 1960s greatly increased the momentum of decolonization. General Assembly Resolution 1541(XV), clarifying the reporting obligations of administering states, was adopted together with Resolution 1514(XV), the Declaration on the Granting of Independence to Colonial Countries and Peoples. This resolution called for the immediate decolonization of all NSGTs through the exercise by the people in such territories of the right of self-determination. No pretext, such as lack of economic or educational preparedness, was to be permitted to retard the process. Although the UN Charter referred to the *principle* of self-determination, it certainly did not refer to a *right* of self-determination. It is, however, now generally accepted that such a right exists in international law, and that view is reinforced by General Assembly Resolution 2625, the Declaration on Principles of International Law Concerning Friendly Relations and Cooperation Among States in Accordance with the Charter of the United Nations, which is regarded as a convenient statement of customary international law, and a common Article 1 to both interna-tional covenants which provide that 'all peoples have the right to self-determination'. The underlying rationale for inclusion of this right, which is clearly a collective right, is that a people which is under alien domination through the institution of colonialism is not free, thus any notion of the enjoyment of individual or other rights within that context is meaning-less. Whether the right to self-determination extends beyond a right to decolonization or to the right of minority secession is an open question, although a reading of Resolution 2625 would seem to support this where the minority in question is subject to discriminatory treatment by the govern-ment of the state. Certainly, the effects of large-scale decolonization by the former colonial powers has had a massive impact on the structure of inter-national society. New states, largely in the developing world, have trans-formed the context of international political and legal debate by an insistence on the restructuring of the international system to respond to their needs. It is largely from these developing states that third-generation rights have emerged.

The Helsinki process

An International development that occurred during the period of *detente* between the West and Communist blocs during the early 1970s, and which deserves mention, was the Conference on Security and Cooperation in Europe, otherwise known as the Helsinki Process, since the Conference was convened in the Finnish capital of that name in 1973. Although the primary function of the Helsinki Process was to establish a framework for the development of peace and security in Europe, it also resulted in formal consideration of human rights issues. While the Soviet Union was concerned to have its western borders recognized, the West sought to exact human rights commitments from the Eastern bloc in exchange. The Final Act of the Conference,[35] which, significantly, was stated to be non-binding, declared the participating governments' determination to respect and put into practice respect for human rights and fundamental freedoms including the freedom of thought, conscience, religion or belief. They also resolved that they would respect the rights of peoples and their right to self-determination. Although the Final Act was clearly not a legally binding instrument, it did contribute in a significant way to state practice in the field of human rights, since it was declaratory of accepted human rights norms. In this way, it might be said to have contributed to customary international law in the human rights field. Of considerable importance in the Helsinki Process was the fact that the Final Act of the Conference provided for assessment of the commitments established by a series of review conferences. This created the institutional structure whereby the declared intentions of the parties, including observance of respect for human rights, could be measured. The Helsinki Process continued in Madrid and more recently Paris (1990). At the latter meeting, the 'Charter of Paris for a New Europe' was adopted in which it was declared by the 34 participating states that:[36]

> Human rights and fundamental freedoms are the birthright of all human beings, are inalienable and guaranteed by law. Their protection and promotion is the first responsibility of government. Respect for them is an essential safeguard against an over-mighty state.

There then followed a commitment to democratic government and political pluralism and a list of individual civil and political rights to which all are entitled without discrimination. Although the Paris Charter is, again, not legally binding, it nevertheless reaffirms the juridical significance of the stated rights under international law. It also marks the fact that the former Communist bloc states have demonstrated their commitment to the liberal-democratic ideal.

REGIONAL HUMAN RIGHTS SYSTEMS

There are at present three regional human rights systems. These are the European human rights system, the inter-American human rights system and the Organization of African Unity's Charter of Human and Peoples' Rights. There have been proposals for the establishment of an Islamic human rights treaty, the most recent being the Cairo Declaration in 1990 by the Organization of the Islamic Conference, but as yet no concrete results have occurred. A regional human rights treaty for South-East Asia and the Pacific has also been proposed, but this emanated from LAWASIA, a private lawyers' group and has, as yet, had no discernible impact on the governments of the region.

The European system

Of the three systems currently in existence, the European Convention on Human Rights and Fundamental Freedoms (1950)[37] is the most developed in terms of its longevity and the quantity of its jurisprudence. Created by the Council of Europe (an international institution designed to facilitate European cooperation, which should not be confused with the European Community), the European Convention was designed to fulfil a three-fold purpose: first, to strengthen democracy and commitment to the rule of law by the member states; second, to sound an alarm against incipient totalitarianism; and, third, to act as a bulwark against the perceived threat of encroaching communism. While the Convention has performed these functions tolerably well, the experience of the Greek Coup and its aftermath in 1967 demonstrated the limits of the Convention's effectiveness. Here, a military coup by a *junta* of army colonels resulted in totalitarian government and the large-scale denial of human rights. In particular, political opponents of the junta were arbitrarily imprisoned and subjected to torture. Despite its denunciation of the Convention and its withdrawal from the Council of Europe, Greece remained responsible under the Convention for its actions. Although this caused difficulty and considerable embarrassment for Greece in the conduct of its international relations, it provided little protection for those whose rights had been violated. None the less, in the 1970s, the newly democratized states of Greece, Spain and Portugal ratified the European Convention as a means of strengthening their domestic democratic processes.

The main achievement of the European Convention, however, has been to provide a mechanism by which individuals who believe that their rights have been violated by their states can petition the European Commission in an attempt to secure redress. As will be seen subsequently, the Commission's main function is to secure a friendly settlement between the individual and his or her state, but if this is not forthcoming the matter may be remitted to the European Court of Human Rights, whose rulings and awards of damages are binding on the state. Through this mechanism, substantial numbers of individuals have secured redress for both major and comparatively minor violations of their rights.

The European Convention and its ten protocols are concerned primarily with the protection of civil and political rights, although Protocol 1 does seek to protect the right to private property. Protection of economic and social rights in Europe is sought to be achieved by the procedures established by the European Social Charter (1961).[38] This instrument, which was also adopted by the Council of Europe, is intended to be complementary to the European Convention. Like ICESCR, it is drafted in a way that makes it clear that the realization of economic and social rights is to be achieved progressively. Supervision under the Social Charter is to be achieved simply by a state reporting system to the Council of Europe by a Committee of Independent Experts. While it might have been reasonable to expect that Europe would have been much more dynamic than other regions of the world in implementing fully economic, social and cultural rights, this has not proved to be so, and the Charter has been something of a disappointment.

The inter-American system

The inter-American human rights system is distinctive since it is formed by two separate but clearly interrelated mechanisms of protection. First, all member states of the Organization of American States (OAS), a regional organization whose objectives are similar to those of the UN, are committed to human rights obligations under the OAS Charter.[39] Like the UN Charter, the OAS Charter, which was adopted in 1948, does not contain a list of protectable rights. Nevertheless, through the processes of amendment of the OAS Charter and institutional adaptation, the American Declaration of the Rights and Duties of Man (1948),[40] which may be regarded as the analogue of the Universal Declaration, has been recognized by the Inter-American Court of Human Rights in an advisory ruling as an authoritative interpretation of the OAS Charter which is binding on all OAS member states.[41] Furthermore, the Inter-American Commission on Human Rights is obliged by its Statute to apply the American Declaration when dealing with human rights issues under its country report, on-site investigation or individual petition procedures.

The second pillar of the inter-American human rights system is the American Convention on Human Rights, otherwise known as the Pact of

San José (1969).[42] This is modelled on the European Convention, but since it was drafted at a later date, its framers were able to take account of some of the defects of the European Convention and correct them. The American Convention, like its European counterpart, is concerned almost exclusively with civil and political rights, although a protocol, the Pact of San Salvador (1989),[43] has added a list of economic, social and cultural rights which are to be implemented progressively by the states' parties. A novel feature of the Protocol is that it creates a right of individual petition to the Inter-American Commission in cases where the right to join a trade union or the right to education is denied.[44]

As with the European Convention, supervision of the rights protected by the American Convention is to be achieved through a commission and a court. The Commission screens all individual applications to ensure they comply with the Convention's admissibility requirements and, in the case of admissibility, attempts to secure a friendly settlement between the parties. If no friendly settlement is achieved, the case is remitted to the Court, which has the power to make binding rulings and award compensatory damages against a delinquent state. Under the Convention, the Inter-American Court is given a very wide power to render advisory opinions or judgments relating not just to the Convention itself, but also to the OAS Charter and 'other treaties concerning the protection of human rights in the America States'. While this power of the Court has been utilized considerably by the Commission and member states of the OAS, it is significant that the contentious procedure of the Court, that is, its procedure where individual violations of human rights have been alleged, has hardly been employed. There are, perhaps, a number of reasons for this, which will be considered in a later chapter.

The African Charter

The third and most recent of the regional systems for the protection of human rights is the African Charter on Human and Peoples' Rights (1981), which is sometimes known as the Banjul Charter after the Gambian capital where it was drafted.[45] The Charter, which like other human rights instruments takes the form of a multilateral treaty, was adopted by the Organization of African Unity in Nairobi in 1981 and it entered into force in 1986. While it enumerates the traditional list of civil and political rights, it differs from the other regional treaties by including within it economic, social and cultural rights and, more controversially, third-generation rights or rights of solidarity. Thus, the right to self-determination, the right to peace and the right to a good environment are all included in the text. Implementation of these rights is to be achieved solely through the functioning of the African Commission on Human Rights, since there is no provision for the creation of an African human rights court. The African Commission has now been in existence for some four years and it has received a number of state reports on the implementation of the protected rights and a small number of individual communications. As yet, no decisions have been reached on these communications.

Non-Governmental Organizations (NGOs)

Much of the foregoing has been devoted to action taken in the sphere of human rights at a governmental level. Discussion of human rights would be incomplete, however, without some reference to the role played by NGOs or groups of private individuals concerned with such issues. The earliest of these NGOs might be said to have been the International Committee of the Red Cross, founded in 1863 following a private initiative by Swiss physician Henri Dunant who was appalled by the suffering of the wounded following the battle of Solferino in which 70 000 men were killed or wounded. In the twentieth century, however, the number of NGOs concerned with human rights has proliferated, as the directory of Human Rights Internet (itself an NGO) will testify. Among the more well-known are the International Commission of Jurists, Amnesty International, the Anti-Slavery Society, Article 19 and the World Council of Churches. Some of these NGOs have been granted a degree of recognition by international organizations. ECOSOC, for example, is empowered by Article 71 of the UN Charter to make suitable arrangements for consultation with NGOs interested in its spheres of activity, and ECOSOC has conferred 'consultative status' on a number of such groups. Perhaps the most important work of NGOs is, however, their actions in exposing to public view violations of human rights within states. In many cases, adverse publicity about their human rights record is what states fear most. It should also be noted that NGOs are able to make communications to competent international institutions on behalf of victims of human rights abuses where those victims themselves are incapable of engaging the appropriate procedures because, for example, they are being held incommunicado.

CONCLUSION

From this brief historical excursus, it is perhaps apparent that both instruments and institutions for the protection of human rights on a universal and regional basis have developed exponentially since the end of the Second World War. There now exists a confusing plethora of treaties, conventions, covenants, charters and declarations dealing with human rights and related humanitarian issues. The proliferation of competent institutions under these instruments is no less confusing. Furthermore, a great many activities in the human rights field take place at a bureaucratic level, largely through the modification of existing institutions and institutional procedures, which are hardly apparent to the majority of casual observers. Much of the remainder of this book will therefore be devoted to a systematic analysis of the existing instruments and institutions concerned with human rights protection, and it will also attempt to illuminate the less accessible areas of international bureaucratic activity in the field.

Before this task can be undertaken, however, there are two important preliminary matters which must be considered. First, considerable reference has been made so far to various groups of rights, especially the two major categories of civil and political rights and economic, social and cultural rights, without any attempt to define what they are. Furthermore, it might be said that the term 'rights' itself demands some analytical enquiry in an attempt to determine exactly what is being considered in this book. Second, since the protection of human rights is in the last resort a matter for international law, it is desirable that some description of the nature, problems and attributes of that legal system are considered. Both these issues will be analysed in the following chapters.

FURTHER READING

Early Developments in Human Rights

Henkin, L., *The Rights of Man Today* (London: Stevens, 1979), pp. 1–30.

Kamenka, E., 'The Anatomy of an Idea', in Kamenka, E. and Tay, A.E.-S., *Human Rights* (London: Edward Arnold, 1978), pp. 1–12.

Szabo, I., 'Historical Foundations of Human Rights and Subsequent Developments', in *Vasak*, Vol. 1, pp. 11–20.

Vincent, R.J., *Human Rights and International Relations* (Cambridge: Cambridge University Press, 1986), pp. 7–57.

Weissbrodt, D., 'Human Rights: An Historical Perspective', in Davies, P. (ed.), *Human Rights* (London: Routledge, 1988), pp. 1–20.

Weston, B., 'Human Rights', (1986) 6 *HRQ* 257–82.

Pre-Second World War Humanitarian Developments

The Position of the Individual
Lauterpacht, Sir H., 'The Subjects of the Law of Nations', (1947) 63 *LQR* 438–60 and (1948) 64 *LQR* 97–119.

Norgaard, C.A., *The Position of the Individual in International Law* (Copenhagen: Munksgaard, 1962), esp. chs 1 and 2.

Oppenheim, L., *International Law*, Vol. 1: *Peace* (London: Longmans-Green, 2nd edn, 1912), pp. 362 *et seq.*

Starke, J.G., 'Human Rights and International Law', in Kamenka, E. and Tay, A. E.-S., *Human Rights* (London: Edward Arnold, 1978), pp. 112–31.

Humanitarian Intervention

Brownlie, I., *International Law and the Use of Force by States* (Oxford: Clarendon Press, 1963), pp. 338–42.

Brownlie, I., 'Humanitarian Intervention', in Moore, J.N., *Law and Civil War in the Modern World* (Baltimore, MD: Johns Hopkins University Press, 1974), pp. 217–28.

Klintworth, G., *Vietnam's Intervention in Cambodia in International Law* (Canberra: AGPS Press, 1989).

Oppenheim, L., *International Law*, Vol. 1: *Peace*, edited by H. Lauterpacht (London: Longman, 8th edn, 1955), pp. 312–20.

The Red Cross

Boissier, P., *History of the International Red Cross: From Solferino to Tsushima* (Geneva: Henri Dunant Institute, 1984).

Dinstein, Y., 'Human Rights in Armed Conflict', in *Meron*, pp. 345–68.

Dominice, C., 'The Implementation of Humanitarian Law', in *Vasak*, Vol. 1, pp. 427–50.

Forsythe, D.B., 'Human Rights and the International Committee of the Red Cross', (1990) 12 *HRQ* 263–89.

The ILO

Jenks, C.W., 'The Revision of the Constitution of the International Labour Organization', (1946) 23 *BYIL* 303–17.

Jenks, C.W., *Human Rights and International Labour Standards* (London: Stevens, 1960).

Valticos, N., 'The International Labour Organisation (ILO)', in *Vasak*, Vol. 1, pp. 363–99.

Wolf, F., 'Human Rights and the International Labour Organization', in *Meron*, pp. 273–306.

The League of Nations and Minorities

Northedge, F.S., *The League of Nations: Its Life and Times 1920–46* (Leicester University Press, 1986).

Stone, J., *International Guarantees of Minority Rights: Procedure of the Council of the League of Nations in Theory and Practice* (London: Stevens, 1932).

Thornberry, P., *International Law and the Rights of Minorities* (Oxford: Clarendon Press, 1991), esp. pp. 25–54.

Zimmern, Sir A.E., *The League of Nations and the Rule of Law* (London: Macmillan, 1936).

The UN Charter

Humphrey, J.P., 'The Universal Declaration of Human Rights: Its History, Impact and Character', in B.G. Ramcharan (ed.), *Human Rights Thirty Years after the Universal Declaration* (Dordrecht: Martinus Nijhoff, 1979), pp. 21–37.

Humphrey, J.P., *Human Rights and the United Nations: A Great Adventure* (Dobbs Ferry, NY: Transnational Publishers, 1984).

Humphrey, J.P., 'The Magna Carta of Mankind', in P. Davies, (ed.), *Human Rights* (London: Routledge, 1988).

Szabo, I., 'Historical Foundations of Human Rights and Subsequent Developments', in *Vasak*, Vol. 1, pp. 20–40.

The Helsinki Process

Bloed, A. and van Dijk, P., *The Human Dimension of the Helsinki Process* (Dordrecht: Martinus Nijhoff, 1991).

The European Convention

Beddard, R., *Human Rights and Europe* (London: Sweet and Maxwell, 2nd edn, 1980), pp. 17–30.

The American Convention

Buergenthal, T., Norris, R. and Shelton, D., *Protecting Human Rights in the Americas* (Kehl-am-Rhein: Engel, 3rd edn, 1990), ch. 1.

The African Charter

Bello, E.G., 'The African Charter on Human and Peoples' Rights', (1985–6) 194 *Hague Recueil* 13–268.

Umzozurike, U., 'The African Convention on Human and Peoples' Rights', (1983) 77 *AJIL* 902–12.

THEORIES OF HUMAN RIGHTS

INTRODUCTION

The central concern of this book is to examine the broad array of universal and regional instruments and institutions for the protection of human rights. Already the term 'human rights' has been employed generously with little attempt to define it. From the preceding chapter, however, the reader may have glimpsed that the phenomenon known as human rights is connected not only with the protection of individuals from the exercise of state or governmental authority in certain areas of their lives, but that it is also directed towards the creation of societal conditions by the state in which individuals may develop to their fullest potential. This description may reveal what human rights are intended to *achieve* in a teleological sense, but it does not reveal *which* human rights exist or *what* they are. This, of course, begs the question whether it is necessary in an enquiry into the institutions and the instrumentalities of human rights protection to attempt to define the nature of the phenomena under consideration. Surely it is appropriate simply to acknowledge that there now appears to be almost universal acceptance of human rights as identifiable, concrete, legal norms? Indeed, commentators such as Weissbrodt[1] and Vasak[2] state unequivocally that human rights have become a universal ideology. If this were so, it would seem that the need for theoretical enquiry into the nature of human rights begins and ends here.

Even if one were to accept uncritically the proposition put forward by Weissbrodt and Vasak, it is none the less clear that their assertions raise a number of acute problems. Some of the problems may be posed in the form of the following questions: Are all three generations of rights 'human rights' in the true sense? If they are, are they all co-equal or is there some hierarchical relationship between them? Even within the category of civil and political rights, are all rights of an equal standing or are some more important than others? What differentiates civil and political rights from other kinds of rights anyway? Are *human* rights different from other kinds of rights? What is the relationship of rights to other kinds of rules? Are rights defeasible? Upon whom lies the obligation to 'prove' or 'disprove' the existence of a right? Can their existence be proved objectively in any event? Do different cultures really have the same understanding of human rights? Are Chinese concepts of human rights the same as Western, Islamic or African concepts? What would be the consequences if the concepts were shown to be fundamentally different?

All of these questions, and many more, are of fundamental importance, since perceptions about the existence, worth and relationship of rights one to another, and to legal norms in general, produce practical consequences as far as the protection of human rights is concerned. Take, for instance, the question of whether economic, social and cultural rights are true rights or simply aspirational targets. If they are the latter, then no human being can legitimately claim that his or her government is under an absolute, indefeasible obligation to accord those rights to him or her through a programme of progressive implementation. They are merely claims to a better life to which a government *may* give effect *if* economic conditions become more favourable at some undetermined future date. If they are rights, however, the government is under a positive obligation to accord them through the appropriate implementation mechanisms. Furthermore, do these rights exist independently of their reduction to positive law in an international instrument? If they do, are they inherent to individuals and therefore to be protected despite any unilateral binding commitment by the state?

The way in which we approach questions such as these depends upon our understanding of human rights within some form of theoretical framework. Even those who would deny that it is necessary to look beyond the positive law contained in the vast array of existing legal instruments have already implicitly adopted a theoretical stance, although they may be unaware of having done so. The function of theory, however, is to provide an analytical tool by which important questions such as those above may be posed and tentative answers offered. It permits the construction of paradigms which lend coherence and consistency to any debate about rights and a model against which putative rights may be measured. It also provides mechanisms by which it is possible to determine the precise ambit of the rights upon whose existence there may be agreement.

From the foregoing, it may be evident that two very broad categories of enquiry about human rights are implicit. The first, often referred to as analytical jurisprudence, raises questions about the nature and origin of rights and how it is possible to know that we have any rights at all. The second category of enquiry, which is sometimes called normative jurisprudence, poses questions about the specificities of rights which individuals are acknowledged to possess, and how such rights stand in relation to each other. While a substantial amount of work has been done in these fields by domestic jurists, international lawyers have concerned themselves little with such questions. International human rights theorists have tended to fall into one of two very broad schools of analytical jurisprudence – the natural and positive law schools – which we will examine shortly. It is in the field of normative jurisprudence that international theorists have been more active, but in the absence of sound analytical foundations, normative enquiry has assumed an air of unreality. This may be a reflection of the poor state of international legal theory in general where commentators still have difficulty in adequately explaining the nature of legal obligation in international law.

It should not be thought, however, that domestic jurists are irrelevant to our inquiry into the analytical and normative aspects of human rights. There are two reasons for this. First, the protection of human rights is primarily a matter for domestic law. As we will see in Chapter 3, it is only when domestic law falls short of the standards imposed by international law, that international mechanisms for individual protection become engaged. Thus, what domestic commentators say about rights within domestic systems has direct relevance to international lawyers. Second, the majority of human rights instruments create institutions to supervise the systems of which they are part. Very often these institutions function either in a judicial or quasi-judicial manner. The decision makers within these bodies are therefore required to apply what might be called traditional techniques of legal reasoning to questions concerning the rights under consideration and, in a sense, to behave like judges in domestic courts and tribunals. Indeed, many of the people who staff these international institutions concerned with human rights supervision are themselves lawyers and judges trained in the craft of domestic law who bring with them all the legal theories, assumptions and methodologies of their national systems. In analysing how these people make decisions, it is therefore appropriate to apply, by analogy, the theories of domestic jurists. One needs only to examine the extensive and detailed jurisprudence of the European Court of Human Rights to see the accuracy of this assertion.

In this chapter, it is possible to do little more than provide a cursory examination of some of the major theories which are of relevance to human rights. A caveat should be entered that such a brief treatment of these theories will inevitably lead to some inaccuracies and distortions and a loss of subtlety possessed by much of the writing under consideration. This chapter should, therefore, be taken only as a route map and must in no way be considered a complete topographical guide.

NATURAL LAW AND NATURAL RIGHTS

There can be little doubt that human rights or the rights of man as they were known at first are progeny of the natural law school. As we saw in Chapter 1, the American Declaration of Independence and the French Declaration of the Rights of Man and the Citizen both had their origins in natural rights theory.

While precepts of natural law may be traced back to classical times, for present purposes it may be said that the modern school of natural law emerged in medieval times with the writings of the early Christian philosophers, foremost among whom was Saint Thomas Aquinas. The Thomistic view of natural law postulated that it was that part of God's perfect law which could be divined through the application of human reason. Part of early natural law philosophy was the idea that each person's station in life was determined by God, but that all people – whatever their status – were subject to the authority of God. From this it was possible to state that not only was the royal authority of monarchs constrained by divine rules, but that all human beings were endowed with a unique individual identity which was separate from the state. Indeed, this latter facet of natural law doctrine may be seen as containing the seeds of the natural rights idea that each person constituted an autonomous individual.

Of course, the basis of early natural law was entirely theistic, that is, it required belief in the Deity to render it coherent. The next stage in the development of natural law, however, was to sever it from its theistic origins and to make it a product of enlightened secular rational thought. This task was undertaken by Dutch jurist Hugo de Groot, who is usually known by his Latin name, Grotius, and who is generally acknowledged to be the 'father of international law'. In his treatise *De Iure Belli ac Pacis*,[3] Grotius argued that it was possible to rationalize the existence of natural law, which was the basis of all positive or written law, on a non-empirical basis by examining the axioms of geometry. Such a mathematical approach to the question of law demonstrated that all rules were ascertainable by the application of 'right reason' and did not depend on the Deity for their validity. This rationalistic, secular approach to law appealed to post-Renaissance scholars, and from the application of Grotian 'right reason' it is possible to discern the development of individual or natural rights theory.

Throughout the seventeenth century, the Grotian view of natural law was refined and, eventually, transmuted into natural rights theory through which subjective, individual rights came to be recognized. Foremost among the proponents of natural rights doctrine was John Locke.[4] Locke argued that all individuals were endowed by nature with the inherent rights to life, liberty and property which were their own and could not be removed or abrogated by the state. However, Locke also postulated that in order to avoid the uncertainties of life in a state of nature, mankind had entered into a social contract or voluntary association by which the exercise of their inalienable rights was transferred to the ruler of the state. Where the ruler of the state broke the social contract by violating the natural rights of the individual, subjects were free to remove the ruler and replace him or her with a government which was prepared to respect those rights.

As we saw in Chapter 1, Locke used his social contract theory to explain, and as an apology for, the English Glorious Revolution of 1688. King James II, by violating the natural rights of his subjects, had forfeited his right to rule and had legitimated the consequent change in government. From the Lockean view of natural rights, two things are evident: first, the individual is an autonomous being capable of exercising choice and, second, the legitimacy of a government depends not only upon the will of the people, but also upon the government's willingness and ability to protect those individual natural rights. While Lockean natural rights theory was clearly an artificial construct designed to explain the nature of man in political society, it nevertheless exercised a profound influence over political thinking in the seventeenth and eighteenth centuries. The language of both the American and French Revolutions, and the writings of French *philosophe* Jean-Jacques Rousseau[5] and German moral philosopher Immanuel Kant, demonstrate the philosophical pedigree of natural law and natural rights.

While Rousseau followed the main thrust of Locke's social contract theory, he declared that far from creating individual natural rights, natural law conferred inalienable sovereignty on the citizens of a state as a whole. Thus, whatever rights were derived from natural law dwelt within the people as a collectivity and could be identified by reference to the 'general will'. It will be readily apparent that the general will was not an absolute quality and could either transform itself or be transformed by a persuasive leader. While Rousseau's theory was therefore derived from natural law precepts, it is obvious that it could be employed to justify demagoguery and totalitarianism. Indeed, it may be argued that the Terror of the French Revolution might be traced to a perversion of the 'general will' thesis.

Kant developed his ideas from a more general appreciation of the non-empirical natural law and natural rights tradition. The basis of Kant's theory was the categorical imperative, that is, the absolute moral good which is identifiable in the exercise of the virtuous will by all rational individuals. In Kant's theory, the categorical imperative operates on three levels: first, it specifies universal acts of duty on all individuals; second, it provides systematic rules for determining these duties; and, third, it specifies the relationship between freedoms and duties. Underlying the categorical imperative, however, is the idea that individuals are under a duty to develop their rational capacities and to employ them for the promotion of happiness in others. While the categorical imperative might be seen to be primarily duty-based, it has, as its correlative, a system of rights. Unlike the old natural law tradition, however, such rights are not prescribed, but flow from the consequences of the Kantian duty-based system. In a society of rational, self-determining human beings, Kant postulated that freedoms or rights would emerge as a consequence of the application of the categorical imperative. Such rights may therefore be described as consequential and non-relational in that they do not depend upon each other for their existence or worth. Unfortunately, because of the non-relational nature of rights in Kant's theory, it is particularly difficult to apply to concrete situations.

Although there has been something of a revival in the post-Second World War period, natural rights theory fell into general disrepute during the nineteenth century. The major criticism directed at natural rights theory was that it was not scientifically verifiable. How was it possible to know where rights came from, what they were and what content they had? Critics pointed to the *a priori* moral or value structures and assumptions derived from the personal preferences of the various theorists and declared that natural rights could have no objective existence. As English utilitarian Jeremy Bentham argued: 'Right is with me the child of law; from real laws come real rights, but from imaginary law, from "laws of nature", come imaginary rights . . . Natural rights is simple nonsense: natural and imprescriptible rights, rhetorical nonsense, – nonsense upon stilts.'[6]

Despite these criticisms of natural law and natural rights, however, sight must not be lost of the powerful influence which they have exercised over the emergence and development of human rights. Natural rights theory has the merit of providing the basis for a system of law which is allegedly superior to the law of the state and to which appeal may be made if it appears that the latter is unjust, arbitrary or oppressive. It may even be argued that the early revolutionary constitutional documents were 'natural rights' documents, and that following the barbarous excesses both prior to and during the Second World War, a revived natural rights movement led to the drafting of the major international human rights instruments. Of course, the view might be taken that although human rights had their origin in natural law, it took a system of positive law to provide a definite and systematic statement of the actual rights which people possessed.

POSITIVISM

While natural law theorists derived their ideas of rights from God, reason or *a priori* moral assumptions, positivists argued that the existence and content of rights could be derived only from the laws of the state. While the approach of the natural law and natural rights theorists was essentially non-empirical, the empirical methods adopted by the positivists reflected the scientific milieu of the 'Age of Enlightenment' of eighteenth-century Europe.

It was Scotsman David Hume who first raised the dichotomy between the 'is' and the 'ought' which has permeated discourse between the naturalist and positivist schools of jurisprudence. Hume argued[7] that inquiry into social phenomena could be divided into two distinct categories: First, the category of facts which could be proved to exist empirically and which could be demonstrated to be true or false. This was the 'is'. Second, there was the category of morality which could not be proved to exist objectively and about which people might have legitimate differences of opinion. This was the 'ought'. In Hume's view, it was only the 'is' – those matters which were empirically provable – that formed the basis of valid scientific enquiry. This had the consequence of severing the discussion of morality from the analysis of legal systems. Once this had been done, natural law appeared to be simply an argument about which moral position was better than another. Furthermore, while natural law failed to demonstrate how a systematic legal system could be constructed from its precepts, positive law took as its starting point the existence of formal legal systems.

The apparent amoral starkness of Hume's position was given a humanitarian face by the development by Jeremy Bentham of a school of positivism known as utilitarianism.[8] The central thesis of utilitarianism was that human existence was dominated by pleasure and pain, and that by increasing the former and diminishing the latter, the lot of mankind would be improved. The aim of utility, therefore, was to increase the overall stock of human pleasure, which could be calculated on a mathematical basis. The ultimate test of utility, therefore, was the implementation of rules which gave the greatest happiness to the greatest number of people – the maximization of felicity. It will be apparent that Bentham's utilitarianism was not amoral, but its morality was derived not from a metaphysical source; rather, its origins lay in the expression of the majority's personal preferences. Clearly this had the potential to lead to a tyranny of the majority and to the oppression of the minority in any given state. It is perhaps paradoxical, therefore, that Bentham and his followers employed utilitarianism as a potent vehicle for English law reform.

The main achievement of Hume and Bentham was to make law an autonomous field of scientific study separate and distinct from natural law inputs, and to pave the way for the more systematic approach of John

Austin.[9] Austin's empiricism led him to conclude that the only valid laws were the commands of the sovereign, or the ruling political power, which were accompanied by appropriate sanctions or remedies. From this position, it was possible to construct a rational system of interlocking and scientifically verifiable rules. The Austinian legacy, however, has been, rightly or wrongly, to suggest that rights are simply those rules which the state has enacted for the protection of individuals and their property interests. In terms of Hohfeldian linguistic analysis of legal rights,[10] it might be said that the Austinian position is that the state grants an *immunity* to individuals with a corresponding *disability* on the part of the state which prevents it from interfering with those immunities. The main criticisms directed at this form of positivism are that it places no moral constraints on the rules adopted by states and individuals only enjoy such rights as the state is prepared to grant them. Thus, the Nazi Nuremburg Laws on racial purity may have been immoral, but from a positivist point of view they were laws none the less, having been adopted by the government in power. Similarly, within a positivist framework, a law requiring all prisoners to be tortured would be legitimate despite its immoral quality.

The positivist position does, however, have certain advantages. It enables individuals to point to concrete norms and prescriptions that allow them to vindicate their rights. Professor H.L.A. Hart, a prominent and influential moral philosopher, has attempted to remove from positivism the less palatable aspects of its Austinian legacy. He has argued that although law and morality stand independently of each other, nevertheless the laws which a government adopts have been recognized and accepted by the community as a whole.[11] This, therefore, provides legitimacy for the laws passed. Of course, Hart's theory is only as good as the system of government in power, so that the community standards and laws of Nazi Germany will be different to those of present-day Britain. It is also true of positivist approaches that it may be possible to identify substantive rules for the protection of human rights within a legal system, but the reality of the situation may be that the social and institutional conditions are such as to deny the effective exercise of those rights.

ANTI-UTILITARIAN THEORIES

The central criticism of utilitarianism is that it sets as its priority the well-being of the majority. Little thought is given to minorities or individuals within a state whose preferences are not represented by the majority and who may, in consequence, be severely disadvantaged or, in rights talk, deprived of their rights. Take, for example, the issue of homosexuality. The majority of people within a state might find the practice of homosexuality so abhorrent or abominable that they would wish to prohibit it by legislation. Clearly, this would satisfy the central axiom of utilitarianism by maximizing the happiness of the majority. The homosexuals, a minority whose practices would be forbidden, would be able to make no argument to gainsay the utilitarian position since, as a minority, their preferences would have to give way to the wishes of the majority. Under a different theory, the treatment meted out to the homosexuals in our fictitious state might look like discrimination, or the consideration of a minority group as having less worth than the majority. Clearly, in a pluralistic, democratic state such a position would be untenable. Because of the tendency to a tyranny of the majority inherent in utilitarian theory, much modern writing has a strong anti-utilitarian focus.

Two of the most notable critics of utilitarianism are Dworkin and Nozick; but it is only in their criticism of utilitarianism that they are united. Each author starts from a different point of departure and arrives at starkly different conclusions. Nozick's rights theory flows from his general political philosophy which demands an ontological commitment to a particular species of morality and social organization.[12] In his theory, he postulates a group of men and women in a state of nature who combine to form the minimal state. The minimal state is not only based on certain moral precepts but is itself one of those moral precepts. To have more than a minimal state whose functions are limited to those of a 'night-watchman' would be to deprive its citizens of more liberty than necessary, which would in itself be immoral. The other moral bases of the minimal state are the right not to be killed, assaulted, robbed or defrauded; the right to acquire, retain and dispose of property; the right to performance of contracts and the right to do as one pleases so long as it does not violate the self-same rights of others. Wrongdoing, therefore, corresponds only to violation of these rights. The role of the minimal state in such circumstances is limited to the enforcement of the moral bases of the state by punishing violators, settling disputes and awarding compensation: the 'night-watchman' role. If the state were to transgress into other areas of activity such as providing welfare or redistributing wealth, it would exceed its function and become immoral by depriving citizens of their liberty to act. Nozick's main criticism of utilitarianism, therefore, is that it sacrifices liberty of the individual for the sake of the majority: it takes no account of the fact that an individual's life is the only one she or he possesses.

Nozick's thesis is, of course, highly theoretical and its application to forms of liberal democratic and capitalist state organization would simply have the effect of entrenching existing social inequalities. But what Nozick is seeking to do, is to construct a theory which would maximize the liberty available to all individuals without accepting the anarchist critique that maximum individual liberty is only possible without the state. With Nozick, the state remains a necessity, but one which must hardly encroach upon its citizens' freedom of action.

If Nozick's minimalist state strikes one as theoretically harsh and potentially populated by bleakly self-interested individuals, one might consider the other major contemporary critic of the utilitarian school whose anchor is firmly set in the Anglo-American liberal tradition: ~~Gerald~~ Dworkin.[13] In Dworkin's view, rights are defined as political 'trumps' held by individuals 'when, for some reason, a collective goal is not a sufficient justification for denying them what they wish as individuals, to have or to do, or not a sufficient justification for imposing some loss or injury upon them'.[14] In other words, rights perform the same function as trump cards in a game of bridge or whist where any trump card will always possess a higher value than the highest card of any other suit. In the same way, a right will always defeat a policy designed to promote general welfare unless a good argument can be adduced for it not doing so. This definition of a right clearly counters the utilitarian thrust that individual preferences must always give way to those of the majority, since it says that in some circumstances the interests of the individual must take priority over those of society as a whole.

As a definition of rights, Dworkin's approach is unobjectionable, but it tells us nothing of where rights come from, what they are or where they stand in relation to each other. To answer these questions, it is necessary to understand that they are constructed on the foundation of Dworkin's commitment to the political doctrine of liberalism, one of the central tenets of which is that governments must treat individuals within their populations with equal respect and concern. In this system, he argues, rights are needed not in order to maximize happiness, but to maintain the principle of equal respect and concern. Thus, although Dworkin's theory is anti-utilitarian in this respect because the individual cannot be sacrificed for the benefit of overall social welfare, he none the less accepts the Benthamite utilitarian credo that everybody counts for one, but nobody counts for more than one. What he argues is that in aggregating the preferences of individuals, the utilitarians deviate from the central liberal proposition that individuals must be treated as individuals. It is therefore not the principle of one person one vote which is wrong, it is the mechanics of aggregation which are flawed. This is so, Dworkin argues, because in making decisions individuals are swayed by two types of preference; the first of which is acceptable, the second of which is not. First, individuals have *personal* preferences which rest on individual taste – a preference for Coke over Pepsi, for example. Such preferences are innate and do not involve preferences about other people's preferences. It is this second – preferences about other people's preferences – which, Dworkin argues, distorts the utilitarian hedonic calculation. This is so because, although in theory we would wish to assign the greatest number of liberties to everyone, our choices would be constrained by external preferences; by giving preference to those people whose preferences we would wish to see satisfied. This distinction leads, in Dworkin's view, to a kind of double counting in favour of those whom we would wish to have their preferences fulfilled, which, in turn, leads to a violation of the principle of equal respect and concern. Since, however, external preferences – preferences about preferences – cannot be excluded from the calculation, but since they clearly violate the principle of equal respect and concern, a system of rights is necessary to 'trump' potential deviations in the hedonic calculation.

Dworkin's distinction between different kinds of preferences is extremely subtle, and it is doubtful whether it can be sustained in practice. Nevertheless, it is crucial to his understanding of rights in a liberal democratic society. At this point, it is possible to discern why rights are necessary and ought to be taken seriously in Dworkin's schema, but it still does not tell us what rights we have, that is, the analytical side of the equation. Here Dworkin argues that there is no general right to liberty as such, since this would be meaningless, but that there are rights to specific liberties such as freedom of expression, association and religion, and freedom in personal and sexual relations. From whence, however, are these specific rights derived? In Dworkin's view, they all derive from the fundamental right that everybody is entitled to 'treatment as an equal', which in turn is derived from the central tenet of liberalism that everybody must be treated with equal respect and concern. In what sense, however, is the right to treatment as an equal fundamental? It is because, argues Dworkin, 'it is the source both of the general authority of collective goals and of the special limitations on their authority that justify more particular rights'.[15] Thus when a right is claimed it must be demonstrable that it is supported by the fundamental right to equal treatment.

While one can take issue with Dworkin's theory of rights at a number of levels, it is none the less useful because it attempts to reconcile societal goals with individual preferences and to establish a hierarchical order of rights. The major problem with Dworkin in attempting to apply his theory to the international human rights field, however, is that his thesis is applicable only to the conditions of a liberal democracy possessing strong democratic institutions. In most states where gross human rights violations occur, they are not always endowed with either that form of political system nor strong democratic institutions. This does not mean that Dworkin's thesis is wrong, but simply that it has limited application. Nevertheless, both the Council of Europe and the inter-American systems for the protection of human rights explicitly require the prior existence of forms of representative democracy within their member states. It may well be that Dworkin's theory of rights might be fruitfully adopted and adapted to explain both the existence and application of rights within these systems at least.

Consideration of anti-utilitarian jurists cannot be deemed complete without a brief examination of Rawls *Theory of Justice*.[16] In this work, he argues that justice is a way of distributing the rights, duties, benefits and burdens among individuals within society. He further posits, as distinct from utilitarians, that every person is inviolable and that even the welfare of society cannot displace this inviolability:

Justice denies that loss of freedom for some is made right by a greater good shared by others. Therefore, in a just society liberties of equal citizenship are settled; the rights secured by justice are not subject to political bargaining or to the calculus of social interest.[17]

Like Nozick, but with starkly different results, Rawls starts with the familiar social contract theory in which all persons are in an original position of equality as regards the distribution of freedom and power. Each, however, is endowed with a 'veil of ignorance' about his or her own personal qualities and attributes. In this state, the rational person who is ignorant of their own potential will, in Rawls' view, choose two principles of justice. The First Principle will be that everyone has an equal right to the most extensive total system of equal basic liberties compatible with the same system for others. The Second Principle is that social and economic inequalities are to be organized so that they are to the greatest benefit to the least advantaged and so that they provide a system of equal access to all offices and equality of opportunity. Thus, in Rawls' system, there is a general conception of fairness and equality in which all social primary goods such as liberty and opportunity, income and wealth are to be distributed equally unless an unequal distribution actually operates to the advantage of the least favoured.

Unlike Dworkin, who does not concede a general right to liberty, Rawls argues to the contrary, that liberty is the pre-eminent right and that all other rights are subsidiary to it. Within such a system, rights may only be restricted if, first, that would strengthen the total system of liberty shared by all or, secondly, if less than equal liberty were acceptable to the citizens so deprived. What, then, are the rights comprehended by the First Principle? Among these Rawls would include political liberty, freedom of expression, conscience and thought, and freedom to integrity and inviolability of the person – including the freedom to hold property. All such rights would be held equally by citizens in a just society. Rawls recognizes, however, that some citizens, although actually possessing the most extensive system of equal rights within society, might because of other factors, such as ignorance or poverty, be unable to take full advantage of their rights. Clearly, this does not affect the intrinsic value of rights possessed by individuals but it does hinder their enjoyment of those rights. In Rawls' terms, it affects the worth or value of the liberties held. How, then, is this disparity in the worth or value of liberty to be compensated for? Rawls' answer to this is by the application of the Difference Principle. This principle states that an equal distribution of resources is to be preferred unless it can be demonstrated that an unequal distribution would make both the advantaged and disadvantaged better off. Thus, this form of distributive justice should be implemented to ensure that each person enjoyed the full worth of his or her liberty.

Again it may be argued that Rawls' theory is acceptable in so far as it applies to liberal democratic societies, but that its application to other forms of political organization make it unrealistic. None the less, it is clear that even at a cursory glance Rawls' concepts could be applied to arguments in favour of the third-generation right to development which demands a reallocation of the world's resources to maximize the well-being of those in the developing world.

LEGAL REALISM

The explosion of regulatory activity in the USA following President Roosevelt's economic 'New Deal' led a number of American jurists to consider new methods of attempting to explain the functions of law within a complex, highly regulated industrial society. In this task they were aided by the input of social scientific perspectives, particularly that of the then relatively modern discipline of sociology. Foremost among the legal realists were Karl Llewellyn[18] and Roscoe Pound.[19] Their major concern was, to paraphrase Llewellyn, to discover what law *does* rather than what law *is*. Because of their empirical framework, the legal realists had no general theory of rights as such, but considered them as forming part and parcel of their study of the processes and interaction of policy, law and legal institutions. Within this framework, rights might emerge as the end-product of such a process of interaction, thereby reflecting the prevailing moral values of society at any given time. In this sense, the realists provided a kind of 'snapshot' of rights as a temporary manifestation of an ongoing process. Although Pound devised a prescription for the validation of human wants, human demands and social interest through the principle of social engineering, he did not identify a mechanism or method by which individual rights might be prioritized both in relation to each other and in relation to societal goals. As Shestack points out, this lack of 'goal identification' renders Pound's approach deficient in assisting normative enquiry.[20]

None the less, a contemporary development within the realist school perhaps addresses some of the criticisms directed at Pound. This is the Yale School of International Law, whose main proponent is Myres McDougal.[21] He and his colleagues have developed a value-explicit and policy-orientated approach to human rights based on the 'super-value' of the protection of human dignity. Like other legal realists, McDougal, Lasswell and Chen argue that demands for the satisfaction of human rights derive from a broad-based international sharing of values. These values are manifested by demands relating to such social goods as respect, power, enlightenment, well-being, health, skill, affection and rectitude. All of these values contribute towards, and are validated by, the super-value of human dignity. The objective of the value-explicit policy-orientated approach is to offer a prescription for the world community in which all the values identified are shared through the application of democratic principles.

While the Yale School might be criticized on the ground that the concept of the 'super-value' of human dignity might not mean the same thing for all cultures at all times, nevertheless it does seem to represent an idea upon which a large core of consensus might be secured, especially since the humanitarian drive for many international human rights instruments has its origins in seeking protection and redress for individuals who are the subjects of inhumane treatment. Furthermore, the identification of a common goal or goals, again, as represented by the major human rights instruments, provides evidence of a minimum of shared values within the world community. This kind of approach avoids problems of metaphysical abstractions which characterizes a substantial amount of theoretical debate about human rights, but it still does not answer the question of whether human rights are immutable or whether – and this is a dangerous argument – they simply reflect prevailing social interests.

MARXISM

Before leaving our consideration of the theoretical schools which might help us to think in a coherent way about human rights, it is probably pertinent to mention Marxist approaches to the issue. Marx, arguing from a scientific basis, claimed that the alleged law of nature was both idealistic and ahistorical, and as such the claim by seventeenth- and eighteenth-century bourgeois revolutionaries to the effect that rights were both inalienable and imprescriptible was unsustainable and indefensible. Rights, Marx argued, were simply bourgeois concepts and a product of bourgeois-capitalist society, designed to maintain and reinforce the pre-eminent position of the ruling class. None the less, Marx was prepared to concede that even within the early stages of a communist revolutionary state, rights, of a particular species, might still have an important role to play in the transformation of society. In order to understand this argument, it is necessary to consider the Marxist approach to the nature of the individual within both the capitalist and the communist state.

In Marxist theory, the essence of an individual is that of a social being who uses his or her abilities to satisfy his or her needs. The fulfilment of these needs in capitalist society, where the means of production are controlled by the ruling class, is impossible since it results in the alienation of the working class. The true potential of human beings, in Marxist doctrine, can only be realized if they are enabled to return to their true nature as social beings. This, however, can only be achieved in a truly communist society where all means of production are held in common and there is an absence of class conflict. Such a communist society can only come into being, however, by a revolution of the industrial proletariat. This, in turn, will transform itself into a dictatorship of the proletariat and, through historical and economic forces, lead to the withering away of the state. Until the state withers, however, the revolutionary party must occupy a vanguard position using the state and its institutions for the transformation of society. It is at this point that Marxist concepts of rights emerge. During the period of transformation there are no individual rights, since these are egoistic, bourgeois property-based 'rights'; there are only legal rights, which are granted by the state and which are directed towards the transition from the communist state to communist society. These legal rights are, however, only contingent in that they are concerned simply with the mechanics of transformation. As such, these rights can only be social and economic, since they are directed towards the reduction of the means of production to common control. It is only this species of rights which contributes towards the Marxist objective of returning individuals to their status as social beings. Once the process of transformation has taken place, the need for rights disappears, since each individual will be in a free and spontaneous relationship with all other individuals. Within Marxist theory, therefore, rights are simply instruments or tools to achieve a particular end. Once that end has been achieved, the tools are no longer needed and may be conveniently disposed of. Furthermore, rights have no transcendental or eternal value; they are positivistic in the sense that those rights which are deemed to exist are fixed solely by the state.

While some states such as China and North Korea still hold firm to teaching based on Marxist principles, other erstwhile communist states such as those comprising the Commonwealth of Independent States have abandoned not only Marxist economic theories, but also Marxist theories of rights. Indeed, a number of the old former communist bloc states, such as Hungary and Czechoslovakia, have become parties to human rights instruments that clearly give effect to individualistic civil and political rights. Nevertheless, the contribution of Marxist thought to the development of international instruments on social, cultural and economic rights has been pronounced and should not be dismissed lightly.

CLASSIFICATION OF RIGHTS IN INTERNATIONAL LAW

It was indicated earlier in this chapter that a great deal of debate about the juridical nature of human rights in international law has tended to focus on the normative relationship between various alleged categories of rights. Some commentators, such as Cranston,[22] take the view that only civil and political rights can properly be called human rights, and that economic and social rights are simply claims against the state which it is not obliged to fulfil. Others jurists, such as Tunkin,[23] who are more predisposed to a socialist orientation, argue that only economic and social rights have any real meaning, since civil and political rights serve to reinforce the present unequal distribution of all social and material goods and impede the process of development. Such dogmatism tends to produce unfortunate effects, since, as we shall see below, it hinders appreciation of the fact that just as not all civil and political rights are individualistic, not all economic and social rights are collectivist in orientation. However, even within supposed categories of rights, there is debate about whether the more fundamental rights and freedoms can be separated from those which are less fundamental.

The position of the UN General Assembly is clear on this issue. It has stated on a number of occasions that '*all* human rights and fundamental freedoms are indivisible and interdependent and that equal attention and urgent consideration should be given to the implementation, promotion and protection of both civil and political and economic, social and cultural rights'.[24] This statement, however, is not particularly useful, since it does not reflect the actual position as regards the different goals and implementation programmes of the various human rights instruments which we will be considering in detail later in this book. Furthermore, it might be questioned whether such an approach is also intellectually compelling, since different societal conditions might demand the setting of different priorities with regard to different classes of human rights. This is not to argue that certain rights may be regarded as less important than others on some kind of arbitrary hierarchical scale, rather that in an imperfect world with an imperfect allocation of resources, the priorities within different states may dictate a different allocation of such resources. None the less, it is possible, both as an intellectual exercise and as a matter of practicality, to adduce weighty arguments in favour of the contention that between different classes of rights, and even within classes of rights, there is some kind of hierarchical classification of rights.

Fundamental rights

Are there some rights that might be regarded as more fundamental than others? Certainly, there is some support for this view in the wide variety of international human rights instruments now in force. The UN Charter, for example, states in its Preamble that the peoples of the UN are determined 'to reaffirm faith in fundamental human rights . . .', apparently indicating that these *fundamental* human rights enjoyed an existence prior to their recognition by the Charter and prior to their reduction to positive law by the various UN instruments. Such rights have also been described as 'supra-positive' or 'elementary' rights by Theodoor van Boven, who argues that their validity 'is not dependent on their acceptance by the subjects of law but which are at the foundation of the international community'.[25] In referring to 'supra-positive' rights, the immediate impression is that van Boven is claiming some kind of natural law origin for his fundamental rights, but throughout his discussion there is constant reference to human rights as a manifestation of international social order, thereby implying that rights, including supra-positive rights, have a sociological basis for their existence. As he says: 'These rights lie at the foundation of the international community *as presently represented* in the United Nations and, in a more limited sense, in other important world-wide and regional organizations.'[26] This statement would seem to suggest that fundamental rights are not static but dynamic and that other human rights may be exalted to such a status. Indeed, van Boven claims that this has been the case for such rights involving the prohibition of race and sex discrimination, since nearly all international human rights instruments take as their point of departure the need to ensure the absence of discrimination on these grounds.

Perhaps the most compelling argument in favour of treating some rights as fundamental lies in the fact that in the ICCPR and in the European, American and African regional human rights conventions, certain rights are characterized as inviolable in that they may not be derogated from even in times of war or other national emergency. Included in this list are the right to life; freedom from torture, inhuman and degrading treatment; freedom from slavery or servitude; freedom from *ex post facto* laws and freedom of thought, conscience and religion.[27] Other rights, however, may be derogated from under defined conditions. This would seem to imply that there is a difference between rights which may be derogated from and those which may not, the natural conclusion being that the former are to be regarded as more fundamental than the latter. Furthermore, the UN Convention Against Torture makes it clear that there can be no justification under any circumstances for the commission of the prohibited acts in that Convention. It would therefore seem that an argument could be made that these non-derogable rights have the characteristics of *ius cogens*, that is, norms which can never be derogated from,[28] and must, in that sense, be seen as fundamental both within the realm of international human rights law and international law in general. And if these non-derogable rights are indeed fundamental and do bear the characteristics of *ius cogens*, then it is possible to argue, as van Boven does, that these rights are 'binding on States, even in the absence of any conventional obligation or of any express acceptance or comment'.[29]

Civil and political rights vs economic, social and cultural rights

It may be recalled from Chapter 1 that although the UDHR included references to all categories of rights – civil, political, economic, social and cultural – within the framework of a single instrument, it proved impossible to secure agreement between the member states of the UN upon the drafting of a legally binding document embracing all of the rights contained in the Declaration. While some states argued that all types of right constituted an indivisible and mutually self-supporting whole, others – particularly the US and the UK – took the view that whereas civil and political rights were immediately enforceable and justiciable, economic, social and cultural rights depended upon positive, programmatic implementation. These Western states, whose political and economic structures had been heavily influenced by the revolutionary constitutionalism of the seventeenth and eighteenth centuries, argued that only first-generation rights – freedoms from state interference – were all that international law could reasonably be expected to protect as a matter of immediacy. Economic, social and cultural rights were not amenable to such immediate protection and were best fulfilled through a progressive reporting system. The ultimate drafting of two separate Covenants dealing with the two broad categories of rights would seem to support the contentions adduced by the Western states. While the ICCPR provides for immediate protection by requiring states to 'respect and ensure to all individuals within its territory and subject to its jurisdiction the rights recognized',[30] the ICESCR on the other hand requires only that states 'undertake to take steps . . . to the maximum of their available resources, with a view to achieving progressively the full realization of the rights recognized'.[31] The conclusion which is drawn by some commentators, such as Cranston, from this differential implementation structure, is that whereas civil and political rights are human rights properly so-called, economic and social rights do not enjoy such a status. If this position were taken to its logical conclusion, it would also mean that these second-generation rights do not require protection or implementation because they are not 'real' rights.

It is questionable, however, whether the drafting history and the arguments about implementation of the perceived categories of rights should determine decisively whether or not one category should be regarded as 'real' rights and the other not. At the theoretical level, it might be possible to argue that the right to education (which is classified as a social right) is of a different moral order to freedom of expression (a civil right), but this is an argument about the relational value of rights and not about the existence of such rights. Of course, whether we choose to accept economic, social and cultural rights as rights properly called, will depend upon our own preferred theoretical standpoint.[32]

If we descend to the level of pragmatism, it also becomes clear that alleged distinctions between the two categories of rights often verges upon the arbitrary. Take, for instance, the argument that civil and political rights are capable of immediate protection, whereas economic, social and cultural rights require progressive implementation. While it is undeniable that the latter group of rights will probably require the spending of a higher proportion of a state's gross domestic product (GDP) on such items as education, social security and health care, it is still obvious that civil and political rights also require a reasonably substantial element of public spending in order to ensure adequate protection. The right to a fair trial, for example, requires the maintenance of an effective justice system, the provision of publicly financed defenders, the payment of interpreters for individuals whose language is not that of the state in which they are being tried, the provision of adequate security systems to enable the courts to be open to the public and so on. While the costs associated with the implementation of such a system are probably not of the order of providing comprehensive social security for individuals within a state, none the less they will not be negligible and may impose a significant burden upon the treasuries of some states.

It should also be noted that the alleged division between civil and political rights on the one hand and economic, social and cultural rights on the other, is largely arbitrary and cannot be entirely sustained by reference to the two UN Covenants. Both Covenants, for example, deal with rights involving freedom of association and family matters which may be categorized as hybrid rights, since they exhibit characteristics of both classes of rights. If one takes a selection of provisions from the ICCPR, it is possible to discern that they are not the 'freedom from' rights, which are normally associated with that Covenant, but 'rights to', which are usually regarded as second-generation rights. Article 24(1), for example, requires state intervention in order to ensure that a child is accorded 'the right to such measures of protection as are required by his status as a minor, on the part of . . . the State'. Conversely, the ICESCR has a substantial number of provisions which would appear not to require state intervention for their protection. These are more of the 'freedom from' than the 'rights to' species and include the right to strike, the prohibition of the use of children in harmful work and so on.

The existence of these hybrid rights makes it apparent that any classification and hierarchical ranking of rights in international law is not easy and that, indeed, it may be questionable whether there is any real utility in attempting to do so. Putting rights into particular categories tells us little about the value of a right *qua* right; it simply provides fodder for moralizing or choosing a preferred political position in debates about human rights. This is not to deny that there may well be a certain utility in differentiating between the implementation measures attached to certain rights, since it permits determination of the varying degrees of state obligation with respect to all rights in general. Ultimately, however, whether rights are civil, political, economic, social or cultural in orientation makes little difference to their qualitative status as rights, but it may make a difference to the speed with which they are implemented by states.

Third-generation rights

The emergence of third-generation or solidarity rights is closely identified with the rise of Third World nationalism and the perception of developing states that the existing international order is loaded against them. It may also be seen as a claim by developing states for fairer treatment and for the construction of a world system that will facilitate distributive justice in the broadest Rawlsian sense. The basis for these claims is not, however, simply moral, but can be identified as having a legal basis in a number of existing international instruments.

The UN Charter itself places human rights in a pivotal position to assist in the creation of a peaceful international order and economic development. Article 1(2) of the Charter provides that one of the purposes of the UN is 'to develop friendly relations among nations based on the principle of equal rights and self-determination of people'. Article 1(3) further provides that another purpose of the organization is 'to achieve international cooperation in solving international problems of an economic, social, cultural or humanitarian character, and in promoting and encouraging respect for human rights and fundamental freedoms . . .'. These purposes are further reinforced by the substantive provisions of the Charter, particularly Articles 55 and 56, which clearly demonstrate that the creation of suitable international conditions is a prerequisite to the full social development of all individuals.

A number of other international instruments also support the view that the international community is obliged to establish a favourable global system for securing the better participation of developing states. The common Article 1 of the two International Covenants, for example, provide for both the political and economic right to self-determination. Article 1(2) provides:

All peoples may, for their own ends, freely dispose of their natural
wealth and resources without any prejudice to any obligations arising
out of international economic cooperation, based upon the principle of
mutual benefit, and international law. In no case may a people be
deprived of its own means of subsistence.

Article 2(1) of the ICESCR also provides that states parties are to 'take steps
individually and through international assistance and cooperation,
especially economic and technical, to the maximum of available resources,
with a view to achieving progressively the rights recognized in the present
Covenant by all available means'. These provisions, it is argued by some
jurists, provide a clear basis for a number of claimed solidarity rights.

What, then, are these third-generation or solidarity rights? Burns Weston
identifies at least six categories of solidarity rights:[33]

1 The right to economic, political, social and cultural self-determination.
2 The right to economic and social development.
3 The right to participate in and benefit from the Common Heritage of
   Mankind and other information and progress.
4 The right to peace.
5 The right to a healthy environment.
6 The right to humanitarian relief.

It is immediately apparent that these rights have two dominant characteristics: first, they are collective in nature and, second, they depend upon international cooperation for their achievement. It is also apparent that these
rights build upon and develop existing categories of rights and in that sense
they are, as Weston suggests, historically cumulative.

The fact that third-generation rights are collective in nature does not
automatically mean that they should be thought of as less than 'real' rights
for that reason alone. While traditional liberal conceptions of rights
emphasize their individualistic quality, it is none the less apparent that even
within the category of rights which might be described as civil and political,
certain rights are collective in nature. These include the right to exercise
one's religion in community with others, the right of peaceful assembly and
the right to freedom of association. The rights categorized as economic,
social and cultural, which are contained in a variety of international
instruments, are also largely collectivist in nature, but are nevertheless
recognized by the parties to those instruments as positive rights. The fact,
however, that the new generation of rights depends for its implementation
on international cooperation leads some authors to assert that they are little
more than aspirational claims which do not possess the binding quality
which is the hallmark of rights proper. Others, such as Alston, however,
argue that there is no need to resort to claiming new rights which may be

categorized as third generation, since by and large the problems which they seek to address are dealt with by existing instruments. Alston has also argued that claims for novel rights such as the 'right to tourism' obscures the need to properly develop existing rights, and more particularly, implementation programmes. He has also argued that there should be a system of procedures for granting a kind of approved origin mark to any 'new' rights proclaimed by the General Assembly.[34]

CONCLUSION

As the foregoing discussion amply demonstrates, there is considerable debate about what rights are, where they come from, what their content is, how they relate to each other and how new rights might be properly identified. The proposed solutions to these questions are as numerous as the questions themselves. It is, however, the identification of the questions which is of importance, since they act as signposts towards a coherent method of thinking about human rights. What is also apparent is that debate about human rights is not static, but is part of a continuing dialectic process through which progress in the field might be, and manifestly has been, made.

Having spent the last two chapters providing the historical and theoretical foundations of human rights, attention is now focused upon the rather more pragmatic issues of the system of international law by which human rights are protected and the precise nature of the international instruments which both contain in concrete form the rights to be protected and the institutions through which this is achieved.

FURTHER READING

Introductory

Cotterell, R., *The Politics of Jurisprudence* (London: Butterworth, 1989), esp. chs 4 and 5.

Rosenbaum, A.S., 'Introduction: The Editor's Perspective on Human Rights', in Rosenbaum, A.S., *The Philosophy of Human Rights* (Westport, CN: Greenwood, 1980), pp. 4–41.

Shestack, J.J., 'The Jurisprudence of Human Rights', in *Meron*, pp. 69–113.

Simmonds, N.E., *Central Issues in Jurisprudence* (London: Sweet and Maxwell, 1986).

Waldron, J., 'Introduction', in Waldron, J., *Theories of Rights* (Oxford: Oxford University Press, 1984), pp. 1–20. This book also contains useful essays by Dworkin and Hart.

General

Alston, P., 'Development and the Rule of Law: Prevention versus Cure as a Human Rights Strategy', in International Commission of Jurists, *Development and Human Rights and the Rule of Law* (Oxford: Pergamon Press, 1981), pp. 31–108.

Cranston, M., *What are Human Rights?* (London: Bodley Head, 1973).

Daniels, N., *Reading Rawls: Critical Studies on Rawls'* A Theory of Justice (Oxford: Blackwell, 1975).

D'Entreves, A.P., *Natural Law* (London: Hutchinson University Library, 1972).

Dworkin, R., *Taking Rights Seriously* (London: Duckworth, 1978).

Finnis, J., *Natural Law and Natural Rights* (Oxford: Oxford University Press, 1980).

Gavison, R. (ed.), *Issues in Contemporary Legal Philosophy: The Influence of H.L.A. Hart* (Oxford: Clarendon Press, 1987).

Hart, H.L.A., *Law, Liberty and Morality* (Oxford: Oxford University Press, 1962).

Hart, H.L.A., *The Concept of Law* (Oxford: Clarendon Press, 1971).

Humphrey, J.P., 'Political and Related Rights', in *Meron*, pp. 171–203.

Kartashkin, V., 'Economic, Social and Cultural Rights', in *Vasak*, Vol. 1, pp. 111–33.

Lillich, R.B., 'Civil Rights', in *Meron*, pp. 115–70.

McDougal, M.S., Laswell H.D. and Chen, L.-C., *Human Rights and World Public Order* (West Haven, CN: Yale University Press, 1980).

McLellan, D., *The Thought of Karl Marx* (London: Macmillan, 1971).

Nozick, R., *Anarchy, State and Utopia* (New York: Basic Books, 1974).

Paul, J. (ed.), *Reading Nozick: Essays on Anarchy, State and Utopia* (Totowa, NJ: Rowman and Littlefield, 1974).

Rawls, J., *A Theory of Justice* (Oxford: Clarendon Press, 1972).

Skubik, D.W., 'Two Models for a Rawlsian Theory of International Law and Justice' (1986) 14 *Denver Journal of International Law and Policy* 231–74.

Szabo, I., *Cultural Rights* (Leyden: Sijthoff, 1974).

Tay, A.E.-S., 'Marxism, Socialism and Human Rights', in Kamenka E. and Tay, A.E.-S. (eds), *Human Rights* (London: Edward Arnold, 1978), pp. 104–12.

Trubek, D.M., 'Economic, Social and Cultural Rights in the Third World: Human Rights Law and Human Needs Programs', in *Meron*, pp. 205–71.

van Boven, T., 'Distinguishing Criteria of Human Rights', in *Vasak*, Vol. 1, pp. 43–59.

Vasak, K. and Newman, F., 'Civil and Political Rights', in *Vasak*, Vol. 1, pp. 135–73.

Waldron, J., *Nonsense upon Stilts: Bentham, Burke and Marx on the Rights of Man* (London: Methuen, 1987).

Wolff, R.P., *Understanding Rawls* (Princeton, NJ: Princeton University Press, 1977).

HUMAN RIGHTS AND INTERNATIONAL LAW

INTRODUCTION

International human rights law is a branch of public international law, that is, the law which has been developed to regulate relations between entities having international personality, such as states, international organizations and possibly individuals.[1] In order to understand the functioning of the various institutions charged with the supervision of human rights, it is necessary to have a basic appreciation of the salient aspects of the international legal system. In the human rights context, international law possesses a dual quality, since it creates both the obstacles to effective human rights protection and provides the means for overcoming such obstacles.

SOVEREIGNTY

This has been described by Brownlie as 'the basic constitutional doctrine of the law of nations'.[2] It is also sometimes regarded as synonymous with the term 'independence'. In essence, it represents the totality of a state's rights in the conduct of its external relations and in the ordering of its internal affairs. This does not mean, however, that states are completely free to exercise their sovereignty or independence on both the external and internal planes, since they are subject to various limitations imposed on their activities by international law.

The main feature of the sovereign state is that it is entitled to exercise exclusive governmental control over its territory and persons therein subject to any contrary rules of international law. It is important to note, however, that states, being the pre-eminent subjects of the international legal system and the creators of law within that system, have the primary task of participating in the formulation of rules by which their conduct is limited.

One particular consequence of state sovereignty which should be noted here is that since all states are sovereign equals, a state is not bound to submit itself to international adjudication unless it has first signified its consent that it is prepared to do so. Thus, the popular notion that a state can be taken to the International Court of Justice (ICJ) or the European Court of Human Rights (ECHR) for an infraction of the law by another state almost at whim, does not reckon with the impediment of the necessity to procure the delinquent state's consent that it be required to submit to such a course of action.

NON-INTERVENTION

The rule against intervention is the necessary corollary to the doctrine of state sovereignty. If a state has the right to exclusive jurisdiction over its internal affairs, then it would clearly run counter to this to permit other states to intervene in those affairs. But what exactly is intervention? There has been considerable debate about this. Intervention clearly means something stronger than simple meddling or interference in the way the government of a state orders its internal affairs. It would, for example, have to be more than a critical comment on the pursuit of some domestic policy by another state. Lauterpacht, for instance, stated that in order to constitute intervention, an act must amount to a dictatorial interference in the affairs of another state without lawful justification.[3] A more precise way of putting this might be that it must amount to an attempt by one state to perform state-like functions within the territory of another state. This view is reinforced by the language of the 1970 UN General Assembly Declaration on Principles of International Law Concerning Friendly Relations and Cooperation Among States in Accordance with the Charter of the United Nations, which states:[4]

> No State or group of States has the right to intervene directly or indirectly, for any reason whatever in the internal or external affairs of any other State. Consequently, armed intervention and all other forms of interference or attempted threats against the personality of the State or against its political, economic or cultural elements, are in violation of international law.

This formula, although contained in a General Assembly resolution which is technically not legally binding, has been relied upon to such an extent since 1970 that it is now regarded as a precise statement of the rule of non-intervention in customary international law.[5]

The combined effect of the doctrine of sovereignty and the rule against intervention would seem to preclude the taking of any meaningful action by the international community in the context of human rights abuses by states. If persons within states are subject to the local laws, then surely other states cannot come to their aid if those local laws appear to violate human rights, since this would infringe the sovereignty of the other state and constitute an intervention in its internal affairs. This view would also seem to be confirmed by Article 2(7) of the UN Charter, which provides that the organization is prohibited from intervening in matters essentially within the domestic jurisdiction of any state.

As we have seen, however, sovereignty is not absolute, but is itself limited by international law. Thus, once human rights have been elevated to a matter of international rather than national concern, states may no longer plead that human rights are a matter essentially within their domestic jurisdiction. It then becomes legitimate for states to make diplomatic protest about human rights violations and to institute sanctions against delinquent states. Some commentators have even argued, as a variation of the nineteenth-century doctrine of humanitarian intervention, that military force may be used against states which violate human rights, since one of the purposes of the UN is to promote and protect such rights. Such an argument runs counter to the major thrust of the UN Charter, which is to facilitate peaceful settlement of disputes and to outlaw the use of force in international relations, and it has also been explicitly rejected by the ICJ in *Nicaragua v United States of America*.[6] It is not difficult to see that any modern notion of 'humanitarian intervention' would be bedevilled by the same subjectivity and potentially self-serving designs of militarily powerful nations as was the case in the nineteenth century.[7]

THE INDIVIDUAL IN INTERNATIONAL LAW

As we saw in Chapter 1, before 1945 the individual was simply an object of the law within the international legal system. Individuals were characterized in terms of nationality, that is, the bond which created legal ties between them and their state. States were therefore not generally constrained by international rules concerning the treatment of their own nationals, but they were, as we have also seen, obliged to treat the nationals of other states in accordance with certain international standards if they were not to violate international law. But even here, the individual was merely the vehicle by which an international claim originated: it was the state which suffered the wrong through the maltreatment of its national.[8] Within the international legal system, therefore, individuals were characterized as objects and not subjects of the law. Rules might be made for the benefit of individuals, but they did not confer substantive rights that could be enforced by procedural mechanisms which might be initiated by those same individuals. Exceptionally, however, the Permanent Court of International Justice recognized in the *Danzig Railway Officials Case*[9] that certain rights created by treaty could, where such an intention was expressly stated, permit individuals to enforce those rights in the domestic, or as they are known by international lawyers, municipal courts of the states parties. This, however, was a different matter to conferring procedural rights to individuals for enforcement of positive rights by an international tribunal.

In the post-Second World War era, the position of the individual has changed considerably. No longer are individuals seen as rightless objects of international law with no procedural capacity, rather, they are seen as the bearers of rights and correlative duties within the context of the international legal system. To some extent, therefore, they may be classified as limited subjects of international law. Although it had long been recognized that individuals were under a duty not to commit acts of piracy or war crimes under international law, it was not until the judgment of the International Military Tribunal at Nuremburg that it became fully established that international law placed direct obligations on individuals not to commit crimes against humanity, and that superior orders were no defence to the commission of those crimes. As the Nuremburg Tribunal itself observed: 'Crimes against international law are committed by men, not by abstract entities, and only by punishing individuals who commit such crimes can the provisions of international law be enforced.'[10]

Now under international law, individuals may be held personally responsible for war crimes, genocide, torture and furthering apartheid. It is irrelevant that these individuals were following orders by implementing the policies of the state. By making individuals responsible under international law for their acts demystifies the claims that such international crimes are simply an expression of the 'collective will' of the state.

THE LOCAL REMEDIES RULE

The post-Second World War period is also significant in the development of the individual as a partial subject of international law, not only because of the clear articulation of human rights in an increasing number of legally binding instruments, but also because of the conferring of procedural capacity upon individuals to enforce their rights before a variety of international tribunals. Individuals may now, under certain conditions, initiate proceedings before UN, European, American and African institutions.

While the methods by which individuals may bring applications, petitions or communications, as they are variously known, before the appropriate universal or regional institutions to secure remedies for the alleged violations of human rights will be considered in the appropriate places in subsequent chapters, it is worth remarking here that there is one factor which is common to all such procedures: individuals must in all cases attempt to secure redress of their grievances internally. This is known as the exhaustion of local remedies rule and is of fundamental importance in international human rights law.

The local remedies rule has its origin in the law of state responsibility or the law which governs the circumstances and consequences of a violation of international law by states. Violation of the law by a state may be direct as, for example, when a state breaches a treaty, or indirect, such as when a host state fails to afford appropriate redress to an alien who has been injured by the agents of the state. It is in the latter circumstances in which the local remedies rule operates. Until an individual attempts to exhaust all available local remedies, the state of which he or she is a national is prevented from taking up or espousing the claim at the international level. As noted above, when a state decides to espouse a claim, it does so for itself and not on behalf of the individual, since it is the state which is injured through the wrongful treatment of one of its nationals. In a sense, the identity of the individual is irrelevant, as long as he or she is a national of the claimant state.

In its traditional international law guise, the rule has both theoretical and pragmatic bases. First, it is designed to ensure respect for the sovereignty of other states by not casting premature aspersions on the ability of that state's institutions to afford appropriate redress to the individual in question. As the International Court of Justice said in the *Interhandel Case*:[11]

> . . . the rule requiring the exhaustion of domestic remedies as a condition of the presentation of an international claim is founded upon the principle that the responsible State must first have an opportunity to redress by its own means within the framework of its own domestic legal system the wrong alleged to be done to the individual.

Second, the rule is designed to prevent the proliferation of international claims by aggrieved individuals. Before a claim can be pursued on the international plane, therefore, individuals must attempt to exhaust all *effective* remedies whether they be judicial, arbitral or administrative. Remedies which are ineffective or illusory need not be pursued. Furthermore, if it is obvious that there are no remedies to exhaust or that the provision of a remedy is likely to be unduly tardy, the need to comply with the rule is obviated.

In its human rights guise, the local remedies rule operates in a slightly different context. Here, concern is not with the rule as a precondition to a state pursuing its own claim against another state on the international plane, rather it is with the rule as a precondition to the admissibility of a claim by an individual before an international tribunal against his or her *own* state. The rationale for the rule is, however, substantially the same: the state must be given the opportunity to redress by means of its own legal procedures any wrong claimed to have been done to the individual concerned before international mechanisms of protection are engaged. A review of all of the international instruments which provide a right of individual application will demonstrate that exhaustion of local remedies by the applicant is a necessary prerequisite to securing legal standing. What the instruments do not disclose, however, is the attitude taken by the various competent institutions to the interpretation of the provision. Each institution has developed its own approach on such issues as upon whom the obligation lies to prove exhaustion and, indeed, what constitutes exhaustion. Although these matters will be dealt with in detail later, it is appropriate to note here that the requirement to demonstrate the exhaustion of local remedies is much more rigorous in the European Convention system than it is under the universal and inter-American systems. Possibly the major reason for this is that while the social and political conditions in the Council of Europe states are generally conducive to the protection of human rights, in the Americas and certain parts of the world covered by the universal system they are not. The enforced disappearances of large numbers of individuals within Latin and Central American states in the recent past tends to demonstrate this point.

MAKING HUMAN RIGHTS LAW

As human rights law is a branch of international law, the means of its creation are identical to that of international law in general. Thus, in order to determine the origins of human rights law, it is necessary to examine the traditional sources of international law. Here, Article 38 of the Statute of the International Court of Justice is generally accepted as the authoritative statement of such sources. It provides:

> The Court, whose function is to decide in accordance with international law such disputes as are submitted to it, shall apply:
>
> (a) international conventions, whether general or particular, establishing rules expressly recognised by the contesting states;
> (b) international custom as evidence of a general practice accepted as law;

(c) the general principles of law recognised by civilised nations;
(d) subject to the provisions of Article 59 [which provides that the previous decisions of the ICJ have no binding force except in the decided case itself] judicial decisions and the teachings of the most highly qualified publicists of the various nations, as subsidiary means for the determination of rules of law.

Before briefly examining each of these sources of law, it is appropriate to point out that since the international legal system is a decentralized and horizontally integrated legal system having no central legislature, rules are created largely by agreement or emerge through the process of interaction between states. Thus, the law-creating processes of the international system have much in common with *gemeinschaft* societies, although it is doubtful whether the international system is able to demonstrate the cohesion of such societies.

Treaties

The principal method of making international law in the modern world is by way of convention or treaty. A treaty is essentially an agreement between two or more states establishing legally binding rules in a particular area. Article 2(1)(a) of the Vienna Convention on the Law of Treaties 1969[12] defines a treaty for the purposes of that Convention as 'an international agreement concluded between States in written form . . . whatever its particular designation'. While there is a requirement that a treaty be in writing, the definition makes it clear that it is the form of the instrument which is important, not its title. Treaties are given a variety of names – conventions, charters, covenants, protocols and so on – but their essential quality is that they are consensual agreements between two or more states under international law. A treaty between two states is generally known as a bilateral, contractual or particular treaty, whereas a treaty between more than two states is known as a multilateral or general treaty, since it seeks to establish rules for a significant number of states parties. Multilateral treaties are also sometimes referred to as international legislation, but this is misleading given the absence of any legislature in the international system. Such a designation simply seeks to convey the idea that a large number of states are party to a particular treaty and conform to the same rules. Treaties have one major advantage over other methods of international law creation: they are accessible and the rules established are more or less clear.

It will already be apparent that the greater part of international human rights law is contained in multilateral treaties. And while it is true that these treaties comprise an accurate index of the individual rights that are protected and the obligations that are assumed by the states which have become parties to the relevant instruments, there are also a number of other matters which must be considered. First, multilateral treaties often allow states to condition their obligations by the entry of reservations. A reservation is defined by Article 2(1)(d) of the Vienna Convention as 'a unilateral statement, however phrased or named, made by a State . . . whereby it purports to exclude or modify the legal effect of certain provisions of the treaty in their application to that state'. This does not mean that a state may modify its obligations at will. Treaties will often lay down the precise extent to which reservations may be entered. Article 75 of the American Convention on Human Rights provides, for example, that: 'This Convention shall be subject to reservations only in conformity with the provisions of the Vienna Convention on the Law of Treaties . . .'. Even where a treaty is silent on the question of reservations, both the Vienna Convention and customary international law demand that a reservation must, if it is to be lawful, be compatible with the object and purpose of the Convention. Thus, for example, an attempt to derogate by way of a reservation from a right in a human rights treaty which is expressed to be absolutely non-derogable, would clearly not be compatible with the object and purpose of such a treaty.[13]

Second, the notion of derogations from certain treaty provisions is one of the distinctive hallmarks of human rights instruments. In nearly all instruments states may, by unilateral declaration, derogate from their obligations under certain clearly prescribed conditions. Such derogations are not only rigorously defined within the particular instruments, but they are also subject to supervision by the institution charged with responsibility for protecting the rights in question. Certain rights, such as freedom from torture, are classified as non-derogable under any circumstances.[14]

A third point to note is that whereas the fundamental breach of a treaty will usually result in the termination of obligations under such an instrument, this is not so in the case of human rights treaties. Article 60(5) of the Vienna Convention provides that the rules concerning termination 'do not apply to provisions relating to the protection of the human person contained in treaties of a humanitarian character'. The rationale behind this rule is clear – if a state could simply discharge its obligations under a human rights treaty by a single violation, it would defeat the continuing protective purpose of such instruments.

Another distinctive feature of human rights treaties, as opposed to other treaties in international law, are provisions which permit denunciation. Here states may withdraw unilaterally from their obligations under a treaty, as long as the procedure established by the treaty is complied with. While most human rights treaties provide for the possibility of denunciation, they also provide that states parties will by responsible for any violations of the treaty committed prior to the denunciation. In so doing, the treaties ensure that states are not able to avoid their legal responsibilities simply by choosing to opt out of the instrument when its obligations become burdensome.

Finally, some mention should be made here of the methods by which treaties may be interpreted. The traditional rule is the literal rule, which is expressed in Article 31 of the Vienna Convention. This provides that 'a treaty shall be interpreted in good faith in accordance with the ordinary meaning to be given to the terms of the treaty in their context and in the light of its object and purpose'. Where, however, a literal interpretation of the instrument leaves the meaning ambiguous or obscure or leads to a result which is manifestly absurd or unreasonable, recourse may be had to supplementary material such as the preparatory works or the drafting history of the instrument.[15] Institutions which are charged with interpreting human rights instruments seldom adopt such a straightforward approach and frequently apply other techniques of interpretation either separately or in conjunction with those enumerated above. Here, the process combines with a number of other factors. Of particular importance is the role of the institution, the context within which it functions, the legal, political and social traditions from which the members of the institution are drawn and their perceptions of their own and their institutions' functions. Thus, for example, the European Court of Human Rights has a predominantly teleological or end-orientated approach to interpretation of the Convention. This does not mean that the Court does not apply the standard techniques when occasion demands, simply that they have a conception of their role as that of maximizing the protective function of the Convention. Critics of the teleological approach, including some past judges of the Court, have argued that it leads to judicial legislation.[16] This is undoubtedly true, since the Court has, on occasion, read rights into the Convention which are not automatically evident at first sight. However, since judges, as a category of decision maker, enjoy a broadly legislative function anyway, the only objection to the teleological approach might be the extent of their creativity.

Having pointed out some of the distinctive features of human rights treaties, it might legitimately be questioned whether or not they are qualitatively different to other kinds of treaties. Certainly there is a school of thought which argues that they are, and this school of thought is supported by statements of both the European and Inter-American Courts of Human Rights. The former, for example, declared in *Austria v Italy*[17] that the obligations undertaken by the parties to the Convention were 'essentially of an objective character being designed rather to protect the fundamental rights of individual human beings from infringements of any of the . . . Parties than to create subjective and reciprocal rights for the . . . Parties themselves'. The Court went on in the same case to say that the purpose of the parties to the Convention 'was not to concede to each other reciprocal

rights and obligations in pursuance of their individual national interests but
. . . to establish a common public order of the free democracies of Europe
with the object of safeguarding their common heritage of political traditions,
ideals, freedoms and the rule of law'. In similar vein, the Inter-American
Court of Human Rights declared in *Effect of Reservations* that 'the object
and purpose of the [American Convention on Human Rights] is not the
exchange of reciprocal rights between a limited number of States, but the
protection of the human rights of all individual human beings within the
Americas, irrespective of their nationality'.[18] Thus, as far as the regional
systems are concerned, the competent institutions appear to be claiming that
their constituent instruments provide the basis for supra-national legal
systems or systems of law superior to national law which can be invoked
by individuals within those states.

Custom

Although the majority of international transactions are now conducted
through the medium of treaties, custom still remains an important source
of law. Indeed, some authors would argue that custom is qualitatively more
important than treaties, since it is custom which forms the bed-rock of the
international legal system. Even treaties derive their binding force from a
prior customary rule which states that treaties are binding and must be
observed in good faith. Furthermore, while states must signify their consent
before they can be legally bound by treaties, this is not a necessary prerequisite to a state becoming bound by a customary rule of international law.

What then is custom? The description in Article 38(1)(b) gives a hint of
its nature. There it is described as a 'general practice accepted as law', which
indicates that it is created by patterns of interaction between states accompanied by an underlying sense of legal obligation. Thus, custom is tradi-
tionally said to consist of two elements: a material element and a
'psychological' element. The material element is evidenced by what is called
state practice or the conduct of states. Such conduct may be evidenced by
a variety of factors which impact on a state's international relations. These
might include statements by the competent organs of state in a variety of
domestic and international fora such as the UN, domestic legislation, the
decisions of local courts and so on. Conduct alone, however, is not sufficient
for the creation of a binding rule of customary international law; it must
also be accompanied by a sense on the part of the relevant state organ that
the conduct is underpinned by a sense of legal obligation. This is usually
known by its Latin name, *opinio iuris sive necessitatis* or, more commonly,
simply *opinio iuris*. There has been much debate about whether *opinio iuris*
needs to be proved in any given case or whether it can be inferred from a

consistent pattern of conduct. The ICJ, however, still insists that it needs to be proved.[19]

There are a multitude of theoretical difficulties associated with proving the existence of customary international law. Many of these arise because customary law is more frequently associated with the development of law within small, tightly integrated human communities, usually known by German sociologist Tönnies' term *gemeinschaft*, rather than the development of law between complex corporate entities such as the modern state. Rather than talking of custom in international law, perhaps it would be more appropriate to coin a new term representing the realities of the situation. Nevertheless, 'custom' remains a potent source of contemporary international law. A state which seeks to rely on custom must prove the rule by demonstrating the existence of state practice which is definite, extensive, which has been extant for an appropriate period of time, and which is supported by the necessary *opinio iuris*.

Two matters which are associated with custom should be mentioned here: the legal status of UN General Assembly resolutions and the concept of *ius cogens*.

United Nations General Assembly resolutions

The legal status of resolutions passed by the General Assembly, the plenary organ of the UN, is frequently misunderstood. 'Housekeeping' resolutions dealing with General Assembly internal organization are legally binding on Assembly members, but resolutions covering other matters are not legally binding *per se*.[20] None the less, the latter may have certain legal effects depending on their subject matter and manner of drafting. Here a distinction should be made between resolutions dealing with issues of a general nature, such as those urging member states to promote research into environmental degradation, and those of a 'legal' nature which seek to set down the member states' understanding of the appropriate rules of law in a particular area. The precise legal effect of such latter resolutions is controversial and open to a number of characterizations. Some states such as the USA deny that General Assembly resolutions have any normative effect, and assert that they are simply statements of political aspiration. Others argue that resolutions may, in appropriate circumstances, be authoritative interpretations of the UN Charter by the General Assembly. Thus, for example, the Universal Declaration might be regarded as an authoritative interpretation of the meaning of 'human rights' in a number of Charter provisions.[21] Still further, some states and commentators argue that resolutions, where they deal with broadly 'legal' issues, are a clear statement of state practice and can therefore be regarded as a material element in the formation of customary international law. This indeed has been the position adopted by the ICJ in *Nicaragua v United States*, where a majority of the Court held that the Declaration of Principles Resolution and Resolution 3314(XXIX) 1974, the Consensus Definition of Aggression Resolution, both evidenced the international community's understanding of the appropriate customary rules in both areas. Thus, while General Assembly resolutions in no way amount to a form of international legislation, they are nevertheless capable of providing the constituent elements for the formation of customary international law.

Ius cogens

If one examines Article 38 of the ICJ statute closely, it is apparent that the sources of law appear to be hierarchical, that is, they tend to move from the more specific to the less specific. The hierarchy is not, however, immutable. Although under normal circumstances a treaty setting down precise rules of law would override customary international law, there are occasions when the customary rule is of such fundamental importance to the structure of the international system that it cannot be overridden by any contrary agreement. An example of this would be a treaty between two states to commit an act of genocide, a treaty which international law could not possibly sanction. In many ways, this is analogous to a contract for illegal or immoral purposes under domestic contract law which domestic courts would not enforce on the grounds that it would be contrary to public policy to do so. Indeed, *ius cogens* is occasionally called the international doctrine of public policy or, to use the more precise French term, *ordre public*. Article 53 of the Vienna Convention on the Law of Treaties provides a definition of *ius cogens* and indicates the effects of a treaty which is concluded in violation of such a norm. It states:

> A treaty is void if, at the time of its conclusion, its conflicts with a peremptory norm of general international law [*ius cogens*] . . . [A] peremptory norm of general international law is a norm accepted and recognized by the international community of States as a whole from which no derogation is permitted and which can be modified only by a subsequent norm of general international law having the same character.

When this particular provision was drafted by the International Law Commission, the latter gave as examples of *ius cogens* norms the rule prohibiting the use of force in international law, and criminal acts under international law such as the commission of acts of slavery, genocide and piracy. Certain members of the Commission also voiced their opinion that the conclusion of treaties which envisaged human rights violations might also be contrary to *ius cogens*. The view that human rights have a *ius cogens* character also finds some support from the ICJ in the *Genocide Convention Case*[22] and the *Barcelona Traction Case*[23] and from the Inter-American Court of Human Rights in a number of cases.[24] On a general scale, however, it seems clear that treaties which violate rules having a general humanitarian character run the risk of being classified as a breach of *ius cogens*, with the corresponding sanction that such treaties may be declared void by a competent tribunal.

General principles of law

The third potential source of international law is 'the general principles of international law recognized by civilized nations'. This was included in the ICJ's statute in order to deal with the circumstances where the Court might not be able to decide a dispute because of the absence of any treaty or customary law dealing with the issue before it. This situation is generally known as *non-liquet*, a situation which is more likely to arise in the decentralized international legal system than it is in hierarchically integrated domestic legal systems. As with the other sources of international law, there is some dispute over exactly what the phrase means. Some writers take the view that it simply means procedural rules of national or municipal law which have been incorporated into international law, whereas others, such as Waldock,[25] claim that the phrase means that the ICJ is competent to draw from a well of immutable principles of law which are common to all major legal systems. Certainly, the latter view would render this particular source of law more dynamic and better suited to the judicial decision-making process than would the former. It also means that when faced with a *non-liquet*, both the ICJ and other bodies charged with interpreting and applying international law would be able to apply a form of juridical calculus by which they might determine whether or not certain principles possess the necessary qualifications for application at the international level.

Subsidiary sources of law

It is clear from the phraseology employed in Article 38 that judicial decisions and the opinions of writers are little more than subsidiary means for the determination of law. None the less, these can be particularly useful, particularly in determining the existence of customary international law. An example of this 'source' of law in action is a Californian court decision in the case of *Filartiga v Pena Irala*,[26] in which the judge, after reviewing the appropriate international instruments, declared that the commission of acts of torture was contrary to the customary international law, and as such could be applied by the court in pursuance of the US Alien Tort Claims Statute.

DOMESTIC APPLICATION OF INTERNATIONAL HUMAN RIGHTS NORMS

The creation of international human rights law is, as we have seen, primarily a function of the international legal system, and the supervision of human rights is largely undertaken by international institutions created for this purpose. It should be noted, however, that domestic tribunals may also have a substantial role to play in the application of international human rights law. Much depends here upon the nature of the domestic constitution under which the local courts function. Some constitutions permit their domestic courts to apply norms of international law origin directly, whereas others require international law to be transformed into domestic law by legislation before the domestic courts can take note of it. Constitutions in which international law can be applied directly are known as monist constitutions, since national and international law are regarded as a single integrated system, whereas constitutions in which transformation of international legal obligations into domestic law is required are called dualist constitutions, since domestic and international law are perceived as two separate and distinct systems. The main feature of monist constitutions is that there is usually some form of direct democratic or legislative control over the transaction of international relations by the executive branch of government, while there is an absence of such direct control in dualist constitutions.

Of course, the monist–dualist dichotomy is seldom as simple in actuality as the definition would suggest. Even in dualist constitutions, a distinction is often drawn between international rules of customary law origin and those of treaty-based provenance. Moreover, states with dualist constitutions will often differ in their approach to the question of whether international rules of direct application or municipal laws take precedence in the event of conflict between them. Some constitutions, such as that of Germany, give clear precedence to both customary and treaty rules over domestic federal law, whereas others, such as that of the USA, will only give precedence to particular categories of treaty. The main point to note from this discussion, however, is that some states' constitutions facilitate the direct application by the municipal courts of international human rights law, whereas others do not. In each and every case, the constitution of the state in question must be considered, as indeed must the approach of the municipal courts to the interpretation of the constitution.

Examples of two constitutions might serve to demonstrate the points made above. First, the British constitution, which is often regarded as the archetypal monist constitution. This is perhaps something of a misnomer, since the English courts have always applied rules of customary international law origin where there is no legislative provision to the contrary.[27] However, the appellation 'monist' clearly indicates that, in general, rules emanating from the competent institutions of the European Community excepted, Parliamentary legislation takes precedence over rules of international origin. Thus, as far as treaty-based obligations are concerned, they will have no domestic application in the UK unless they have been transformed into domestic law by legislation. In the absence of statutory transformation, rules contained in an international treaty have no legal force in the UK.[28] The English courts have adopted certain canons of interpretation to deal with the relationship between statute and treaty, such as, where possible a statute will be construed to give effect to the UK's international legal obligations,[29] but in all cases rules emanating from a treaty will give way to a contrary intention expressed by Parliament in its legislation.[30] In the human rights field, the English courts have consistently refused to allow provisions of the European Convention on Human Rights to take precedence over domestic law, even when the latter has clearly been contrary to the rules of the Convention.[31]

This position has recently been reaffirmed by the House of Lords in *Brind and Others v Secretary of State for the Home Department*.[32] This case concerned certain directives issued by the Home Secretary prohibiting the direct broadcasting of statements made by representatives of proscribed organizations in Northern Ireland. The measures adopted by the Home Secretary were in the form of delegated legislation which the appellants complained violated Article 10 of the European Convention (freedom of expression). The appellants further contended that the Home Secretary did not take the Convention into account when he made the directives and that he had been wrong in law in not doing so. This argument was rejected by the House of Lords, which held that although the UK courts would interpret domestic legislation in a manner which conformed to the Convention where this was possible, there was no corresponding presumption of domestic law that the courts would review the exercise of an administrative discretion on the basis that such a discretion had to be exercised in conformity with the Convention. In responding to a submission that Article 10 of the Convention was a relevant factor to which the Home Secretary ought to have had regard when exercising his discretion in making the directives, Lord Ackner said: 'If the Secretary of State was obliged to have proper regard to the Convention, ie to conform with art 10, this inevitably would result in incorporating the Convention into English domestic law by the back door.'[33] It is apparent, therefore, that the UK constitution, as a form of dualist constitution, is not particularly well suited to giving effect to treaty-based international human rights obligations.

An appropriate example of how a broadly monist constitution gives effect to human rights of international law provenance is the constitution of the USA. Article II(2) of the US Constitution provides that the President has the power to make treaties 'by and with the advice and consent of the Senate . . . provided two thirds of the Senators present concur'. Article 4 of the constitution further provides that treaties made in such a way 'shall be the supreme law of the land; and the judges in every state shall be bound thereby'. The treaty can therefore be an important legislative device in the USA, but unlike the UK, the treaty-making power of the executive, in the person of the US President, is subject to clear and direct democratic control. Moreover, treaties which are adopted in conformity with the constitution may produce rules which are directly enforceable by individuals before the municipal courts. These are known as self-executing treaties. However, in order for a treaty to be self-executing, it must have a precise quality which is capable of giving rise to individual rights. As the Supreme Court of California pointed out in *Sei Fujii v California*,[34] the human rights provisions contained in the UN Charter lacked 'the mandatory quality and definiteness which would indicate an intent to create justiciable rights in private persons immediately upon ratification'. If such qualities are in existence in a particular treaty, then the potential for individual protection in the USA would be considerable. Unfortunately, the USA has steadfastly refused to participate in any international human rights instruments, claiming that its domestic system for human rights protection is more than adequate.

FURTHER READING

The following list represents only a fraction of the number of public international law texts available. Only those which are appropriate for introductory purposes have been included here.

Akehurst, M., *A Modern Introduction to International Law* (London: Allen and Unwin, 6th edn, 1987), esp. chs 3, 4, 7 and 10.

Brownlie, I., *Principles of Public International Law* (Oxford: Clarendon Press, 4th edn, 1990), esp. chs I, II, III, XIII, XX, XXIII and XXV.

Ott, D.H., *Public International Law in the Modern World* (London: Pitman, 1987), esp. chs 2, 3, 4, 10 and 11.

Shaw, M.N., *International Law* (Cambridge: Grotius, 3rd edn, 1991), esp. chs 3, 4, 5, 6, 13 and 15.

Starke, J.G., *Introduction to International Law* (London: Butterworth, 10th edn, 1989), esp. chs 2, 3, 4, 10 and 16.

Wallace, R.M.M., *International Law* (London: Sweet and Maxwell, 2nd edn 1992), esp. chs 2, 3, 4, 9 and 10.

THE UNITED NATIONS AND HUMAN RIGHTS

INTRODUCTION

Although the institutions and procedures established under the auspices of the UN are sometimes referred to as the universal system for promoting respect for and observance of human rights, the term is somewhat misleading, for although there are a number of supervisory systems established under the umbrella of the UN, none of them enjoy participation by all the states of the world. None the less, the term is convenient for distinguishing those instruments and systems of potentially global application from those which are simply regional in their operation.

There is a bewildering variety of institutions and supervisory systems established within the framework of the UN. Some of the institutions and systems are discrete as they have been created by treaties which, while adopted within a UN context, nevertheless apply to specific fields and possess autonomous implementation machinery. An example of this is the ICCPR, which stands as a separate treaty, has an autonomous supervisory body in the Human Rights Committee, but which was drafted and adopted within the UN Organization. Other institutions and supervisory mechanisms have been developed under the Charter either because their creation was mandated by that instrument or because they have evolved under the Charter on an *ad hoc* basis.

THE UN CHARTER

The UN Charter, which is a multilateral treaty and therefore creates legally binding obligations for all UN member states, contains a number of provisions concerning human rights. The Preamble states the determination of the peoples of the UN 'to reaffirm faith in fundamental human rights, in the dignity and worth of the human person, in the equal rights of men and women and of nations large and small', and Article 1(3) includes as one of the purposes of the UN 'promoting and encouraging respect for human rights and for fundamental freedoms for all without distinction as to race, sex, language, or religion'. Moreover, under Chapter XI of the Charter, which is entitled 'International Economic and Social Cooperation', Article 55 provides that the UN 'shall promote . . . universal respect for, and observance of, human rights and fundamental freedoms for all without distinction as to race, sex, language, or religion'. This is further buttressed by Article 56 by which all members 'pledge themselves to take joint and separate action . . . for the achievement of the purposes set forth in Article 56'.

As might be expected, there is a diversity of views on the nature of the human rights obligations imposed on members under the Charter. Some jurists argue that the requirement to 'promote' respect for and observance of human rights is simply hortatory and incapable of being defined with the precision necessary to impose legal obligations on members. They further argue that the obligation to *promote* human rights in Article 55 does not necessarily infer an obligation to *protect* human rights. In addition to the imprecision of the Charter obligations, they draw attention to the fact that there is no indication of which human rights are protectable nor any mechanisms for their actual protection.

Other commentators adopt sharply divergent views to those expressed above. They argue that Article 56 imposes a clear obligation on all members to take positive action to achieve respect for and observance of human rights. Thus a state which denies human rights cannot be said to be taking action to respect or observe human rights. The criticism that there is no index of protectable rights is also not insuperable. If one takes a natural law standpoint similar to that of Judge Tanaka in the *South West Africa Cases*,[1] the reaffirmation of faith in human rights in the Preamble would seem to assume that such rights enjoyed an existence both prior, and superior, to the positive law of the Charter. Such an argument, however, raises the difficulties associated with the natural law school in general; namely, which rights should be included in any potential list? Happily, this particular problem can be overcome by the pragmatic expedient of examining the Universal Declaration, which might be said at the very least to contain an index of what is meant by the term 'human rights' in the Charter. This is a view which will be addressed in further detail below.

These theoretical arguments have in many ways been overtaken by the actual practice of the UN. Within debates of the various organs of the organization it is now generally agreed that the human rights provisions of the Charter create legally binding obligations on members to protect human rights. It is also apparent that early objections by some states to the competence of the UN and other members to comment on human rights violations based on Article 2(7), the non-intervention provision of the Charter discussed above, are now seldom raised.

THE UNIVERSAL DECLARATION OF HUMAN RIGHTS[2]

It will be recalled that the Universal Declaration was adopted to remedy the failure of the UN members to agree on the incorporation of a catalogue of protectable human rights within the body of the Charter itself. The Declaration was adopted as a simple resolution of the General Assembly and therefore it was not legally binding in a technical sense. Furthermore, although there were no votes against the Declaration, Byelorussia, Czechoslovakia, Poland, Saudi Arabia, South Africa, Ukraine, the Soviet Union and Yugoslavia abstained. While the abstentions were primarily based on conflicting ideologies to those expressed in the individualistic categories of rights contained in the Declaration, both South Africa and Saudi Arabia also expressed anxiety that the Declaration might eventually be used to interpret the Charter. This was a particularly prescient assumption.

What, however, is the legal status of the Declaration today? There are a number of potential answers to this question, each of ascending normative importance. First, it is possible that the Declaration has simply retained its status as a non-binding resolution. However, because of subsequent developments in both UN and state practice, which will be addressed below, this minimalist position is unlikely to be correct. Second, it is arguable that the Declaration is an authoritative interpretation of the Charter by one of its competent organs: the General Assembly. This is a highly plausible argument since the Preamble to the Declaration makes it clear by its language that it was adopted to give effect to the obligations contained in Articles 55 and 56 of the Charter. Third, it may be posited that the Declaration is now part of the general principles of law recognized by civilized nations.[3] This proposition would be difficult to gainsay, since nearly every written constitution in the modern world contains a commitment to the protection of human rights and a list of the rights to be protected. Fourth, and this is an argument that a significant number of authors find persuasive, it may be said that after forty years, the Declaration has become part of customary international law.[4] A great deal of evidence is available to support this view. There is a large amount of state practice which indicates that the Declaration is the benchmark against which human rights standards within states is measured. This state practice includes resolutions of international organizations and institutions, ministerial statements, participation in a variety of human rights treaties, domestic legislation and so on. It is also apparent that the necessary *opinio iuris* is available, since the bulk of state practice is supported by a belief that human rights obligations, as enunciated in the Declaration, are legally binding. Perhaps the most telling point, however, is that the UN Commission on Human Rights (a body whose functions will be discussed later) is empowered to employ the Declaration in determining whether there have been widespread and gross violations of human rights in states under whose human rights record is being scrutinized by it. A small number of commentators would also advance beyond the basic proposition that the Declaration represents customary international law and state that it now possesses the characteristics of *ius cogens*,[5] that is peremptory norms from which no derogation is permitted. As Lillich points out,[6] while certain of the rights contained in the Declaration, such as the prohibition of slavery, do possess a *ius cogens* character, this is not true of all the provisions, especially those which permit derogations under specified conditions.

If the argument that the Declaration represents customary international law were to be accepted, this would mean that all states are legally bound to afford to individuals within their jurisdiction the human rights set forth.[7] While this might be a happy theoretical position to adopt, it does pose a number of practical problems. First, the rights in the Declaration include a mixture of first-, second-and third-generation rights. All of these rights are formulated as precise and immediate commands to states. Article 3, for example, simply states: 'Everyone has the right to life, liberty and security of person.' As a general statement of a fundamental right, this formulation is unobjectionable. What, however, is the content of such a right? Does it preclude abortion, euthanasia or the death penalty following conviction and sentencing by competent courts? Is it absolute? Can exceptions to the right be invoked in times of emergency? None of these questions are answered by the Declaration.

The second problem is intimately linked to the first. There is no obvious institution which is specifically empowered to interpret or apply the Declaration. Notwithstanding these objections, it seems that both a number of UN organs, international bodies and domestic courts have been sufficiently convinced that some of the rights stated in the Declaration, as exiguous as those statements might be, are endowed with sufficient precision for application in a general sense. Nor should the political and moral potency of the Declaration be neglected. It has not only formed the basis for the drafting of two international covenants and three regional human rights treaties, but it has also been the paradigm for the drafting of the human rights provisions of over 25 domestic constitutions. The Declaration is also very often perceived by states, international institutions, NGOs and individuals alike as the touchstone of human rights; indeed, John Humphrey has referred to the Declaration as the 'Magna Carta of Mankind'.[8]

UN ORGANS AND HUMAN RIGHTS

There are a plethora of UN organs and institutions which have a greater or lesser degree of responsibility within the general field of human rights. This section will simply attempt to paint a broad picture of the organs and their various competences.

The General Assembly

The General Assembly is the plenary organ of the UN and has broad competence under the Charter to consider questions concerning human rights. These questions may be dealt with by the General Assembly of its own motion or they may be referred to it by one of its seven Main Committees.[9] Under Article 13(1)(b), the major obligations of the General Assembly with respect to human rights are to initiate studies and to make recommendations for the purpose of assisting in the realization of fundamental rights and freedoms for all. A number of studies has been commissioned by the General Assembly, and it has made a large number of recommendations on human rights issues. Such recommendations are not legally binding on members,[10] but when taken in conjunction with the obligations contained in Articles 55 and 56 of the Charter, they assume considerable legal significance, and may even be said to create legal obligations where they are stated with sufficient precision. Perhaps the most important contribution of the General Assembly to human rights has been the significant number of international instruments adopted by it in the field following reference from the Commission on Human Rights and ECOSOC. These have included the Universal Declaration, the two International Covenants and a number of UN conventions in specialized human rights fields, the most important of which are considered below. It should also be noted that under these UN-sponsored human rights conventions, the General Assembly is the ultimate destination of all reports made on questions of implementation and on any special procedures to be followed.

The General Assembly has also established, in accordance with its powers under Article 22, a number of subsidiary organs to deal with human rights issues. Some of these have enjoyed substantial longevity, whereas others have simply been of a short-term *ad hoc* nature. Among the more notable of these organs have been the UN Children's Emergency Fund (UNICEF), the Office of the High Commissioner for Refugees, the Decolonization Committee and the Special Committee on Apartheid. Each of these has had a significant impact upon the matters within its purview.

The Economic and Social Council (ECOSOC)

The Economic and Social Council is a political organ of the UN consisting of 54 members. In the field of human rights, it is charged with making recommendations for the purpose of promoting respect for and observance of human rights and fundamental freedoms and, as we have seen above, submitting draft conventions to the General Assembly. ECOSOC is also the organ which is responsible for receiving reports from, co-ordinating activities with and concluding agreements with UN specialized agencies having certain human rights competences such as ILO, Unesco and WHO. ECOSOC is also responsible for co-ordinating activities with NGOs.

Much of ECOSOC's work is undertaken by commissions which it is required to establish under Article 68. The most important of these commissions, as far as human rights are concerned, are the Commission on Human Rights, the Sub-Commission on Prevention of Discrimination and Protection of Minorities and the Commission on the Status of Women.

The Commission on Human Rights (CHR)

The establishment of a CHR was recommended in 1945 by the Preparatory Commission of the UN in order to deal with the outstanding human rights issues which could not be resolved during the original drafting of the Charter. At its first session in 1946, ECOSOC established the CHR. The Commission, which has grown in size over the years, now consists of 43 persons chosen from the UN members who serve the CHR in their capacity as governmental representatives.[11] In this sense, the CHR may be regarded as a political body, and it is therefore not surprising that the debates within the Commission frequently take on an overtly political dimension. The CHR's terms of reference were established by ECOSOC in 1946. These were that the Commission should submit proposals, recommendations and reports to ECOSOC regarding:[12]

(a) An international bill of rights;
(b) International declarations or conventions on civil liberties, the status of women, freedom of information and similar matters;
(c) The protection of minorities;
(d) The prevention of discrimination on grounds of race, sex, language or religion;
(e) Any other matter concerning human rights not covered by items (a), (b), (c), and (d).

In 1979, ECOSOC added the following term to the above: 'The Commission shall assist [ECOSOC] in the coordination of activities concerning human rights in the [UN] system.'[13] This addition clearly reflected the transition by the UN to an integrated and holistic approach to human rights matters as reflected in a 1977 General Assembly resolution on the subject.[14]

Despite the fact that the Commission is clearly a political organ of the UN, it has in fact undertaken much useful work in developing the human rights agenda within the organization. In pursuit of its mandate, the CHR has not only drafted the Universal Declaration and the two Covenants, but also a large number of standard setting declarations and a large number of conventions concerned with human rights.

The Sub-Commission on Prevention of Discrimination and Protection of Minorities

The Sub-Commission, which was established by ECOSOC in 1947, works closely with the CHR. It consists of 26 members who are independent and who serve in their own individual capacities. The terms of reference under which the Sub-Commission functions are:

(a) to undertake studies particularly in the light of the Universal Declaration . . . and to make recommendations to the [CHR] concerning the prevention of discrimination of any kind relating to human rights and fundamental freedoms and the protection of racial, national, religious and linguistic minorities; and
(b) to perform any other functions which may be entrusted to it by [ECOSOC] or the [CHR].

While the Sub-Commission has performed much valuable work on the question of the protection of minorities, has drafted a number of instruments relevant to human rights standards and has encouraged bodies such as Unesco and the ILO to undertake studies appropriate to their spheres of competence, it is, perhaps, the protective function of the Sub-Commission in conjunction with the CHR and ECOSOC which deserves particular mention.

ECOSOC procedures

When the CHR was established, it received a large number of complaints from individuals alleging human rights violations. The Commission, however, decided that it had no power to take any action in respect of individual human rights violations notified to it. This position was confirmed by ECOSOC Resolution 75(5) in 1947 and reconfirmed in 1959 by Resolution 728(XXVIII). This latter resolution, however, provided for the production of a confidential list of petitions which, although providing useful information, could not be used as a basis for action by the CHR. In 1967, however, ECOSOC changed its position. Under Resolution 1235(XLII), ECOSOC authorized the CHR to:

> . . . examine information relevant to gross violations of human rights and fundamental freedoms *as exemplified by the policy of apartheid* as practised in the Republic of South Africa . . . and to racial discrimination . . . contained in the communications listed . . . pursuant to . . . Resolution 728F(XXVIII) . . . [emphasis added].

Pursuant to this, the CHR was empowered to make thorough studies of situations which revealed a 'consistent pattern of violations of human rights, *as exemplified by the policy of apartheid . . . and racial discrimination . . .* and report with recommendations thereon to [ECOSOC]'. While it is clear that Resolution 1235 appeared to have as its main concern discriminatory policies, the prime example of which was *apartheid*, it is also apparent that, by implication, the CHR was to examine other gross abuses of human rights. The expansion of the CHR's mandate to examine all gross violations became clear in Resolution 1503(XLVIII).

Resolution 1503 empowers the Sub-Commission to establish a five-member working group whose task is to screen all incoming communications. Communications which 'appear to reveal a consistent pattern of gross and reliably attested violations of human rights and fundamental freedoms' are considered by the Sub-Commission together with any replies from the relevant governments. A confidential report is then sent to the CHR. On the basis of this report, the CHR may decide whether to act, and if so, whether it should undertake a 'thorough study' in accordance with Resolution 1235 or whether to make the matter a subject of study by an *ad hoc* committee. If it decides on the latter course of action, not only must the consent of the relevant government be obtained, but it must also ensure that individuals involved in making the complaints have 'direct and reliable knowledge of the violations', have exhausted all local remedies and that the communication is not being considered under another form of international procedure, such as a communication to the Human Rights Committee under the ICCPR First Optional Protocol or any of the regional systems. A number of *ad hoc* committees have been brought into being and have functioned with varying degrees of success. The more important cases in which such committees have operated have been Equatorial Guinea, Chile, Namibia and the Israeli occupied West Bank.

Two points should be noted about the Resolution 1503 procedure. First, it is engaged solely by the accretion of individual communications which reveal 'a consistent pattern of gross and reliably attested violations'. The procedure is not one which results in individual remedies, but simply draws the attention of the UN to states in which the human rights situation is already dire. Second, the procedure is entirely confidential until the CHR decides to make recommendations to ECOSOC. All the CHR's meetings are held in private, and no documents are released until ECOSOC is informed of the CHR's recommendations. None the less, once ECOSOC has received a thorough study under the procedure, it – and the General Assembly to whom it is responsible – may discuss the reports and adopt resolutions calling upon states to comply with their human rights obligations under the Charter.

The 1503 procedure has a number of obvious defects. First, confidentiality ensures that states are not put 'in the dock'. While this might facilitate state cooperation in proceedings, it denies the UN institutions the power and leverage which accompany adverse publicity. Second, the accumulation of evidence by which gross violations are identified means that the institutions are always working 'in arrears' and may be unable to exercise their influence until it is too late. Third, the procedure is open to abuse by states who may be able to place political pressure on the various institutions involved. To some extent, these criticisms have been circumvented by the CHR by relying on a new thematic rather than a country-orientated approach to violations. Under Resolution 2325, the CHR has undertaken studies on enforced disappearances, summary executions, mass expulsions and torture. The Resolution 2325 procedure can be engaged more quickly than the 1503 procedure, since it does not depend on an accumulation of events. Furthermore, it does not suffer the defects of excessive confidentiality, since investigations and discussions take place in public. This helps focus public attention directly and immediately upon some of the worst violations and reduces the opportunity for political interference.

Commission on the Status of Women

This institution was established contemporaneously with the CHR. It consists of 32 members whose function is two-fold: first, to prepare recommendations and reports to ECOSOC on promoting women's rights in political, economic, civil, social and educational fields and, second, to make recommendations to ECOSOC on urgent problems requiring immediate attention in the field of women's rights with the object of implementing the principle that men and women shall have equal rights and to develop proposals to give effect to such recommendations. The Commission has enjoyed most of its success in the area of setting international standards and has played a major role in the drafting of the Declaration on the Status of Women 1967, the Convention on the Elimination of All Forms of Discrimination Against Women 1979, and the Convention on the Political Rights of Women 1953. Unlike the CHR, the Commission on the Status of Women declared itself competent to receive communications from women alleging violation of their rights from an early stage. Much of this procedure has, however, been overtaken by other, more specific procedures. Nevertheless, it is the organ which is charged with receiving reports from the Committee on the Elimination of Discrimination Against Women under the 1979 Convention.

Unesco

Unesco is a specialized agency of the UN which has its headquarters in Paris. Under Article 1 of its constitution, Unesco's purpose is:

> . . . to contribute to peace and security by promoting collaboration among the nations through education, science and culture in order to further universal respect for justice, for the rule of law and for the human rights and fundamental freedoms which are affirmed for the peoples of the world, without distinction of race, sex, language or religion.

As Saba observes,[15] Unesco has always seen education, the natural and social sciences, and the defence of human rights as 'indissolubly linked to the safeguarding of peace'. In pursuing these objectives, Unesco sets standards for the guidance of governments in matters within its competence (and there has been a great deal of dispute as to exactly what lies within Unesco's competence in recent years) and the drafting of relevant treaties. The organization's Convention and Recommendation against Discrimination in Education is perhaps the clearest example of its dual competence in the human rights and educational fields.

Initially, Unesco took the view that, like the CHR, it had no competence to receive communications from individuals alleging violations of human rights. However, in 1978, it adopted a procedure for considering communications.[16] Like all international procedures, it is predicated upon the exhaustion of local remedies and must disclose violations of human rights which lie within the fields of Unesco's competence. Communications alleging human rights violations are considered by the Committee on Conventions and Recommendations, whose primary function is to secure a friendly solution 'designed to advance the promotion of human rights falling within Unesco's fields of competence'.[17] The procedure is both flexible and confidential. Such confidentiality extends to the Committee's report which is made to Unesco's Executive Board at the end of each session. The Committee's report not only identifies individual and specific cases of human rights violation, but also questions of 'massive, systematic or flagrant violations'.[18] Such questions may be discussed by Unesco's plenary body, the General Conference.[19]

International Labour Organization (ILO)

The ILO which, as we saw in Chapter 1, was founded in 1919 by the Treaty of Versailles, was transformed into a specialized agency of the UN under an agreement with ECOSOC. The objectives of the ILO were restated in the Declaration of Philadelphia 1944, which became part of the Organization's constitution. Its major concerns are those of social justice and social welfare through the promotion of social welfare rights. The ILO has sponsored over 150 international instruments which provide the basis for labour and social welfare law in a significant number of states.

Supervision under the ILO Constitution takes a number of forms. First, under Article 22, member states are bound to submit periodic reports on the measures which they have taken to give effect to the ILO conventions to which they are party. These are examined by a Committee of Experts consisting of 18 independent persons. The Committee may address requests to members for further information and include its observations on the reports and other information gathered through its requests to the annual session of the International Labour Conference, where they are considered by a Conference Committee on the Application of Conventions and Recommendations.

Second, under Article 24, if a representation is made to the International Labour Office by an association of industrial employers or workers that a member has failed to observe the standards set down in any ILO convention to which it is a party, the Governing Body of ILO may communicate this to the affected state, which may respond to the allegation. The Governing Body then delegates the hearing of the case to a committee which reports back with recommendations. The Governing Body can determine whether or not to accept the recommendations and, if a breach is found to have occurred, can publish the original representation.

Third, there exists an inter-state complaints procedure under Article 25 whereby one member state may complain that another has not been observing an ILO convention to which both states are party. The Governing Body may refer such a complaint to a Commission of Inquiry, which investigates the complaint and then reports to the Director-General of the ILO who communicates the report to both parties and to the Governing Body which is obliged to publish the report. Each of the member states must within three months inform the Director-General whether it accepts the report of the Commission and indicate whether, as it is entitled to do, it proposes to refer the complaint to the ICJ for adjudication. The first complaint made under this procedure was a complaint by Ghana against Portugal alleging a violation of the Convention on the Abolition of Forced Labour 1957 in Portugal's African colonies.

Fourth, there is a special procedure concerning complaints about the violation of the right to freedom of association. In 1951, a Committee on Freedom of Association consisting of nine members was established to examine complaints in this area. After examining such complaints, the Committee submits a detailed report to the Governing Body with proposed conclusions and recommendations to be made to the state concerned. In order to deal with serious and politically sensitive cases, a Fact Finding and Conciliation Commission may undertake investigations. The Commission has, however, not been used often, simply because the area in which it operates is too politically sensitive for most of the states concerned.

Other organs

The picture of competent bodies in the field of human rights under the UN Charter would be incomplete without mention of the Security Council and the ICJ. While the Security Council has no specific responsibility for human rights, it has, on a number of occasions, made pronouncements on such matters acting under Chapter VI (disputes and situations likely to endanger maintenance of international peace and security) and Chapter VII (enforcement action) of the Charter. In particular, the Council has considered, *inter alia*, the question of *apartheid* in South Africa and the treatment of Palestinians in the Israeli occupied territories.

The ICJ, which is the principal judicial organ of the UN, clearly has competence to determine questions concerning or involving human rights under its contentious and advisory jurisdictions. This it has done in a number of cases. In the *Corfu Channel Case*,[20] for example, the Court ruled that Albania ought to have had regard to 'elementary considerations of humanity' in warning British warships of the presence of mines in the Corfu Channel which was under its jurisdiction. Questions of political asylum were raised in the *Asylum Case*,[21] issues of apartheid were discussed in a series of cases concerning Namibia or South West Africa,[22] and in the *Genocide Convention Case*[23] the question of genocide as *ius cogens* was touched upon obliquely.

THE INTERNATIONAL COVENANTS ON CIVIL AND POLITICAL RIGHTS (ICCPR) AND ECONOMIC, SOCIAL AND CULTURAL RIGHTS (ICESCR)

At the time the Universal Declaration was drafted, it was recognized that it would not create legally binding obligations but would simply 'set a standard of achievement for all peoples and all nations'. It was therefore agreed that the CHR should undertake the drafting of a legally binding human rights instrument modelled on the Declaration. Although the proposed treaty was to include both economic, social and cultural rights, and civil and political rights within it, problems arose concerning the appropriate methods of implementation for the different categories of rights. It was therefore proposed that two instruments be adopted, one dealing with economic, social and cultural rights and the other dealing with civil and political rights. Two covenants were therefore presented to, and adopted by, the General Assembly in 1966. They did not, however, enter into force until 1976, when the required number of 35 states had ratified them.

Unlike the Universal Declaration, the Covenants create legally binding obligations for the more than 80 states which are now party to them. Thus it is no longer possible, if it ever were, for these states to argue that protection of human rights is simply a matter within their domestic jurisdiction. Furthermore, while the obligations in respect of the protected rights are contained in treaties which normally give rise to reciprocal rights and duties between the parties, these human rights treaties are more in the nature of unilateral legally binding commitments by the states parties to be supervised by international institutions.

Only two provisions are common to both Covenants. The first of these provisions is Article 1, which provides for the self-determination of peoples, that is the right of a cognate group to determine their own political destiny. The common Article 1 also provides for the right of peoples to dispose of their own natural resources and wealth, and not to be deprived of their own means of subsistence. These are clearly third-generation rights, and the rationale for their inclusion in a separate part which lies at the head of both Covenants would seem to be that if a people is subject to alien domination and subjugation and is thus denied the right of self-determination, all other rights become meaningless. The second common provision is the rule prohibiting discrimination on grounds of race, colour, sex, language, religion, political or other opinion, national or social origin, property, birth or other status.[24] This broad prohibition of discrimination, which is a constituent central element of the rule of law, is clearly a necessary prerequisite to the proper enjoyment of all other substantive rights.

ICCPR

Whereas the Universal Declaration was drafted in the form of peremptory commands to states to protect certain rights, the ICCPR was drafted to meet the practical problems of protecting human rights. Thus, the Covenant elaborates the protectable rights more specifically and indicates with a reasonable degree of clarity the limitations which may be imposed upon the exercise of certain of the rights in given situations. Furthermore, the rights contained in the ICCPR do not correspond exactly with those in the Universal Declaration.[25] Included in the Covenant is the obligation on states to allow individuals who are members of an ethnic, religious or linguistic minority 'to enjoy their own culture, to profess and practice their own religion or to use their own language' in community with other members of the group (Article 27). Also included is the right to be free from imprisonment for failure to fulfil a contractual obligation (Article 11); the right of all prisoners to be treated with humanity and respect for the inherent dignity of the human person (Article 10(1)); and the right of special protection for children (Article 24). Excluded from the Covenant is the right to asylum, the right to a nationality and, largely as a result of ideological differences between the East and West blocs, the right to own property.

Although a number of rights protected by the Covenant may not be derogated from under any circumstances,[26] Article 4 provides that the remaining rights may be derogated from 'in time of public emergency that threatens the life of the nation' as long as such derogations are proportionate to the threat to be met and non-discriminatory. Derogations must also be communicated immediately to the other states parties through the intermediary of the UN Secretary-General, together with the reasons for which they were taken. Certain rights are also subject to what Professor Rosalyn Higgins calls 'claw-back' provisions, which permit limitations to be imposed on rights for the protection of public safety, order, health or morals or the fundamental rights and freedoms of others.[27] While this gives a margin of discretion to states, a discretion which possesses the potential for abuse, it is nevertheless counterbalanced by Article 5(1) which introduces an element of proportionality. This provides that the rights in question should not be limited to 'a greater extent than is provided for in the present Covenant'.

Under Article 2(1) of the Covenant, states parties are obligated to 'respect and to ensure to all individuals within its territory and subject to its jurisdiction the rights recognised in the present Covenant' without discrimination of any kind. Where such rights are not already respected and ensured within a state's jurisdiction, it is required by Article 2(2) to introduce the necessary legislative or other measures in order to give them effect. It should be noted that these obligations are absolute and immediate. It should also be noted that the rights are to be accorded to all individuals, whatever their nationality, who find themselves under the jurisdiction of the state. This not only includes the state's territorial jurisdiction, but also the state's personal jurisdiction over its own nationals who might be located overseas.[28]

The Human Rights Committee (HRC)

The body which is charged with supervising the states parties' obligations under the ICCPR is the Human Rights Committee (HRC), which sits either at the UN Headquarters in New York or at Geneva, which is the location of the Human Rights Division of the UN Secretariat.[29] The HRC is a creature of the Covenant[30] and is composed of 18 members who must be nationals of the parties to the Covenant and 'persons of high moral character and recognised competence in the field of human rights'.[31] Although members need not necessarily be lawyers, Article 28(2) provides that 'consideration should be given to the usefulness of the participation of some persons having legal experience'. In fact, the Committee has, since its inception, been staffed entirely by lawyers, usually of some distinction. Committee members are elected for a four-year period by secret ballot from nominations by the states parties.[32] No two persons elected may be from the same state, and each serves in their individual capacity, not as state nominees.[33] The personal nature of the duties performed by Committee members is reinforced by the requirement that each must, on appointment, make a solemn declaration that they will perform their functions impartially and conscientiously.[34] Committee members, therefore, owe their allegiance not to their nominating state but to the Committee alone. Committee members are also paid by the UN, thus eradicating one particular major source of potential government interference. In order to ensure the widest representation of legal cultures, Article 31(2) requires that in the election of the Committee, consideration must be given to equitable geographical distribution and to the representation of different forms of civilization and of legal systems. Given the diverse origins of the Committee members, it might be thought that political and ideological differences would have come to the fore in its proceedings and discussions. As Nowak has indicated, however, the Committee works on the basis of consensus, and although the inevitable disputes over legal doctrine and methodology have occurred, there has been little political confrontation.[35]

Supervisory mechanisms

The ICCPR and its First Optional Protocol provide one mandatory and two optional mechanisms to enable the HRC to supervise the states parties' obligations. The mandatory means of supervision is a system of periodic reports under Article 40(1), under which states parties undertake 'to submit reports on the measures they have adopted which give effect to the rights recognised [in the ICCPR] and on the progress made in the enjoyment of those rights'. The Committee has now received a large number of state reports, and has developed guidelines both for their presentation and for its follow-up procedure. Briefly, the practice is this.

Within a year of becoming party to the ICCPR and at periods specified thereafter by the Committee,[36] states parties are required to submit their reports to the Committee via the UN Secretary-General. The Committee then studies the reports and draws up a list of questions requesting the state to clarify or elaborate various parts of the report. A representative of the state is then required by the Committee's Rules of Procedure to make a final presentation to the HRC in person in order to deal with the general and specific issues raised by it. The HRC then forwards its comments to the state party which is entitled to submit observations on those comments. The main advantage of this procedure is that it enables the Committee to engage in a 'constructive dialogue' with the state party, but it also allows it to investigate the state parties' submissions by probing weaknesses, resolving ambiguities and illuminating obfuscation in reports. Copies of reports and comments are forwarded to ECOSOC for consideration, and the HRC itself is also required to submit an annual report to the General Assembly on its activities. This enables the Committee to isolate particular problems and difficulties identified in any of the country reports studied. It also makes public any matters of concern, and opens the way for possible debate in the General Assembly in respect of certain states. While this procedure might appear anodyne, the Committee has on occasion raised the ire of certain states of whose reports it has been critical. The report by Iran in 1982, the Committee's comments and the Iranian response bear witness to the sensitivity of certain states put under the spotlight of this procedure.[37]

The second, optional, method of supervision is an inter-state complaint procedure under Articles 41 and 42. This procedure requires acceptance by individual state parties, and it can be utilized only against other states which have also agreed to submit themselves to the procedure. Assuming the condition of reciprocity applies, the procedure operates as follows. A state which considers that another state is violating the Covenant brings that fact to the attention of the state party concerned. That state party must respond to the allegation within a period of three months. If, within six months, the states cannot resolve their differences, either state may bring the matter to the attention of the HRC. The Committee must decide whether all local remedies have been exhausted before considering the case in closed session. It may then offer its good offices with a view to achieving a friendly settlement between the states. If a friendly settlement is reached, the HRC must make a report on its terms, but if no friendly settlement is forthcoming, the Committee may appoint an *ad hoc* Conciliation Commission consisting of five members acceptable to the disputing states. The Conciliation Commission has the power to make recommendations after hearing the submissions of the parties, but these recommendations are not binding on the parties. In all cases, however, the matter will be referred to the General Assembly via ECOSOC by the Committee in its annual report.

The inter-state complaint procedure is most unsatisfactory. Like inter-state procedures in the regional conventions, it is subject to potential abuse since it may be used for overtly political purposes. The emphasis on friendly settlement of the dispute also renders the procedure unsuitable for protecting individuals, the violation of whose rights may have prompted the original complaint. Since there is no adjudicative power either in the Committee or the *ad hoc* Conciliation Commission, objective determination of the issues is not possible. Finally, the absence of binding decisions does not ensure the rectification of breaches. It is perhaps not surprising that this procedure has never been invoked.

The third, optional, method of supervision and enforcement of the rights contained in the Covenant is the individual communication procedure contained in the First Optional Protocol. This has undoubtedly been the most significant development in the universal system of human rights protection, since it allows individuals direct access to an impartial international body, the Human Rights Committee, which has the power to determine whether or not a state has violated the rights protected under the Covenant. Given the significance of the communication system under the Protocol, it is appropriate to consider it in some detail.

Admissibility and procedure under the individual application system

The conditions for admissibility of a communication and the procedures to be followed in dealing with it are contained in the Protocol, the Committee's Rules of Procedure and the jurisprudence of the Committee. Under Article 1, a state party to the Protocol must recognize the competence of the Committee to receive communications from individuals subject to its jurisdiction who claim to be victims of a violation of any of the rights protected by the Covenant. In order to declare a communication admissible, a number of conditions must be met:

1 The communication must be from an *individual* who claims to be a *victim* (Articles 1 and 2(1) Protocol).

2 The communication must not be under consideration under any other procedure of international investigation or settlement (Article 5(1)(a) Protocol).
3 The victim must show that he or she has exhausted all *local remedies* (Articles 2 and 5(2)(b) Protocol).[38]
4 The communication must not be *anonymous, abusive of the right of submission* or *incompatible with the provisions of the Covenant* (Article 3 Protocol).
5 The communication must not be manifestly ill-founded. This requirement is derived from the jurisprudence of the HRC.

There are no definitions of the admissibility criteria contained in the Protocol, but the Committee has developed these through its own jurisprudence. Similarly, there is no time limit for making a communication, but this does not appear to have concerned the Committee to date. Although the Covenant is silent on its temporal scope, the Committee has decided that it cannot take account of violations which took place before the entry into force of the Covenant for the state in question, unless those violations have a continuing character or have produced continuing effects.[39]

Procedure of the Committee

Unless a case is rejected by the HRC, all communications must be brought to the attention of the affected state party.[40] Rule 91(2) of the HRC's Rules of Procedure further provides that no communication may be ruled admissible until the state party concerned has been given opportunity to comment upon it. Once a communication is declared admissible, however, the state party must within six months furnish the Committee with written explanations or statements clarifying the matter and any remedial action which it has taken.[41]

The major characteristics of the Committee's procedure both at the admissibility and merits stages is that it is written and confidential with all HRC meetings being held *in camera*.[42] Once the Committee has examined the written evidence before it, it makes its views known to the state and the individual concerned in accordance with Article 5(4) of the Protocol. Although Article 6 envisages that the Committee should simply include a summary of its activities under the Protocol in its annual report to ECOSOC and the General Assembly of the UN, it has, in fact, published complete versions of its procedures and views in the case of every communication.

1. Communications from 'individuals' who are 'victims'
This requirement raises a number of issues of interpretation:

(a) Must the author of the communication always be the victim of the alleged violation?

If this requirement were taken too literally, it could lead to a denial of the right of communication in certain circumstances. A person arbitrarily arrested and held incommunicado, for example, would not, on a strict reading of the Protocol, be able to avail him or herself of the right of communication. To permit the right of third-party communication on their behalf would not only accord with the overall object and purpose of the Protocol, it would also ensure that states were not able to evade their obligations under the Covenant by 'disappearing' victims.

This view is supported by Rule 90 of the HRC's Rules of Procedure, which states that a communication should 'normally be submitted by the individual himself or by his representative'[43] and that it may be submitted on behalf of an alleged victim 'when it appears that he is unable to submit [it] himself'. The Committee has had no difficulty in accepting third-party communications in a number of cases. In *Massera v Uruguay*,[44] for example, the Committee accepted a communication from a woman alleging the arbitrary detention and torture of her husband, mother and stepfather in Uruguay saying: 'The author of the communication was justified by reason of close family connexion in acting on behalf of the . . . alleged victims' (para. 5.a).

This formula, which has been reiterated in subsequent cases, does not mean that the third-party representative of an alleged victim need necessarily be a family member, but it is clear that the author will need to prove an interest in the proceedings. It will be easy to show an interest where the representative has the express consent of the alleged victim, as in the case of a lawyer representing him or her,[45] but rather more difficult where consent is to be implied. A friend would probably have legal standing, but a member or representative of an organization of which the alleged victim was also a member would probably not.[46]

It is certainly clear that there is no possibility of a class action, or *actio popularis* as it is known, under the Protocol. In the *Mauritian Women Case*,[47] a number of women complained about the discriminatory effect of a 1977 immigration law which affected the residence rights of the foreign husbands of Mauritian women, but not the foreign wives of Mauritian men. Many of the women complainants refused to be named in the communication, and it was brought on their behalf by some women who were willing to identify themselves. The Committee declared:

> A person can only claim to be a victim if he or she is actually affected. It is a matter of degree how concretely this requirement should be taken. However, no individual can in the abstract, by way of an *actio popularis*, challenge a law or practice that has not already been

concretely applied to the detriment of that individual, it must in any event be applicable in such a way that the victim's risk of being affected is more than a theoretical possibility (para. 9.2).

The Committee decided in this case that there were a number of women who were not affected by the law, whereas others were affected even though the law had not been applied to their husbands. The Committee's reasoning here was that the mere existence of the law created uncertainty as regards the residence status for the foreign husbands of these women.

(b) Must the victim be an individual?
The majority of rights contained in the Covenant are of an individual nature, but Article 1 is a third-generation or group right which guarantees the right to self-determination. The question, therefore, that arises in this connection is whether a group may submit a communication complaining of a denial of this right. It is clear that the HRC has set its face against this, ruling in a number of cases[48] that, on the wording of the Protocol, communications may only be accepted from individuals and not from groups. It would seem, therefore, that the right of self-determination is an unenforceable right under the individual complaints procedure of the Protocol.

(c) Must the author be within the territorial jurisdiction of the state against which the complaint is made either (i) at the time the violation occurred or (ii) at the time of submitting the communication?
Before considering these questions, it should be noted that under Article 2 of the Covenant and Article 1 of the Protocol individuals may complain of a violation of their rights by a state even though they are not citizens of that state, as long as they are subject to its territorial jurisdiction.

(i) There have been a number of communications from individuals who have been victims of violations by the states of which they are citizens, although they have been resident in the territory of another state at the time. Examples of this have ranged from kidnap of victims by the agents of their own state acting in violation of the sovereignty of the state of residence at the more serious end of the spectrum, to refusal to renew a passport at the less serious end. In an early communication involving the latter,[49] Uruguay refused to renew the passport of one of its citizens who was resident in Mexico. Uruguay claimed that the HRC lacked competence to consider the communication lodged by the complainant, since he was not within its territorial jurisdiction. The Committee, however, took a wider view, indicating that the issue of a passport was a matter which was entirely subject to the jurisdiction of the state, since it alone was competent to determine whether or not it should be issued.[50]

This personal nature of the jurisdiction referred to in Article 1 of the

Protocol and Article 2 of the Covenant was stated unequivocally by the HRC in *Celiberti v Uruguay*.[51] Here a Uruguayan citizen had been abducted by agents and returned to Uruguay where he was arbitrarily imprisoned and tortured. Uruguay, contesting the admissibility of the communication, complained that the act had not taken place within Uruguay's territorial jurisdiction. The Committee rejected this contention, stating that the reference in Article 1 of the Protocol was 'not to the place where the violation occurred, but rather to the relationship between the individual and the State in relation to the rights set forth in Covenant wherever they occurred'.[52]

(ii) There is no requirement in the Protocol that the author of a communication must be within the state complained of at the time it is submitted. A glance at the origin of many communications indicates that they have been made by refugees or the relatives of victims who are themselves refugees. A number of the early communications involving Uruguayan citizens were authored in Mexico, to which they had fled from Uruguay's right-wing military regime. The HRC has accepted such communications without question since the Protocol demands no residential requirement.

2. *Overlapping systems of international investigation*

Under Article 5(2)(a) of the Protocol, a communication may not be considered by the HRC if it contains the same matter as that which is being examined under another procedure of international investigation. This is to prevent proliferation of proceedings among the various human rights institutions now in existence. In most cases, the Committee will have no difficulty in determining whether or not this requirement has been fulfilled. In a number of cases, applications have been submitted to the American Commission on Human Rights or the European Commission on Human Rights and this has led to inadmissibility before the HRC. In some circumstances, however, the Committee has shown a willingness to be flexible. In *Millan Sequeira v Uruguay*,[53] for example, a two-line reference to the author of a complaint in a list of over one hundred named persons who had been arbitrarily detained by Uruguayan authorities which had been submitted by a third party, was not held to breach the non-duplication requirement. Further, in *Celiberti*,[54] the Committee held that it was not precluded from examining a communication by reason of the subsequent opening of a case before the American Commission by a third party who was unrelated to the alleged victim. The HRC showed itself to be even more creative in *Grille Motta*,[55] where it found that a communication which was before the American Commission could not contain the same matter as that currently before it, since the communication before the American Commission concerned events which had taken place prior to the entry into force of the Covenant for the state in question.

Difficulties of another kind have arisen for the Committee in cases where the subject matter is the same as that which has been considered previously by either the Inter-American or European Commissions and rejected. Here the question has been whether the HRC is competent to reconsider such a case? In the communications which have come before it, the Committee has decided that it possesses the competence to consider cases *anew*, but has declined to do so because of particular reservations to the Protocol made by the state parties in question. These reservations precluded it from considering cases which had already been considered by the European Commission.[56] The HRC's views in these cases have, however, turned very much on the precise language used by the reserving states. On a different but related issue, it should be noted that the Committee itself will not generally review its own admissibility decisions, but if new information comes to light which might have affected its decision, Rule 93(4) of its Rules of Procedure give it the power to do so.[57]

3. Exhaustion of local remedies

As indicated in Chapter 3, all human rights instruments require complainants to exhaust local remedies before international proceedings may be initiated. The Protocol is no exception to this requirement, and although Article 5(2)(b) does not expressly state a complainant must exhaust local remedies 'in accordance with the accepted rules of international law', the HRC has implied this condition. Thus, remedies which are unduly tardy or which do not provide redress for violations, will not be a bar to admissibility on this ground.

Since the HRC's procedure is written, problems arise in determining whether a complainant has exhausted all possible local remedies. It would seem that a state which wished to contest admissibility need only allege that a complainant has not taken the necessary steps to secure redress in domestic institutions. The Committee has not, however, been prepared to accept such general statements as conclusive and has placed the burden of demonstrating that domestic remedies have not been exhausted upon the state. It is not enough for the state to respond simply by referring to general categories of remedies; it must indicate in detail the specific remedies available to the complainant in his or her particular case. This was made clear in *Lanza v Uruguay*,[58] where the HRC said:

> Specific responses and pertinent evidence (including copies of the relevant decisions of the courts and findings of any investigations which have taken place into the validity of the complaints made) in reply to the contentions of the author (para. 15).

This device has been remarkably effective in securing fuller cooperation with the Committee by states.

4. Further conditions for admissibility

Article 3 provides that the Committee shall consider inadmissible any communication which is anonymous or which it considers to be abusive of the right of submission of communications or to be incompatible with the provisions of the Covenant. There have been few communications which have been declared inadmissible on the grounds of abuse of process or incompatibility, but one such is *Taylor v Canada*.[59] Here Taylor complained of an infringement of his right to hold opinions freely and freedom of expression under Article 19 of the Covenant in that he had been prohibited from transmitting recorded messages over his telephone warning of the dangers of international Jewry. The Committee found that this communication was clearly incompatible with the provisions of the Covenant, since states parties were under an obligation by virtue of Article 20(2) to prohibit any advocacy of national, religious or racial hatred.

It is apparent that the HRC has also extended its competence to declare inadmissible communications which are not well-founded. This has been developed by the Committee's jurisprudence, for there is no such explicit admissibility requirement in the Protocol. In adopting this course of action, the Committee has of necessity been obliged to examine the merits of a case as a preliminary to determining its admissibility. While this again is not specifically provided for in the Protocol, it is a necessary consequence of its decision to extend its competence and mirrors closely the practice of other human rights bodies. There are a number of examples of the Committee's approach in recent communications. In *J.D.B. v The Netherlands*,[60] a communication by an unemployed television repair man that Dutch law discriminated against him by punishing him for failing to take employment not related to his trade was held inadmissible on the grounds that no facts had been stated which substantiated the applicant's claim that he had suffered a violation of any of the rights guaranteed by the Covenant. Perhaps a clearer case of rejection on the grounds that a communication was manifestly ill-founded was that of *L.T.K. v Finland*,[61] in which the author of the communication alleged that the failure of the Finnish authorities to recognize him as a conscientious objector, thus leading to his criminal prosecution and imprisonment, violated Articles 18 and 19 of the Covenant. In finding the claim inadmissible, the Committee simply declared that 'the Covenant does not recognise the right to conscientious objection'.[62]

Assessing evidence

Under Article 5(1), the Committee is required to consider communications 'in the light of all written information made available to it by the individual and by the state party concerned'. It is apparent, however, that the written procedure has a number of defects. One major problem is the lack of appropriate mechanisms to enforce state party compliance with the obligation to provide information under Article 4(2) of the Protocol. The effective operation of the procedure depends entirely on the cooperation of states and the provision of detailed information by them. Unfortunately, a number of states have been less than cooperative with the HRC, and in its early days, Uruguay, in the words of Tomuschat, 'demonstrated a deplorable lack of cooperation'.[63] This included the failure to respond to the Committee's requests for information, tardiness in the provision of information and the supply of very general information. In order to deal with this lack of cooperation, the HRC developed a number of practices. In the case of non-provision of requested information, the HRC in the first communication with which it dealt, *Massera v Uruguay*,[64] simply compiled its final views by accepting all the evidence that had been supplied by the complainant. The HRC took the view that by non-compliance Uruguay had not contradicted the evidence which the Committee had in its possession.

Where there has been a lack of information or information of a general nature has been supplied by the state, the HRC has proceeded rather more cautiously. It has pointed out that Article 4(2) implies that states are under an obligation to provide the most detailed information possible within the given time limit of six months.[65] It has further been argued that it is only natural to place the burden of disproving the alleged victim's allegations upon the state, since it is the state which generally has access to the appropriate information. Thus, in *Santullo*,[66] the Committee decided to accept as proved, '. . . facts which have either been essentially confirmed by the State Party or are unrepudiated or uncontested except for denials of a general character offering no particular information or explanation' (para. 7).[67] The Committee therefore phrased its final views in a negative way and indicated that it 'could not find that there has *not* been any violation [of the Covenant]'.[68]

The HRC has also decided that where specific allegations are made against particular government agents by the author of a communication, those allegations should be fully investigated by the state concerned. This was made clear in *Grille Motta v Uruguay*,[69] where the complainant alleged that he had been subjected to electric shocks, *submarino* (immersion of a victim's head in foul water until the victim is close to drowning), insertion of bottles and the barrels of automatic weapons into his anus, standing hooded and handcuffed with a piece of wood thrust into his mouth for several days and nights by identifiable individuals. Uruguay dismissed these allegations as 'a figment of the imagination of the author'.[70] The HRC found, however, that since the allegations had not been duly investigated by Uruguay, they remained unrefuted. The state should have demonstrated that it had investigated the allegations in accordance with its domestic law and brought those found to be responsible to justice.[71]

Given the limitations inherent in the written procedure, it is arguable that the Committee has been remarkably successful in overcoming the difficulties involved. Its placing the burden of proof on the state to disprove the allegations made by the author of a communication once again finds justification in law and policy. Under the Protocol, which is an optional instrument to which states have freely acceded, states parties are required to comply with certain obligations. The requirement that they provide written explanations or statements clarifying alleged violations of the Covenant to the HRC under Article 4(2) requires cooperation in the utmost good faith. Failure to do so would deprive the Protocol of its efficacy if states were able to avoid their obligations by recalcitrance or tardiness.

While it may be argued that the Committee's procedure favours a complainant, it has none the less maintained that its procedures conform to the standards of natural justice as far as allegedly delinquent states are concerned. In *Quinteros v Uruguay*,[72] it said:

In accordance with its mandate under article 5(1) of the . . . Protocol, the Committee has considered the communication in the light of the information made available to it by the author of the communication and by the State party concerned. In this connection the Committee has adhered strictly to the principle *audiatur et altera pars* and has given the State party every opportunity to furnish information to refute the evidence presented by the author (para. 10.8).

Legal status of final views

The HRC concludes its process of considering a communication by presenting its 'views', usually referred to as 'final views', on the allegations made. This has been criticized as the weakest part of the procedure, since it is argued that the views are not legally binding. Tomuschat[73] has argued that even so, the views have immense authority which 'proceeds from their inner qualities of impartiality, objectiveness and soberness'.[74] While it may be open to a state to challenge the Committee's final views and to refuse to implement them, this would expose it to the criticism that it had disregarded the authoritative pronouncement of an independent tribunal to whose jurisdiction it had freely submitted. Further, there can be no doubt that the HRC's views are authoritative. It alone is given exclusive competence to rule on compliance or breach of the Covenant under the Protocol, and although its views may not be binding in a strict legal sense, a finding of breach is to all intents and purposes a potent declaration of international delinquency.

As the views of the HRC are not legally binding, and in the absence of any provision for remedies in either the Covenant or the Protocol, it would not appear to be open to the Committee to decide that a state must grant compensation to the victim of a violation of any of the rights contained in the ICCPR. However, in line with its practice of declaring breaches, the HRC has also declared that delinquent states are required to grant remedies to victims in order to comply with their obligations under the Covenant. In general, the HRC uses the following formula:

> The Committee . . . is of the view that the State Party is under an obligation to provide the victim with effective remedies, including compensation, for the violations which he has suffered and to take steps to ensure that similar violations do not occur in the future.

While a state is not under a legal duty to comply with the views of the Committee, it is under an obligation to comply with the obligations established by the Covenant. Again, it would be difficult to argue that the ruling of the Committee here is not authoritative.

The practice of the Human Rights Committee under the ICCPR First Optional Protocol is one of the most important developments in international human rights law in the twentieth century. For the first time, it gives individuals direct access to an impartial international tribunal which is competent to rule on the question of violations of a large number of civil and political rights. The way in which the Committee has gone about its task of forging an effective mechanism of near universal application is also to be commended and bears witness to the calibre of the people who serve on it. As some states, particularly Uruguay and Zaire, have discovered to their cost, the HRC is both creative and tenacious and it is certainly not content to be relegated to diplomatic backwaters. If there is a criticism of the procedure, it is the length of time taken to present final views on communications. At present, this takes approximately three years, but this is no fault of the Committee, which must sit as a single body and cannot sit in 'chambers' of lesser numbers. It might also be commented that there are no procedures for the HRC to act in cases of urgency; this, it would appear, must be left to the regional human rights institutions.

ICESCR

Like its analogue ICCPR, ICESCR both elaborates upon and expands the list of rights contained in the Universal Declaration. Unlike ICCPR, however, it does not require states to give immediate effect to the rights recognized, but simply initiates an exhortatory and programmatic approach to their implementation. As we saw in Chapter 2, this approach has led some jurists to argue that economic, social and cultural rights are not real rights, since they do not possess an absolute quality, but are dependent upon economic factors for their implementation. This view is based on Article 2(1) of ICESCR, which provides that each state party 'undertakes to take steps . . . to the maximum of its available resources, with a view to achieving progressively the full realisation of the rights recognized in the present Covenant by all appropriate means . . .'.

There is only one method of supervision under ICESCR and that is the submission of periodic reports to ECOSOC on the measures which the states parties have adopted and the progress made in achieving the observance of the rights recognized. There is no provision for individual communication, but this is currently under consideration by ECOSOC. Although ECOSOC is the formal supervising body, it has effectively delegated its functions under the Covenant to a Committee on Economic, Social and Cultural Rights, which was created in 1985 by Resolution 17. This body mirrors the Human Rights Committee as it consists of 18 experts elected by the states parties who serve in their individual capacities. It considers the periodic reports made by the states parties and forwards its observations to ECOSOC, the UN Commission on Human Rights and to other specialized agencies of the UN concerned with economic, social and cultural rights.

Clearly, the implementation procedures and means of supervision under the Covenant are relatively weak and can do little more than highlight the shortcomings of states in the social welfare rights field. None the less, the Committee on Economic, Social and Cultural Rights has demonstrated in its early sessions a willingness to engage in the same kind of constructive dialogue which has characterized the activities of the Human Rights Committee.[75] A realistic approach to economic, social and cultural rights, however, suggests that difficulties of implementation are only to be expected, since progress depends not only upon the political will of states, but also upon the availability of resources to fulfil the stated obligations. But as Trubek argues, the minimum position tenable for states parties to ICCPR is that it creates a presumption in favour of social welfare rights which they are clearly legally bound to advance.[76]

UN ACTION IN SPECIFIC AREAS OF HUMAN RIGHTS

In addition to action in the broad fields of civil, political, economic, social and cultural rights, the UN has also undertaken a variety of activities relating to narrower, more specific areas of human rights promotion and protection. Only the more important conventions adopted under the auspices of the UN will be examined here.

Genocide

The Convention on the Prevention and Punishment of the Crime of Genocide was adopted by the General Assembly in 1948 and entered into force in 1951.[77] Its drafting and adoption, like the inclusion of the human rights provisions in the Charter, was motivated by the experience of the Nazi extermination of millions of Jews, Gypsies, Slavs and other groups both prior to and during the Second World War. Genocide, which has been described by Whittaker as the 'ultimate crime',[78] is defined by Article II of the Convention as:

. . . any of the following acts committed with intent to destroy, in whole or in part, a national, ethnical, racial or religious group, as such:
(a) Killing members of the group;
(b) Causing serious bodily or mental harm to members of the group;
(c) Deliberately inflicting on the group conditions of life calculated to bring about its physical destruction in whole or in part;
(d) Imposing measures intended to prevent births within the group;
(e) Forcibly transferring children of the group to another group.

Under Article I of the Convention, the parties 'confirm that genocide . . . is a crime under international law which they undertake to prevent and punish'. Not only is the list of acts which constitute genocide punishable, but so too are conspiracy, incitement, attempt to commit and complicity in genocide.[79] Under Article IV, all individuals, whatever their status, are personally responsible for committing genocide, which implies that the position taken in the judgment of the Nuremburg Tribunal that superior orders emanating from high-ranking state officials is no defence[80] applies within the context of the Convention.

Although Article VI of the Convention recognizes that an international tribunal with jurisdiction to try individuals who have committed genocide may be brought into existence by the parties at some future date, it none the less requires the competent tribunals of the contracting states to adopt jurisdiction over the offence in the meantime if the crime is committed within their territories. Subsequent events have also made it clear that genocide is a crime over which the courts of all states are competent to exercise their jurisdiction wherever and by whomsoever the crime was committed. Thus, genocide is said to be a crime under international law which attracts universal jurisdiction, and a norm of *ius cogens*. Support for this view can be found in the *Reservations to the Genocide Convention Case*, the *Barcelona Traction Case*, statements of the International Law Commission[81] and in the practice of a considerable number of states which have given legislative effect to the Convention.

Racial discrimination

The elimination of all forms of discrimination has been one of the major objectives of the UN since its inception. The Charter, the institutions created under the Charter and the International Bill of Rights all have as a predominant theme the equality of treatment of all human beings. It is therefore not surprising that various institutions of the UN have devoted considerable energy to drafting instruments designed to combat the most pervasive of all kinds of discrimination – racial and sexual discrimination.

The first treaty to deal specifically with racial discrimination was the International Convention on the Elimination of All Forms of Racial Discrimination, which was adopted by the General Assembly in 1965 and entered into force in 1969.[82] The Convention both condemns and prohibits racial discrimination, which is defined by Article 1(1) as:

> . . . any distinction, exclusion, restriction or preference based on race, colour, descent or national or ethnic origin which has the purpose or effect of nullifying or impairing the recognition, enjoyment or exercise, on an equal footing, of human rights and fundamental freedoms in the political, economic, social, cultural or any other field of public life.

In its advisory opinion in the 1971 *Namibia Case*,[83] the ICJ held that this definition was authoritative for the purposes of interpreting the non-discrimination provisions of the UN Charter. It might be argued that in view of its widespread acceptance, the definition also forms part of *ius cogens*. It should be noted that under Article 2(2), affirmative action programmes are not prohibited by the Convention, although they are clearly limited in time until the objectives for which they were introduced have been achieved.

States parties are under an obligation by Article 2(1) to take 'all appropriate means' to eliminate racial discrimination within their territory and to ensure that all civil, political, economic and social rights are accorded without discrimination. In order to supervise the Convention, a Committee on the Elimination of Racial Discrimination (CERD) consisting of 18 independent experts elected by the states parties is created by Article 8. The main method of supervision is a system of periodic reporting by the states parties similar to that under the International Covenants,[84] but the Convention also provides for a right of individual communication where states have recognized the competence of CERD to receive such communications.[85] As under the ICCPR First Optional Protocol, complainants must have exhausted all local remedies before their communication may be considered. Once admitted, CERD considers the complaint and may make recommendations to the state party and individual concerned. Although the Convention provides in Article 22 for the compulsory jurisdiction of the ICJ

in cases of unresolved disputes between states parties, the majority of
states have entered reservations to this, effectively rendering nugatory this
important provision.

One of the most important challenges to international human rights law
in recent years has been South Africa's institutionalized policy of racial
discrimination and segregation known as 'apartheid'. While this policy
has been subject to constant condemnation by a number of UN organs concerned with human rights, it was not until 1973 that the UN General
Assembly adopted the International Convention on the Suppression and
Punishment of the Crime of Apartheid. The Convention entered into force
in 1976.[86]

Apartheid, which is declared by Article I of the Convention to be a crime
against humanity, thus placing it on an equal footing with genocide, is
defined by reference to 'similar policies and practices of racial segregation
and discrimination as practised in southern [*sic*] Africa'.[87] Like the
Genocide Convention, the Apartheid Convention then provides a broad
definition supplemented by a list of particular practices. Thus, the crime
of apartheid applies to acts which are 'committed for the purpose of
establishing and maintaining domination by one racial group of persons over
any other racial group'.[88] These acts include murder, infliction of serious
mental and physical harm, arbitrary arrest and illegal imprisonment and the
deliberate imposition of living conditions calculated to cause the physical
destruction of racial groups in whole or in part. The crime of apartheid is
also committed by those who incite, conspire, aid, abet or encourage its
commission.[89] In the absence of any international penal tribunal, states
parties are to take jurisdiction over the prosecution and punishment of the
crime.

Supervision of the Convention is undertaken by the submission of periodic
reports by the states parties on the progress achieved to a group of three
members of the CHR nominated by the Chairman of the Commission.[90]
This group of three must also be representatives of the states parties to the
Convention as well as members of the CHR. The Convention also empowers
the Commission to prepare studies and reports on apartheid and to prepare
lists of individuals, organizations, institutions and representatives of states
that are alleged to be guilty of the crime.[91] These reports and lists have
been made available to the General Assembly via ECOSOC.

Sexual discrimination

As indicated above, the UN and its organs have undertaken a substantial
amount of work in standard setting and taking measures to prohibit
discrimination based on sex. The Convention on the Elimination of All

Forms of Discrimination Against Women, which was adopted by the General Assembly in 1979 and which entered into force in 1981,[92] comprises together with the International Covenants one of the major instruments in this field. Article 1 of the Convention defines 'discrimination against women' as 'any distinction, exclusion or restriction made on the basis of sex which has the effect or purpose of impairing or nullifying the recognition, enjoyment or exercise of women . . . of human rights and fundamental freedoms in the political, economic, social, cultural, civil or any other field'. States parties are not only required to eliminate such discrimination, but under Article 2 are also required to initiate measures to promote equality of women with men in their social, public and political life. Article 5(a) in particular requires states parties to take 'all appropriate measures to modify the social and cultural patterns of conduct of men and women, with a view to achieving the elimination of prejudices and customary and all other practices which are based on the idea of the inferiority or the superiority of either of the sexes or on stereotyped roles for men and women'. Despite the large number of states which are party to this Convention, this particular obligation remains more honoured in its breach than in its observance.

As with other UN-sponsored conventions, this Convention is supervised by requiring states parties to submit periodic reports on the measures adopted to give effect to the Convention's provisions.[93] The reports are studied by a 28-member Committee on the Elimination of Discrimination Against Women elected by the states parties, but who serve in an independent capacity.[94] Observations on the reports studied by the Committee are sent to the Commission on the Status of Women, which then forwards its observations to the General Assembly via ECOSOC. Under Article 29(a), there is provision for the resolution of disputes between the parties by the ICJ, but as with other UN conventions in which a similar provision exists, no recourse has yet been had to this procedure.

Torture

A glimpse at either Amnesty International's annual reports or the US Senate's country reports on human rights practices will confirm that torture remains endemic in the modern world. It is used by governments not only to obtain information from suspected political opponents, but also to oppress their populations. Although both the Universal Declaration and the ICCPR contain prohibitions on torture, inhuman and degrading treatment, these concepts are nowhere defined within those instruments. The UN Convention Against Torture and Other Cruel, Inhuman or Degrading Treatment, which was adopted by the General Assembly in 1984 and which entered into force in 1987,[95] not only seeks to remedy this omission, but also provides a supervisory mechanism.

There are undoubtedly problems in defining what constitutes torture. It can be approached from a subjective point of view, which is inherently difficult to measure, or it can be defined objectively. The Torture Convention takes the latter approach. Article 1(1) of the Convention defines torture as:

> . . . any act by which severe pain or suffering, whether physical or mental, is intentionally inflicted on a person for such purposes as obtaining from him or a third person information or a confession, punishing him for an act he or a third person has committed or is suspected of having committed, or intimidating or coercing him or a third person, or for any reason based on discrimination of any kind, when such pain or suffering is inflicted by or at the instigation of or with the consent or acquiescence of a public official.

Torture does not, however, include pain or suffering 'arising only from, inherent in or incidental to lawful sanctions'. This definition is replete with difficulties, not least of which is what is *severe* pain or suffering? None the less, Article 2 of the Convention makes it clear that there are no exceptional circumstances which will ever justify torture, nor may a torturer ever plead superior orders as a defence to the commission of such an act. If a person is alleged to have committed torture in any state, the state party within whose jurisdiction that person is found is under an obligation either to try or extradite him or her to a requesting state.[96] States parties are also obliged to keep their interrogation rules, instructions and methods under review as a means of preventing torture.[97]

Supervision of the Torture Convention is by a ten-person Committee against Torture which is elected by the states parties but whose members serve in their individual capacities. The methods of supervision under the Convention are a periodic reporting system (Article 19), an optional inter-state complaint procedure (Article 21) and a right of individual petition which is also optional and depends upon state acceptance (Article 22).[98] These by now familiar supervisory mechanisms are supplemented in the Torture Convention by an innovation which allows the Committee to investigate a state party on its own initiative when it receives reliable information that suggests that torture is being systematically practised in the territory of that state party. Such an inquiry is to be confidential and Article 20 requires the Committee to seek the cooperation of the state party under investigation. If such cooperation is not forthcoming, it would seem that the Committee may nevertheless proceed with its inquiry. What is clear, however, is that if the Committee wishes to conduct an investigation within the *territory* of a state party, it must be granted permission, otherwise the state party's sovereignty would be violated. As with the Committee's other supervisory functions, reference is made to the proceedings in its annual report which is submitted both to the states parties and the General Assembly. A state party which does not wish itself to be bound by the inquiry procedure must make a declaration to this effect at the time of becoming party to the Convention. This is also unusual, since treaties generally require states to 'opt in' to rather than to 'opt out' of international supervisory systems. Disputes between states parties may also be referred under Article 30 to the ICJ for adjudication, but states may avoid this obligation by entering a timely reservation.

Children

While it might have been thought that the rights of the child were adequately protected by existing human rights instruments, particularly the ICCPR, it was nevertheless agreed in 1979, the Year of the Child, that a working group of the CHR should draft a convention which would give effect to certain child-orientated rights. The UN Convention on the Rights of the Child was adopted by the General Assembly in 1989 and entered into force in 1990.[99] In addition to the protection of a number of traditional civil, political, economic and social rights, the Convention includes certain rights which apply to the child alone, a child being defined by Article 2 for these purposes as 'every human being below the age of 18 years unless, under the law applicable to the child, majority is attained earlier'. Among the 'new' rights protected are the right to a name, the right to know and be cared for by his or her parents, the preservation of the child's identity, freedom from sexual abuse and exploitation, narcotic drugs and trafficking. A number of provisions also place obligations on states parties to ensure, by the adoption of appropriate measures, that children will be allowed to develop to their maximum potential.

Supervision under the Convention is by a ten-member Committee on the Rights of the Child.[100] The members of the Committee are to be drawn from the states parties and they serve in their individual capacities. As with other UN treaties, supervision is by a system of periodic reports submitted by the states parties which are studied by the Committee. Under Article 45 of the Convention, the Committee is obliged to forward a biannual report of its activities to the General Assembly via ECOSOC. It is also interesting to note that UNICEF and other competent UN organs are entitled to participate in considering the implementation of the obligations under the Convention.[101] As yet, it is too early to speculate on the likely effectiveness of this particular instrument, but it clearly has the effect of strengthening UN institutional cooperation and supervision in this particular area.

FURTHER READING

UN Charter and Universal Declaration

Goodrich, L.M., Hambro, E. and Simons, A.P., *Charter of the United Nations* (New York: Columbia University Press, 3rd edn, 1969).

Humphrey, J.P., 'The Universal Declaration of Human Rights: Its History, Impact and Character', in Ramcharan, B.G., (ed.), *Human Rights Thirty Years After the Universal Declaration* (Dordrecht: Martinus Nijhoff, 1979), pp. 21–37.

Robertson, A.H. and Merrills, J.G., *Human Rights in the World* (Manchester: Manchester University Press, 3rd edn., 1989), chs 2 and 3.

Robinson, J., *Human Rights and Fundamental Freedoms in the Charter of the United Nations* (New York: Inst. Jewish Affairs of the American Jewish Congress and World Jewish Congress, 1946).

Schwelb, E. and Alston, P., 'The Principal Institutions and Other Bodies Founded under the Charter', in *Vasak*, Vol. 1, pp. 231–301.

Sohn, L.B., 'Human Rights: Their Implementation and Supervision by the United Nations', in *Meron*, pp. 369–401.

Commission on Human Rights and Sub-Commissions

Galey, M.E., 'International Enforcement of Women's Rights', (1984) 6 *HRQ* 463–90.

Haver, P., 'The Mandate of the United Nations Sub-Commission on the Prevention of Discrimination and Protection of Minorities', (1982) 21 *Columbia Journal of Transnational Law* 103–34.

Humphrey, J.P., 'The United Nations Sub-Commission on the Prevention of Discrimination and Protection of Minorities', (1968) 62 *AJIL* 869–88.

Reanda, L., 'Human Rights and Women's Rights: The United Nations Approach', (1981) 3 No. 2 *HRQ* 11–31.

Tolley, H, 'Decision-making at the United Nations Commission on Human Rights, 1979–82', (1983) 5 *HRQ* 27–57.

Tolley, H., *The United Nations Commission on Human Rights* (Boulder, CL: Westview Press, 1987).

ECOSOC Procedures

Bossuyt, M.J., 'The Development of Special Procedures of the United Nations Commission on Human Rights', (1986) 6 *HRLJ* 179–210.

Lillich, R. and Newman, F., *International Human Rights: Problems of Law and Policy* (Boston, MA: Little Brown, 1979), pp. 318–87.

Meron, T., *Human Rights Law Making in the United Nations* (Oxford: Clarendon Press, 1986).

Rodley, N.S., 'United Nations Action Procedures against "Disappearances", Summary or Arbitrary Executions, and Torture', in Davies, P. (ed.), *Human Rights* (London: Routledge, 1988), pp. 74–98.

Shelton, D., 'Individual Complaint Machinery under the United Nations 1503

Procedure and Optional Protocol to the International Covenant on Civil and Political Rights', in Hannum, H. (ed.), *Guide to Human Rights Practice* (Philadelphia: University of Pennsylvania Press, 1984), pp. 60–73.

Tardu, M.E., 'United Nations Response to Gross Violations of Human Rights: The 1503 Procedure', (1980) 20 *Santa Clara Law Review* 559–601.

Tolley, H., 'The Concealed Crack in the Citadel: The United Nations Commission on Human Rights' Response to Confidential Communications', (1984) *HRQ* 420–62.

Zuijdwijk, T.J.M., *Petitioning the United Nations* (Aldershot: Gower, 1982).

Unesco

Alston, P., 'Unesco Procedure for Dealing with Human Rights Violations', (1980) 20 *Santa Clara Law Review* 665–96.

Saba, H., 'Unesco and Human Rights', in *Vasak*, Vol. 2, pp. 401–26.

ILO

Jenks, C.W., *Human Rights and International Labour Standards* (London: Stevens, 1960).

Valticos, N., 'The International Labour Organisation (ILO)', in *Vasak*, Vol. 1, pp. 363–99.

ICJ

Schwelb, E., 'The International Court of Justice and the Human Rights Clauses of the Charter', (1972) 66 *AJIL* 337–51.

ICCPR

Fischer, D.D., 'Reporting Under the Covenant on Civil and Political Rights: The First Five Years of the Human Rights Committee', (1982) 76 *AJIL* 142–53.

Ghandi, P.R., 'The Human Rights Committee and the Right of Individual Communication', (1986) 57 *BYIL* 201–51.

Henkin, L. (ed.), *The International Bill of Human Rights: The Covenant on Civil and Political Rights* (New York: Columbia University Press, 1981).

Humphrey, J.P., 'Political and Related Rights', in *Meron*, pp. 171–203.

Lillich, R., 'Civil Rights', in *Meron*, pp. 115–70.

McGoldrick, D., *The Human Rights Committee* (Oxford: Clarendon Press, 1990).

Nowak, M., 'The Effectiveness of the International Covenant on Civil and Political Rights – Stocktaking after the First Eleven Sessions of the United Nations Human Rights Committee', (1980) 1 *HRLJ* 136–70.

Tomuschat, C., 'Evolving Procedural Rules: The United Nations Human Rights Committee's First Two Years of Dealing with International Communications', (1980) 1 *HRLJ* 249–57.

ICESCR

'The Limburg Principles on the Implementation of the International Covenant on Economic, Social and Cultural Rights', (1987) 9 *HRQ* 122–55.

Alston, P., 'Out of the Abyss: The Challenges Confronting the New United Nations Committee on Economic, Social and Cultural Rights', (1987) 9 *HRQ* 332–81.

Alston, P. and Quinn, G., 'The Nature and Scope of States Parties Obligations under the International Covenant on Economic, Social and Cultural Rights', (1987) 9 *HRQ* 156–284.

Alston, P. and Simma, B., 'First Session of the United Nations Committee on Economic, Social and Cultural Rights', (1987) 81 *AJIL* 747–56.

Alston, P. and Simma, B., 'Second Session of the United Nations Committee on Economic, Social and Cultural Rights', (1988) 82 *AJIL* 603–15.

Trubek, D., 'Economic, Social and Cultural Rights in the Third World: Human Rights and Human Needs', in *Meron*, pp. 205–71.

CERD

Buergenthal, T., 'Implementing the United Nations Racial Convention', (1977) 12 *Texas International Law Journal* 187–221.

Lerner, N., *The United Nations Convention on the Elimination of All Forms of Racial Discrimination* (Leyden: Sijthoff, 1980).

Sexual Discrimination

Galey, M.E., 'International Enforcement of Women's Rights', (1984) 6 *HRQ* 463–90.

Havener, N.K., *International Law and the Status of Women* (Boulder, CL: Westview Press, 1983).

Tinker, C., 'Human Rights for Women: The United Nations Convention on the Elimination of All Forms of Discrimination Against Women', (1981) 3 *HRQ* 32–43.

Torture

Boulesba, A., 'The Nature of the Obligations Incurred by States Under Article 2 of the United Nations Convention Against Torture', (1990) 12 *HRQ* 53–93.

Rodley, N., *The Treatment of Prisoners Under International Law* (Oxford: Clarendon Press, 1987), pp. 128–32.

Children

Cerda, S.C., 'The Draft Convention on the Rights of the Child: New Rights', (1990) 12 *HRQ* 115–19.

Davidson, S., 'The United Nations Convention on the Rights of the Child', (1990) 2 *Family Law Bulletin* 121–5.

Freestone, D., 'The United Nations Convention on the Rights of the Child', in Freestone, D. (ed.), *Children and the Law* (Hull: Hull University Press, 1990).

Hammarberg, T., 'The United Nations Convention on the Rights of the Child – And How to Make it Work', (1990) 12 *HRQ* 97–105.

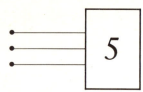

5

THE EUROPEAN SYSTEM FOR PROTECTING HUMAN RIGHTS

INTRODUCTION

The European system for protecting human rights is primarily composed of two major treaties: the European Convention on Human Rights and Fundamental Freedoms (ECHR) and the European Social Charter (ESC). The ECHR, which is focused upon the protection of civil and political rights, was adopted in 1950 and entered into force in 1953.[1] It is thus the oldest specific human rights instrument in existence, its entry into force pre-dating the ICCPR by more than twenty years. The ESC, which covers the implementation of economic and social 'rights and principles', was adopted in 1961 and entered into force in 1965.[2] Both Conventions were drafted under the auspices of the Council of Europe, an inter-governmental organization of 25 European states, the function of which is to facilitate European cooperation across a broad range of subjects. Upon joining the Council, every member must, under Article 3 of its Statute,[3] 'accept the principles of the rule of law and of the enjoyment by all persons within its jurisdiction of human rights and fundamental freedoms . . .'. And, as Vasak points out, the themes of democracy, the rule of law and the protection of human rights permeate the Council's founding document.[4] These principles are also echoed in the ECHR's Preamble, which reaffirms their crucial importance to the High Contracting Parties.

THE EUROPEAN CONVENTION ON HUMAN RIGHTS AND FUNDAMENTAL FREEDOMS (ECHR)

As indicated above,[5] the motivation for the drafting of the ECHR arose from the wish of the participating states to protect against encroaching communism, to sound the alarm against incipient totalitarianism and to strengthen democracy and the rule of law in the member states. It is also clear that the Council of Europe wished to move more quickly than the UN in the drafting of legally binding human rights obligations. In the Preamble to the ECHR, the Universal Declaration is mentioned on three occasions, the third being the most noteworthy in the present context, for there the parties resolve 'to take the first steps for the collective enforcement of certain of the rights stated in the Universal Declaration.'

Much of the work of the Convention's institutions has been directed towards resolving deficiencies in the domestic law of the states parties, rather than dealing with the gross violations of human rights which its drafters originally appeared to envisage. None the less, the ECHR has on occasion had to deal with the eruption of totalitarianism, as in *Denmark, Norway, Sweden and The Netherlands v Greece*,[6] which, as previously remarked, highlighted some of the weaknesses of the Convention's protective system.[7] It is arguable that the Convention has functioned rather better as a kind of quasi-constitutional device, providing an instrument of last resort where domestic institutions and laws have been found lacking. It should also be noted that the Convention has self-executing status in a large number of the contracting parties and is pleaded by lawyers directly before their domestic courts. Several calls on various occasions to make the ECHR part of the UK's domestic law have met with no success, although it is now arguable that certain of the rights protected take effect within the UK's legal system, since they have been held by the European Court of Justice to be part of the general principles of EC law.[8]

The ECHR and its ten additional Protocols protect most of the rights contained in the Universal Declaration, although there are some omissions and some differences in the drafting of the rights in order to take account of European conditions.[9] The contracting parties are required by Article 1 to 'secure to everyone within their jurisdiction' the rights and freedoms protected by the Convention, and they are required to do so on a non-discriminatory basis. In the event of a violation of any of the rights and freedoms, Article 13 declares that persons so affected 'shall have an effective remedy before a national authority notwithstanding that the violation has been committed by persons acting in an official capacity'. It is clear that Articles 1 and 13 impliedly require states to take the necessary legislative measures in appropriate cases both to implement the Convention's rights and to provide means for redress in cases of violation.

The ECHR'S institutions

In order to ensure the observance of the obligations undertaken by the parties to the Convention, Article 19 provides for the establishment of a European Commission on Human Rights ('the Commission') and a European Court of Human Rights ('the Court'). It should also be noted that both the Committee of Ministers, which is the governing body of the Council of Europe, and the Secretary-General of the Council, also have functions assigned to them under the Convention. All these institutions have their seat at the Palais de l'Europe in Strasbourg, an imposing building which is periodically shared with the peripatetic Parliament of the European Community.

The Commission

Commission members must be persons of high moral character and should either possess the qualifications required for appointment to high judicial office or be persons of recognized competence in national or international law.[10] They serve for a period of six years in an individual capacity and may not during their period of office hold a position which is incompatible with their independence and impartiality.[11] The Commission consists of a number of members equal to that of the parties to the Convention. No two members may be from the same state, and there is no requirement that a Commission member should be a national of a contracting party.[12] Whereas, in the past, the Commission was required to sit as a plenary body when considering individual applications submitted to it under Article 25, following an amendment to the Convention by Protocol No. 8 in 1985 in order to expedite its procedures, it may now sit in chambers of seven members. The Commission must still sit in plenary session, however, if it is required to deal with inter-state applications under Article 24 or if one of the chambers considers it necessary in view of the case before it.

   Under Article 24 of the ECHR the jurisdiction of the Commission under the Convention is automatically accepted by states when they become parties to the ECHR. All proceedings before the Commission take place *in camera*,[13] largely to facilitate the conciliatory function which is the central duty of the Commission if an application is found to be admissible.

The Court

The Court is composed of a number of judges equal to that of the Members of the Council of Europe.[14] The Court is not normally required to sit as a plenary body, but sits rather in less cumbersome chambers of seven.[15] In cases of importance, however, there is provision for the full Court to sit.

The difference between the number of members of the Commission and the number of judges of the Court should be noted. While the Commission members must be equal in number to the parties to the Convention, the number of judges is determined by reference to the number of Members of the Council of Europe. The reason for the difference is that, as Beddard writes, the drafters of the Convention wanted the Court to represent a kind of 'conscience of Europe.'[16] The divergence between the number of judges and members of the Commission has fluctuated from time to time according to differing memberships of the Council of Europe and the European Convention.

In order to be judicial candidates, Article 39(3) ECHR requires nominees to be of 'high moral character' and possess the qualifications required for appointment to high judicial office or be jurisconsults of recognized competence. Although no two judges may be from the same contracting party, there is no requirement that judges possess the nationality of the nominating state. Indeed, Liechtenstein nominated Canadian law professor R. St. John MacDonald to sit on the Court rather than one of its own nationals.

Unlike the Commission, the jurisdiction of the Court under the Convention is neither automatic nor compulsory. The parties to the ECHR must declare that they accept the Court's jurisdiction to interpret and apply the Convention.[17] This may be done unconditionally, for a specified period, by special agreement in individual cases or on the basis of reciprocity with other states. The nature of the Court's jurisdiction is two-fold. First, it exercises a contentious jurisdiction, where states have accepted this, to make rulings in inter-state and individual cases initiated under Articles 24 and 25 ECHR. Secondly, under Protocol II to the Convention, the Court has power to render advisory opinions at the request of the Committee of Ministers. This latter jurisdiction is strictly limited to provisions of the Convention which do not relate to the content or scope of the rights or freedoms guaranteed, and it is therefore of marginal utility. It has never been employed by the Court and compares unfavourably with the exceptionally broad advisory jurisdiction of the Inter-American Court of Human Rights which has been frequently utilized.[18]

ECHR enforcement mechanisms

There are two types of enforcement mechanism under the Convention: (1) an inter-state complaint system and (2) a right of individual application.

Inter-state complaints

Under Article 24 of the ECHR, any party may refer to the Commission via the Secretary-General of the Council of Europe, any alleged breach of the Convention by any other party. By becoming party to the ECHR, all states automatically accept the Commission's competence to receive such complaints. This, as we shall see in Chapter 6, is different from the American Convention on Human Rights where states must declare that they accept the jurisdiction of the Inter-American Commission in such matters. It should be noted that the inter-state procedure is not predicated upon the alleged violation of one of the substantive rights protected by the Convention, but can be invoked in relation to any provision of the Convention. Even if an alleged violation does infringe or violate one of the ECHR's substantive rights, it is not necessary for the complaining state to demonstrate that it has a special interest in, or relationship to, the victim. In a technical sense, all that states are concerned with here is ensuring that other parties observe their obligations under the Convention. It has been apparent, however, that in the small number of inter-state cases brought to date, the majority have been motivated by political hostility. In *Greece v UK*,[19] Greece's complaints concerned the treatment of Greek Cypriot (AOKA) terrorists by the British authorities in Cyprus. The case of *Austria v Italy*[20] was motivated by the alleged inhuman treatment by Italian authorities of German-speaking youths in the Italian Tyrol. In *Ireland v UK*,[21] the Irish government objected to the use of certain methods of interrogation known as the 'five techniques' employed against suspected Provisional IRA members by the British security forces which, it claimed, amounted to torture, inhuman and degrading treatment under Article 3 ECHR. Finally, two cases brought by *Cyprus v Turkey*[22] arose from the circumstances surrounding Turkey's invasion and partition of Cyprus, and its treatment of the displaced Greek Cypriot population.

Two inter-state applications, however, stand out as being motivated not by political hostility, but by genuine humanitarian concerns. These are the cases brought by Denmark, Norway, Sweden and the Netherlands against Greece in 1970[23] and by the same states against Turkey in 1982.[24] The first case arose from the aftermath of a *coup d'état* by a number of Greek military officers ('the Colonels') in 1970 in which political opponents to the military regime were imprisoned and tortured. The effect of the case was to lead Greece to denounce the Convention and to withdraw from the Council of Europe a short time before it was due to be expelled. The second case concerned allegations of torture and inhuman treatment of prisoners in Turkey. Unlike the Greek case, the Turkish Case was subject to a friendly settlement.

The Greek case is often held up as an example of the inadequacy of international legal instruments in the face of a totalitarian regime bent on systematically denying human rights to its people. While it is true that a legal instrument by itself can achieve very little without the attendant political will to make it effective, the violation of human rights norms by a state deny its actions legitimacy, damage its international reputation and may lead to diplomatic, political and economic sanctions. Although human rights violations may often appear to be cost-free to states, nevertheless they do damage a state's credibility and make international relations more difficult to sustain, as indeed the Greek 'Colonels' discovered.

Individual applications

Although the term 'petition' is used in Article 25 of the ECHR, the Commission and the Court now use the term 'application' to denote the procedural right of individuals to lodge claims with the Commission that one or more of their rights under the Convention has been violated. The right of application depends, however, upon a declaration of state acceptance. Such declarations may be unconditional or made for a specified period. The UK, for example, adopts the latter approach, making declarations for periods of only five years, the most recent being its declaration of 14 January 1991. The question of renewal of the UK's declaration under Article 25 has occasionally lead to a difference of opinion between government departments. In 1986, for example, it was reported that the Foreign and Commonwealth Office was eager to renew the UK's declaration, whereas the Home Office was apparently reluctant to have human rights issues adjudicated in Strasbourg.

Under Article 25, applications to the Commission may be lodged with the Secretary-General of the Council of Europe by 'any person, non-governmental organisation or group of individuals claiming to be the victim of a violation by one of the parties of the rights set forth in this Convention', provided, of course, that the state in question has accepted the right of individual application. From this it is clear that victims, and hence applicants, may be either natural or legal persons. Indeed, applications have been lodged by a number of corporate groups such as companies, trades unions, churches and other representative organizations. The use of the word 'victim' in Article 25 has been held to mean that an applicant must have been actually affected by the alleged violation, although in *Marckx*[25] the Court held that in certain circumstances it may be enough for an applicant to show that they would be potentially directly affected by the application of a particular measure. What is clear, however, is that there is no possibility of a class action or *actio popularis* under the ECHR. This was stated by the Court in *Klass*,[26] although it is arguable that the judgment in *Marckx* mitigated the rigour of this position to a certain extent. The Commission has also identified a class of individuals who can submit applications who are known as 'indirect victims'. These are persons not immediately affected by an original violation, but who none the less suffer as a result of such a violation or, in the words of the Commission, individuals who have 'a genuine personal interest in the termination of a violation'. An example of an indirect victim might be a spouse whose partner has been arbitrarily imprisoned. The spouse is clearly not a direct victim of the violation of Article 5, but he or she will be an indirect victim because of the consequences of the violation. It should also be noted that in such circumstances the spouse would also be the direct victim of a violation of Article 8, the right to family life, and therefore competent to lodge an application in his or her own right.

There are a number of conditions set out in Articles 26 and 27 which must be fulfilled before the Commission can admit an application and thus proceed to consider the merits of a case.

Exhaustion of local remedies

Article 26 provides:

> The Commission may only deal with the matter after all domestic remedies have been exhausted, according to the generally recognised rules of international law, and within a period of six months from the date on which the final decision was taken.

Article 27(3) further provides that the Commission must reject any application referred to it which does not comply with the exhaustion of local remedies requirement. Although it would seem unnecessary for states to ensure that local remedies have been exhausted, since states are bringing the claim not on behalf of an alleged victim, but in their own right, the Commission has nevertheless examined the question where individual rights within the respondent state have been in issue.[27]

The rationale for the existence of the local remedies rule has been considered in Chapter 3, but it is worth remarking that the both the Commission and the Court have fully accepted the basis of the rule. In *Application 343*, the Commission stated that the rule is 'founded upon the principle that the Respondent State must first have an opportunity to redress by its own means within the framework of its own domestic legal system the wrong alleged to have been done to the individual', and in *De Wilde, Ooms and Versyp* (*Vagrancy Cases*)[28] the Court held that the rule 'dispenses states from answering before an international body for their acts before they have had an opportunity to put matters right through their own legal system'.

Both the Commission and the Court in applying the rule have adhered closely to the international law concerning the exhaustion of local remedies. Thus, since the rule is for the benefit of states, it has been held that it is open to them to waive the rule. Such a waiver may be express, but more often than not it will be implied in cases where states have been tardy in raising the issue. In *DeJong, Baljet and van den Brink*,[29] for example, the

Netherlands raised the question of non-exhaustion of local remedies for the first time before the Court, without having pleaded it before the Commission at the admissibility stage. The Court held that the Netherlands was precluded or estopped from raising the objection at this later stage, when it should have done so in contesting admissibility of the application before the Commission.

The jurisprudence of the Commission and the Court has also demonstrated that, in accordance with international law, applicants are not required to exhaust local remedies if they are not genuine and effective or if they are subject to unreasonable delay. As the Court said in *Van Oosterwijk*,[30] an applicant need only exhaust remedies which 'relate to the breaches alleged and at the same time are available and sufficient'. Thus, where a remedy is shown to have been consistently unsuccessful, it will be deemed not to have been sufficient. This does not mean, however, that if a remedy is uncertain an applicant is absolved from attempting to seek redress through the domestic system of appeals; he or she is required to attempt all reasonable avenues to obtain a remedy.

An important exception to the rule requiring exhaustion of local remedies which has been developed by the Commission and the Court arises in circumstances where there exists an 'administrative practice' within the state in question. An administrative practice has been defined by the Court as 'an accumulation of identical or analogous breaches which are sufficiently numerous and inter-connected to amount not merely to isolated incidents or exceptions but to a pattern or system'. It is unnecessary that such practices be formalized in legislative or quasi-legislative measures; it is enough that there is official toleration of the practice. Such official toleration would, as the Court stated in the Greek case, tend to render judicial remedies ineffective, since it would be practically impossible to obtain evidence through the cooperation of official bodies. Indeed, in the Irish Case, techniques for interrogating Provisional IRA suspects had not been authorized in any official document, but they had been taught to UK security forces at an official training centre. This was enough to signify government toleration of the practices and obviate the need to exhaust local remedies.

The burden of proving that local remedies have been exhausted lies initially with the applicant. If the Commission is not satisfied that the application discloses an attempt to exhaust all available genuine, effective and timely remedies, it must reject the application. The determination by the Commission at this stage that all local remedies have been exhausted is not conclusive, since it is open to the respondent state to raise the question of non-exhaustion later in proceedings before the Commission. If a state does raise this issue as a barrier to admissibility, the burden of proof is then upon the state to demonstrate non-exhaustion.

Intimately linked to the exhaustion of local remedies rule is the requirement that the application must be lodged within six months of the final decision. What, however, is meant by the term 'final decision'? In *Application 214*, the Commission ruled that this 'refers exclusively to the final decision concerned in the exhaustion of all domestic remedies according to the generally recognised rules of international law, so that the six months period is operative only in this context'. Thus, it would seem that where an individual applies to a domestic tribunal which clearly has no power to grant a remedy for a violation, it is the date on which the previous decision was given which will count as the final decision. A potential applicant would therefore have to determine carefully whether or not there was any real likelihood of success before attempting to secure redress before a particular domestic tribunal. If, however, there is a violation of the Convention which is of a continuing nature and there is no domestic remedy available, the obligation to submit an application within a six-month period is clearly otiose. This occurred in *De Becker*,[31] in which a journalist was denied a licence to practise his profession in Belgium. There was no recourse to any tribunal against the decision of the licensing authority, and it was therefore held that the violation of Article 10 (freedom of expression) was of a continuing nature to which the six-month limitation period did not apply.

Article 27 requirements

Once an applicant has demonstrated that local remedies have been exhausted, he or she must also satisfy three further criteria contained in Article 27 before the application can be ruled admissible by the Commission. Article 27 reads:

(1) The Commission shall not deal with any application submitted under Article 25 which
   (a) is anonymous, or
   (b) is substantially the same as a matter which has already been examined by the Commission or has already been submitted to another procedure of international investigation or settlement and if it contains no relevant new information
(2) The Commission shall consider inadmissible any application submitted under Article 25 which it considers incompatible with the provisions of the present Convention, manifestly ill-founded or an abuse of the right of application.

Anonymity
This requirement is not taken too literally by the Commission. As long as the application contains sufficient information to allow the applicant to be identified, it will be admitted.

Substantially the same as a matter which has already been examined by the Commission
The Commission has applied this provision so strictly that it has developed a doctrine of *res judicata*. None the less, the Commission has indicated that it is prepared to be flexible where there is new information forthcoming. It is also clear that where a previous application has been ruled inadmissible because of a failure to exhaust local remedies, the Commission will not subsequently reject the same application if it is re-submitted following the exhaustion of local remedies.

Submitted to another procedure of international investigation
In the first decades of the operation of the Convention, the possibility of duplication of individual application procedures under different international instruments was remote. However, with the entry into force of the First Optional Protocol to the ICCPR, it became apparent that individuals could make applications under both systems. Because of this, the Council of Europe recommended to states which wished to recognize the right of individual application under both systems that they make a reservation when ratifying the Protocol excluding consideration of applications by the Human Rights Committee of matters which had already been considered under the ECHR. As we saw in Chapter 4, reservations by European states to the First Optional Protocol have been pleaded, with mixed results, in an attempt to prevent the HRC from effectively re-hearing a case previously rejected as inadmissible by the European Commission. It would seem that the application of such reservations might, if accepted by the HRC without qualification, work to the detriment of individuals whose applications are rejected on the basis that they concern rights not covered by the Convention. It is arguable that applicants should have the opportunity to correct their error before the Committee.

Incompatible with the provisions of the Convention
The Commission may declare applications inadmissible on this ground under a variety of circumstances. There are a number of potential categories of inadmissibility under this heading:

1 Where an application claims a violation of a right not guaranteed by the Convention, otherwise known as inadmissibility *ratione materiae*. This has often involved the claimed violation of rights protected by the Universal Declaration or the European Social Charter but not by the ECHR, such as the right to holiday pay. Sometimes, however, the right claimed is not covered by any instrument such as the right of prisoners to holidays.[32]
2 Where the applicant is not a victim or an indirect victim, otherwise known

as inadmissibility *ratione personae*. This has already been covered above in the context of Article 25.

3 Where the issue is covered by a reservation properly made under Article 64 ECHR by the respondent state.

4 Where the alleged victim did not fall within the jurisdiction of the respondent state at the time of the claimed violation. This is known as inadmissibility *ratione loci*.

5 Where the violation took place before the entry into force of the ECHR, unless the breach is of a continuing nature as in *De Becker*, known as inadmissibility *ratione temporis*.

6 Where the application violates Article 17, which provides:

> Nothing in this Convention may be interpreted as implying for any State, group or person any right to engage in any activity or perform any act aimed at the destruction of any of the rights and freedoms set forth herein or at their limitation to a greater extent than is provided for in this Convention.

Manifestly ill-founded

This admissibility requirement essentially requires the Commission to determine whether the facts of the application disclose a prima facie breach of the Convention. In order to do this, the Commission must undertake a preliminary investigation of the facts of the case. Sometimes not much more than a cursory investigation is required in order to ascertain whether or not a prima facie breach of the Convention is disclosed. On other occasions, such as in *Klass*,[33] the Commission has been required to undertake an extensive analysis which has come close to a determination of the merits of the case.

Abuse of the right of application

A rough equivalent of this term in domestic law might be the rules prohibiting vexatious litigation. It is primarily designed to prevent applicants from making false claims and allegations, but it has also been used in the case of *Rafael v Austria*[34] to rule inadmissible an application in which the applicant used abusive and defamatory language about certain members of the respondent state's government. This latter decision has been criticized as being contrary to the spirit of the Convention, since the Commission should be concerned with the question of whether protected rights have been violated not with whether an applicant has used objectionable phraseology. The Commission's decisions under this heading also make it clear that the motive of an applicant is irrelevant. In *Lawless*,[35] for example, the Irish government claimed that the applicant's motives were simply political and not primarily concerned with securing a remedy for violated rights. The Commission rightly rejected this contention.

Given the number of hurdles placed in front of a potential applicant, it is not surprising that the majority of applications, approximately 96 per cent, never proceed beyond the admissibility stage. The question may legitimately be asked, therefore, why is it so difficult for an individual to bring a case to the merits stage? The answer to this is probably two-fold. First, the emphasis of the Convention is on respect for national sovereignty and the primary obligation of states to provide the initial avenues of redress by means of their own legal systems. Second, in any international system of protection, it is necessary to sift out applications which clearly have nothing to do with human rights issues either because they claim the protection of rights which do not exist or because they are simply frivolous.

Derogations

As we saw in Chapter 3, the possibility of derogations exists in most human rights instruments. These allow states to modify or opt out of the protection of certain rights in certain specified circumstances. This does not mean, however, that states are given a free hand to do what they like simply by declaring a derogation, since both the circumstances giving rise to the derogation and the operation of the derogation itself will be subject to the supervisory institutions in each instrument. None the less, a derogation may stand in the way of effective human rights protection by precluding or limiting the possibility of redress by an applicant. As in the case of the ICCPR, however, certain rights protected by the ECHR are non-derogable.

Article 15(1) of the ECHR provides:

> In time of war or public emergency threatening the life of the nation any High Contracting Party may take measures derogating from its obligations under this Convention to the extent strictly required by the exigencies of the situation, provided that such measures are not inconsistent with its other obligations under international law.

It is apparent from Article 15(1) that derogations may only be made in circumstances in which the very fabric of the state is under threat, and even then any derogations must be proportionate to the threat. Thus derogations involve a paradox. They demand the denial of rights or aspects of certain rights in order to protect the totality of rights which can only be guaranteed by the continued existence of the state. Derogations also involve balancing the interests of the state in taking measures which it deems necessary for its survival together with the interests of the Convention's institutions which are charged with supervising its observance.

Both the Commission and the Court have developed important jurisprudence under Article 15(1) to determine whether or not a state is entitled to make derogations in particular circumstances. From this it is clear that there must be an actual or imminent crisis of exceptional proportions, which affects the whole population of the state by threatening the organized life of the community. In determining whether or not such a state of affairs exists, a Party enjoys a degree of discretion which is known as the 'margin of appreciation'. The exercise of this margin of appreciation is, however, subject to the supervision of the Commission and, in the final analysis, the Court. It is they which determine whether or not the conditions permitting the making of derogations exist in fact and whether or not the state has properly exercised its discretion. It would seem that where derogations are properly made they excuse parties from breach of the Convention, although Judge Sir Gerald Fitzmaurice argued in a separate opinion in *Ireland v UK*[36] that a derogation properly made actually *nullifies* a technical breach of the Convention. Parties which avail themselves of the right of derogation must make the derogation public and keep the Secretary-General of the Council of Europe fully informed of the measures which they have taken and the reasons giving rise to them.

The majority of derogations under the ECHR have been made by both the UK and Ireland to deal with the terrorist threat in Northern Ireland. In *Lawless*,[37] the Court held that Ireland had legitimately proscribed membership of the IRA by means of a derogation because the extra-constitutional and violent activities of that organization not only affected the fabric of Irish society, but also placed Ireland's relations with the UK at risk. Similarly, in *Ireland v UK*, the Court found that the terrorist activities of the IRA justified the UK in taking the necessary measures by way of derogation. In contrast, the Commission held in the *Greek* case that there was not a public emergency in Greece at the time of the military overthrow of the constitutional government by 'the Colonels.' The Commission found that allegations of a communist takeover and a deterioration in the state of public order following a constitutional crisis in 1967 had not been demonstrated.

The Commission's post-admissibility procedure

Once an application has been declared admissible, the Commission must then perform a number of separate tasks. First, it must act as an investigatory body by undertaking a thorough review of the facts alleged in the application. This is not done by the whole Commission, but rather by use of a *rapporteur* or an individual Commission member who undertakes a review of the facts and reports back to the Commission. If in the course of its investigation of the facts the Commission finds the existence of one of the grounds in Article 27 which would have initially rendered the application inadmissible had it been discovered at the admissibility stage, the

Commission may still reject the application. Such a decision must, however, be taken by a unanimous vote of the Commission. This procedure is clearly designed to deal with those applications which ought not to have been admitted, but where this only becomes apparent on close examination.

Second, once the Commission has established the accuracy of the facts alleged in the application, it must then undertake the role of conciliator. Article 28(b) requires the Commission to 'place itself at the disposal of the parties concerned with a view to securing a friendly settlement of the matter on the basis of respect for Human Rights as defined in this Convention'. All this takes place *in camera*.[38] In the view of one former President of the Commission, Sir Humphrey Waldock, the drafters of the Convention were right to make friendly settlement the central remedy within the Convention structure. He said:

> Investigation of the shortcomings of a State in regard to human rights is a very delicate form of intervention in its internal affairs. The primary duty of the Commission is to conduct confidential negotiations with the parties and to try and set right unobtrusively any breach of human rights that may have occurred. It was not primarily established for the purpose of putting States in the dock and registering convictions against them.[39]

Clearly, the Commission must steer a *via media* and must not be seen to favour one party at the expense of another, although it might be felt that the conciliatory function allows states to escape lightly on some occasions. In *Amekrane*,[40] for example, an application was filed by Mrs Amekrane against the UK on her own behalf and on behalf of her husband. Her husband had been an officer in the Moroccan Air Force who had taken part in an unsuccessful coup against the King of Morocco. Amekrane escaped to Gibraltar where he sought asylum but was immediately returned to Morocco where he was shot and killed. Mrs Amekrane claimed a number of breaches of the ECHR including Article 3 (inhuman treatment) because of the circumstances of her husband's return to Morocco. Mrs Amekrane, however, reached a friendly settlement with the UK in which she was given an *ex gratia* payment of £37 500 without any admission on the part of the UK that it had violated the Convention. The results of all friendly settlements are recorded in a report by the Commission that is published and which contains a brief statement of the facts and the solution reached between the parties.

Third, if a case cannot be settled by friendly means, the Commission must, under Article 31(1), 'draw up a report on the facts and state its opinion as to whether the facts found disclose a breach by the State concerned of its obligations under the Convention'. This phase of proceedings by the Commission may be regarded as quasi-judicial in nature. The report compiled by the Commission is drafted as if it were the judgment of a court and can contain concurring, separate and dissenting opinions. The report is not, however, conclusive, since the Commission is not competent to reach decisions binding upon the parties; that competence lies solely within the purview of the Committee of Ministers or the Court.

When the Commission has drawn up its report it must transmit it to the Committee of Ministers with any proposals that it sees fit. The report is also transmitted to the respondent state and, if the case is an individual application under Article 25, to the applicant. None of the parties is at liberty to publish the report. If the respondent state has not accepted the jurisdiction of the Court or has accepted it with reservations which preclude consideration of the instant case, the case *must* be disposed of by the Committee. If a respondent state has accepted the jurisdiction of the Court but the case has not been referred to the Court within a period of three months, the Committee of Ministers must similarly dispose of it at the end of that period. The decision on whether a case should be referred to the Court is dealt with by Article 48. This provides that the following may refer a case to the Court:

(a) the Commission;
(b) a . . . Party whose national is alleged to be a victim;
(c) a . . . Party which referred the case to the Commission;
(d) a . . . Party against which the complaint has been lodged.

When Protocol No. 9 of 1990 enters into force, a consequential amendment to Article 48 will allow a fifth category of persons to refer a case to the Court. This category will include the person, NGO or group of individuals who lodged the complaint with the Commission. The reason for this additional protocol was to broaden access to the Court by individuals and thus make the system more responsive to the individuals which it is meant to serve. The potential amendment to Article 48(2) makes it clear, however, that individuals will not be entitled to refer a case to the Court as of right, since a procedure is established for screening such referrals. Where a case is referred by an individual, it must first be considered by a panel of three judges, one of whom must be a member of the respondent state. If the panel decides by unanimous vote that the case does not raise a serious question affecting the interpretation or application of the Convention and does not warrant consideration by the Court for any other reason, it may decide that the case should not be considered by the Court. If the panel takes such a decision, then the matter falls to be dealt with by the Committee of Ministers in the usual way under Article 32. Britain has already indicated that it has no intention of becoming party to Protocol 9.

To date, the vast majority of cases has been referred to the Court by the Commission. There are no guidelines contained in the Convention as to how the Commission is to exercise its discretion in deciding whether to refer a case to the Court or whether to leave it to be dealt with by the Committee of Ministers. From the Commission's referrals, however, it is apparent that cases in which difficult points of law emerge or where there are sharp divergences of opinion between Commission members will be referred to the Court if the state concerned has accepted its jurisdiction. It has also been suggested that the Commission prefers to refer cases to the committee that have a political complexion, although, of course, there is no satisfactory definition of what might be considered political in this context.

Decisions by the Committee of Ministers

Where a case is referred to the Committee of Ministers for decision in the circumstances outlined above, the Committee must decide by a majority of two-thirds whether there has been a violation of the Convention.[41] If it is decided by the requisite majority that a Party is in breach, the Committee of Ministers is required to prescribe the remedial action which the state must take and the time within which it must be taken.[42] Such decisions are legally binding on the states to which they are addressed.[43] The representative of the respondent state party may take part in all these decisions, an approach which runs counter to the principle of *nemo iudex in sua causa* (no-one should be a judge in their own cause).

Although it is clear that the Committee has adjudicative power, it is also clear that it is not required to adopt a judicial approach to the Commission's reports. This is because the Committee, being composed of Council of Europe member states' representatives, is a political institution. Scrutiny of the Committee's decisions under Article 32 appears to indicate, however, that it avoids political confrontation and tends to agree with the position taken by the Commission in most cases. There have been exceptions to this, but they are comparatively rare.

Contentious cases before the Court

Article 47 provides that the Court may deal with a case only after the Commission has acknowledged the failure of efforts to secure a friendly settlement and within the period of three months referred to in Article 32. It is also worth reiterating that application of Article 47 is, of course, predicated upon the prior acceptance of the Court's contentious jurisdiction by the respondent state party.

Until Protocol 9 enters into force, only the Commission and ECHR parties enjoy the competence to bring a case before the Court. None the less, the gradual amelioration of the position of the individual under the application system has been one of the noteworthy features of the development of the

Convention. In *Lawless*, which was the Court's first case, it became apparent that the applicant was effectively excluded from proceedings before the Court, since only the Commission was given standing to present the case. Thus, although the applicant initiated the Article 25 procedure, and although it was the applicant who would ultimately be the beneficiary of any decision, he was prevented from making his voice heard directly by appearing before the Court. The Court overcame this particular problem by allowing the applicant to append his own written observations to the Commission's statement, and the Court also reserved the right through its Rules of Procedure to hear at the request of the Commission or state party 'any person whose evidence or statements seem likely to assist it in the carrying out of its task'.[44] Manifestly, this meant that the Court could hear the applicant, if the Commission deemed this appropriate. Since 1983, under Rule 30 of the Court's Rules of Procedure, applicants have been entitled to plead their own case before the Court. This, however, still does not entitle them to become a party to the proceedings.

Once the Court gives judgment in a case it is final and admits of no appeal. Furthermore, if the respondent state is found to be in violation of the Convention, it must, under Article 53, 'undertake to abide by any decision of the Court'. Such a decision may include the award of monetary compensation, but increasingly the Court has taken the decision that a declaration of breach of the Convention is sufficient remedy for the applicant, especially where only moral damage has been suffered.[45] The Court does not have the power to make punitive awards, nor, would it appear, does it have the competence to make orders for specific performance, that is to direct a state to take positive action in a particular area. However, if a state has been found to be in breach of the Convention through the application of a particular piece of legislation, it is clearly incumbent upon that state to take the appropriate remedial action in accordance with its obligations under Article 1 of the ECHR.

Supervision of the execution of the Court's judgments are undertaken under Article 54 by the Committee of Ministers. Once the Court has made a judgment, it is transmitted to the Committee of Ministers which places it as an item on its agenda. The delinquent state must then inform the Committee of the measures which it has taken to give effect to the judgment. This may include a statement to the effect that the state has paid damages awarded by the Court to the applicant, or that it has taken the appropriate legislative measures to remedy the breach. Given delays in domestic legislative procedures, however, it is clear that the Committee needs to keep a watching brief over state activities in this field. It is also arguable that the Committee is not the most effective body for policing this particular aspect of the system, since a determination of whether legislative amendments have indeed remedied the breach and forestalled any potential breaches in the terms of any judgment by the Court, may be a particularly nice question; a question for which the Committee as a political body may not necessarily be adequately equipped to answer. Nevertheless, this does not appear to have caused insuperable difficulties. A number of states has been required to modify domestic legislation both in order to remedy and to foreclose upon future breaches of the Covenant. Britain, following the *Sunday Times Case*,[46] for example, modified its laws concerning contempt of court, and Belgium, in the aftermath of *Marckx*, amended its legislation concerning children born out of wedlock.

Interpreting the rights under the ECHR

It is impossible, given the constraints of space in this book to offer more than cursory attention to the significant and detailed jurisprudence which has been amassed by the ECHR since it heard its first case in 1961. None the less, it is possible to give a flavour of the Court's approach by examining the subject matter of, and the decisions in, some of its more important cases relating to one particular Convention article. At the outset, however, comment should be made about the Court's technique of interpretation. The approach adopted by the Court towards interpreting the substantive rights contained in the Convention is clearly dynamic in nature. The Court has not been constrained by apparent gaps in the protection of certain rights protected by the Convention and has, arguably, engaged in forms of broad judicial legislation in order to achieve results consistent with its overall philosophy. The Convention is seen by the Court as a 'living instrument', the role of which is to deal with the problems of contemporary Europe and not simply the problems which the drafters may have contemplated in the 1950s. In many ways, therefore, the Convention is similar to the Bill of Rights of the American Constitution, not only in the subject matter with which it deals, but also in the way in which the rights protected have been developed through alternating periods of judicial activism and restraint.

In order to give an idea of the way in which the Court decides cases involving alleged breaches of the Convention's substantive provisions, it is intended here to examine, albeit briefly, its interpretation of Article 3. This article, which provides that 'no one shall be subjected to torture or to inhuman or degrading treatment or punishment', has given rise to a series of important cases, the majority of which have involved the UK as respondent. The first of these was an inter-state case, *Ireland v United Kingdom*, in which the Irish government accused the UK of breach of Article 3 by the use of the so-called 'five techniques' by British security forces in Northern Ireland to extract intelligence from detainees who were suspected of being IRA terrorists. The 'five techniques' involved making detainees stand in a painful posture against a wall, depriving them of light by hooding them, subjecting them to prolonged periods of noise, depriving them of sleep and placing them on a severely restricted diet. The Commission found unanimously that these procedures amounted to torture, but the Court departed from the Commission's finding and and held that the acts complained of were not of the 'particular intensity and cruelty implied by the word torture'. None the less, the Court did find that the use of the 'five techniques' violated Article 3, since it amounted to inhuman and degrading treatment. It is interesting to note here that the Court took a very subjective view of what might amount to a breach of Article 3. It was clearly of the opinion that in order to come within the meaning of Article 3, the conduct complained of 'must attain a minimum level of severity', but that this was relative and depended upon all the circumstances of the case, and, in particular, the personal characteristics of the individual involved. Thus what might amount to a breach of Article 3 in the case of a person who was sick and old might not be a breach in the case of a person who was young and healthy.

It is apparent that such a subjective approach may raise more problems than its solves, and that determining the perceptions of the individual might cause acute difficulties for states. It is interesting to note that the specialist torture conventions actually work from an objective definition of torture by concentrating on the intention and motivation of the person inflicting the torture rather than from the point of view of the victim.

In *Tyrer v United Kingdom*,[47] the Court was faced with the question of whether punishment of minors by birching constituted degrading punishment within the meaning of Article 3. Here it held that the infliction of physical violence by one person against another was compounded by its institutionalized nature and the aura of official procedure which was attached to it. This, the Court found, was an attack upon Tyrer's dignity and therefore amounted to degrading treatment. Again, the Court held that the assessment of whether punishment was degrading was relative and depended upon the circumstances of the case and, in particular, 'on the nature and the context of the punishment itself and the manner of its execution'. It also took the view that physical punishment itself was not necessary for a violation of Article 3, and that apprehension of the physical punishment itself might be sufficient to constitute a breach.

A case involving the UK in which a breach of Article 3 was alleged but not found by the Court was that of *Campbell and Cosans*.[48] Here, the applicants were the parents of two children who were being educated in the Scottish school system. The use of corporal punishment was still permitted in Scotland and the parents of the children complained that the threat of the use of such punishment, even though it had not been used upon their children, amounted to a violation of Article 3. While the Court found that there had been no breach of Article 3 in this case, it nevertheless held that the threat of torture might itself amount to inhuman treatment.

Of all the cases recently decided by the European Court of Human Rights in this area, perhaps the most far-reaching has been that of *Soering v United Kingdom*.[49] In this case, the applicant, a German citizen, had been arrested in the UK and was serving a prison sentence for fraud, when a request for his extradition was made by US authorities for a murder he and his girlfriend were alleged to have committed in Virginia in 1985. Soering argued that if the UK were to extradite him to the US, this would amount to inhuman treatment because, if he were convicted of murder (which was likely since his girlfriend accomplice had already been convicted of the crime), he would be exposed to Virginia's 'death row' phenomenon upon conviction, since that state still maintained the death penalty for such crimes. In this landmark judgment, the Court held that there would be a breach of Article 3 if the decision to extradite an individual were made in circumstances where 'substantial grounds have been shown for believing that the person concerned, if extradited, faces a real risk of being subjected to torture or to inhuman or degrading treatment or punishment in the requesting country'. This, said the Court, would hardly be compatible with the 'underlying values' of the Convention nor with the 'spirit and intendment of Article 3'. In *Soering*, the Court also reaffirmed elements of its earlier judgments in *Ireland v United Kingdom* and *Tyrer*. It made clear once again that the treatment concerned must reach a minimum level of severity before Article 3 was violated, but that it also depended on 'all the circumstances of the case', including the characteristics of the victim him or herself. Furthermore, the Court observed, in line with *Tyrer*, that it was not only physical pain with which Article 3 is concerned, but also 'the sentenced person's mental anguish of anticipating the violence he is to have inflicted upon him'. Thus, the Court found that the possible extradition of Soering to the US would amount to inhuman treatment and therefore a breach of Article 3. In the subsequent case of *Cruz Varas v Sweden*,[50] the Court also held that the principles elaborated in *Soering* were equally applicable to cases involving the expulsion or deportation of aliens to states where torture or persecution was likely. In *Cruz Varas v Sweden*, however, the facts found by the Court did not suggest that the applicant was likely to face such circumstances when the Swedish government decided to deport him to Chile.

From the cases referred to above, it will be evident that the Court has a clear conception of its role within the general context of the European Convention, and a clear understanding of the limits and potentialities of the Convention itself. Examination of the Court's extensive case law in other areas would tend to confirm this view. The Court's case law in the fields of protection of freedom of the person (Article 5) and the right to a fair trial (Article 6) has been both voluminous and important. It has also extended the ambit of the substantive rights in question beyond unexpected limits. In *Golder*, for example, the Court held that the right to a fair trial in Article 6 also implied the right of access to courts for the determination of an individual's civil rights and obligations or in answer to any criminal charge. As Sinclair has pointed out,[51] if one examines the plain words of Article 6, it is difficult to escape the conclusion that the Court engaged in judicial legislation in this particular case. Similarly, in *Marckx*, a case concerning the legal disabilities of illegitimate children in Belgium that the right to family life (Article 8) not only prevented the state from intervening in such matters, but also required it to create conditions in which such family life might be enjoyed to its maximum potential. Again, this judicial legislation was criticized by dissenting British judge, Sir Gerald Fitzmaurice, as being 'a misguided attempt to read – or rather introduce – a whole code of family law into Article 8 of the Convention, thus inflating it in a manner wholly incommensurable with its true and intended proportions'. Despite the criticisms of judicial legislation, however, it is clear that the dynamic teleological approach adopted by the Court is consistent with the overall object and purpose of the Convention, which as the Court has pointed out recently[52] is 'for the protection of individual human beings'. This being so, the Court went on to say that the provisions of the Convention must be 'interpreted and applied so as to make its safeguards practical and effective'.

The European Convention on Human Rights is unarguably one of the successes of post-1945 human rights developments. While it may not have fulfilled its original primary purpose in acting as a warning signal against the emergence of totalitarian regimes, nevertheless it has provided an extremely useful and potent mechanism of last resort for large numbers of individuals whose grievances have not been redressed by the relevant institutions in their own states. Citizens of the UK may, in particular, have good cause to look upon the European Convention as a safeguard against a domestic system which is ill-suited to protecting the rights and freedoms of individuals.

THE EUROPEAN SOCIAL CHARTER (ESC)

The primary purpose of the European Social Charter (ESC) is, in the words of the Committee of Ministers, to act as 'the complement to the [ECHR]'. Thus, whereas the ECHR is designed to protect the civil and political rights of individuals from state interference, the primary aim of the ESC is to secure state participation in realizing the rights involved. As we saw in the context of the ICCPR and the ICESCR, the obligations on states concerning the implementation of the different categories of rights varied. Whereas in the case of the civil and political rights protected by the ICCPR, implementation is to be immediate and absolute, in the case of the economic, social and cultural rights recognized by the ICESCR, the implementation is to be programmatic. The same divergence is evident in both the ECHR and the ESC. The ECHR requires the civil and political rights protected to be secured immediately; the ESC demands a progressive approach.

Part I of the ESC states that the parties 'accept as the aim of their policy, to be pursued by all appropriate means . . . in which the following rights and principles may be effectively realised . . .'. A list of 19 rights and principles dealing with a wide variety of economic, social and cultural rights then follows. In a sense, therefore, Part I establishes the policy goals to which the parties commit themselves; it does not, however, at this stage create legally binding obligations for the parties. This is done by Part II of the ESC, which defines both the scope and content of the rights and principles set out in Part I in greater detail.

The obligations assumed by the states parties under the ESC are set out in Article 20. This adopts an unusual formulation by first placing an obligation on states to commit themselves to pursuing the policy goals set out in Part I and then giving the parties a choice as to which of the substantive rights it will consider itself bound. Thus Article 20(1) provides:

Each of the Contracting Parties undertakes
(a) to consider Part I of this Charter as a declaration of the aims which it will pursue by all appropriate means, as stated in the introductory paragraph of that Part;
(b) to consider itself bound by at least five of the following articles of Part II of this Charter: Articles 1 [right to work], 5 [right to organise], 6 [right to bargain collectively], 12 [right to social security], 13 [right to social and medical assistance], 16 [right of the family to social, legal and economic protection] and 19 [right of migrant workers and their families to assistance and protection];
(c) in addition to the articles selected by it in accordance with the preceding sub-paragraphs, to consider itself bound by such a number of articles or numbered paragraphs of Part II of the Charter as it may select, provided that the total number of articles or numbered paragraphs by which it is bound is not less that 10 articles or 45 numbered paragraphs.

The apparently curious method of establishing state party obligations has a number of advantages which relate directly to the practical problems inherent in implementing the ESC. As Vasak points out,[53] the object of committing states to the 'inner nucleus' of five out of the seven articles referred to in Article 20(1)(a) is to secure protection for what are seen as the essential economic and social rights. The remaining 'outer nucleus' must therefore be considered as the foundation for a complete system of social justice. The obligations of the ESC are clearly flexible in nature, allowing account to be taken of the disparities in the economic conditions between the member states of the Council of Europe. States parties are therefore able to undertake their obligations progressively and programmatically, which is in line with rights implementation in the general field of economic, social and cultural rights.

Supervision under the ESC

The present method of supervision under the ESC is the by now familiar system of periodic reports. Unlike the international instruments examined so far, however, the ESC requires two types of reports: first, a biennial report concerning the implementation of the Part II rights which the Party in question has accepted and, second, a report at intervals prescribed by the Committee of Ministers detailing the status of Part II rights not accepted by the Party. These reports are considered by a body known as the Committee of Independent Experts, which consists of seven 'independent experts of the highest integrity and of recognised competence in international and social questions' who are nominated by the parties and elected by the Committee of Ministers.[54] The Committee of Experts is also assisted in its deliberations by a consultant supplied by the ILO. This is an interesting development, since it demonstrates the potential for the cross-fertilization of ideas in the field of economic, social and cultural rights.

The state reports, together with the conclusions of the Committee of Experts, are referred to a sub-committee of the Governmental Social Committee of the Council of Europe.[55] This is a political body, since it is composed of governmental representatives. It is, however, assisted by four consultants, two of whom are representatives of employers' organizations and two of whom are trade union representatives. The Governmental Social Committee, in accordance with Article 27 of the ESC, then forwards its views to the Council of Europe. The state reports and the conclusions of the Committee of Independent Experts are also sent to the Consultative Assembly of the Council of Europe.[56] This body is composed of delegations of elected members of the legislatures of each of the member states, and thus has a degree of democratic influence on the activities of the Council. Not surprisingly, there has sometimes been a divergence of opinion between the Committee of Ministers, which is composed entirely of government representatives, and the more democratic Consultative Assembly as to the course of action which should be taken on the reports of the Committee of Experts. As might be expected, the Consultative Assembly has, in general, favoured specific action by states where there appear to have been short-comings in the implementation of their obligations under the ESC, whereas the Committee of Ministers has preferred to proceed more diplomatically and therefore at a general level. None the less, through the process of discourse between the various Council of Europe institutions and from the recommendations for state action which emerge at the end of it, the progressive implementation of certain economic and social rights does take place. An examination of the reports of the Committee of Experts and the recommendations which follow, clearly indicate an incipient jurisprudence in this field. It must be admitted, however, that the mechanisms for the development of rights in this area is imperfect in comparison to the ECHR. Although there have been proposals to incorporate the ESC as a protocol to the ECHR and make it subject to the enforcement mechanisms of that instrument, no concrete progress has been made to date. A protocol to the ESC has been adopted, but this simply extends the range of rights to be protected under the existing system of implementation.[57]

In order to improve the implementation system under the ESC, the Council of Europe adopted a further Protocol to the Charter in Turin in 1991.[58] While this Protocol is not in force at the time of writing, it is perhaps appropriate to examine its salient features since its entry into force is likely to take place in the near future. Under the Protocol, the membership of the Committee of Independent Experts is increased from seven to nine, but of greater importance is the enhanced role given to the Committee. Here, Article 2 of the Protocol (amending Article 24 of the Charter) gives the Committee exclusive competence to interpret the Charter and to write the reports of the Governmental Committee (the present Governmental Social Committee). The Charter's supervisory system will also be simplified by the Protocol and it will enhance the role of trade unions and NGOs in the process.

Since the major criticisms of the Charter have consistently been the indeterminate status of the Committee of Independent Experts' reports and the poverty of the supervisory system, the Council of Europe hopes that when the Charter is eventually amended by the Protocol, these criticisms will be addressed.

THE EUROPEAN CONVENTION FOR THE PREVENTION OF TORTURE AND INHUMAN OR DEGRADING TREATMENT OR PUNISHMENT 1987

Although the ECHR contains in Article 3 a clear prohibition on the use of torture, inhuman and degrading treatment, it was decided by the Committee of Ministers following a proposal from the Council of Europe's Consultative Assembly in 1983 to consider the adoption of a treaty which would introduce a preventative mechanism in this area. The present Convention, which entered into force in 1989,[59] is the fruit of that proposal. It establishes a European Committee for the Prevention of Torture and Inhuman or Degrading Treatment composed of competent persons of high moral character of a number equal to that of the parties which is given authority to visit and investigate any place in which individuals deprived of their liberty are held.[60] Such visits may be periodic or at times considered necessary by the Committee. Parties must allow the Committee access to its territory, the right to travel freely throughout its territory, full information on the places where persons deprived of their liberty are being held and unlimited access and freedom of mobility within such places.[61] Further, the parties must not hinder the Committee's procedures, including the right to communicate within any person deprived of their liberty or any other person the Committee feels may be able to help it.[62] Parties may in exceptional circumstances make representations to the Committee against a visit on grounds of national defence, public safety or serious disorder, but such representations are not conclusive and the Committee may make proposals to the party to institute different arrangements in order to facilitate fulfilment of its task.[63]

Following a visit, the Committee must draw up a report containing any necessary recommendations which it must then forward to the party concerned.[64] If after consultation with the Committee a party refuses or fails to improve the situation concerning persons deprived of their liberty, then the committee by a two-thirds majority may decide to make a public statement on the matter.[65] This threat of adverse publicity is clearly one of the most potent tools at the Committee's disposal.

The Convention represents an interesting departure from the traditional type of human rights treaty in two major ways. First, it is concerned primarily with the prevention of human rights abuses by taking pre-emptive action rather than relying on *ex post facto* control as is the case with most of the instruments so far examined. Secondly, it makes on-site investigation in the territory of a party the norm. States, by becoming party to the Convention, automatically concede the right to the Committee to undertake investigatory visits without prior approval. There is no question here of a state being able to plead that there has been an intervention in its internal affairs, since this is subject to explicit prior waiver.

FURTHER READING

Beddard, R., *Human Rights and Europe* (London: Sweet and Maxwell, 2nd edn, 1980).

Castberg, F., *The European Convention on Human Rights* (Dobbs Ferry, NY: Oceana, 1974).

Drzemczewski, A.Z., *European Human Rights Convention in Domestic Law* (Oxford: Clarendon Press, 1983).

European Committee for the Prevention of Torture, *First General Activity Report November 1989–December 1990*, (1991) 12 *HRLJ* 206.

Harris, D.J., *The European Social Charter* (Charlottesville, VA: University of Virginia Press, 1984).

Higgins, R., 'The European Convention on Human Rights', in *Meron*, pp. 495–549.

Jacobs, F.G., *The European Convention on Human Rights* (Oxford: Clarendon Press, 1975).

Merrills, J.G., *The Development of International Law by the European Court of Human Rights* (Manchester: Manchester University Press, 1988).

Mikaelson, L., *European Protection of Human Rights* (Leyden: Sijthoff, 1980).

Morrison, C.C., *The Dynamics of Development in the European Human Rights Convention System* (Leyden: Sijthoff, 1981).

Nedjati, Z.M., *Human Rights under the European Convention* (Amsterdam: Elsevier/North-Holland, 1978).

Robertson, A.H. and Merrills, J.G., *Human Rights in the World* (Manchester: Manchester University Press, 1989), ch. 4.

van Dijk, P. and van Hoof, G.J.H., *Theory and Practice of the European Convention on Human Rights* (Deventer: Kluwer, 2nd edn, 1990).

Vasak, K., 'The Council of Europe', in *Vasak*, Vol. 2, pp. 457–542.

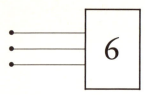

6

THE INTER-AMERICAN SYSTEM FOR PROTECTING HUMAN RIGHTS

INTRODUCTION

Of all the regions in the world, it is perhaps the Americas, sometimes known as the Western Hemisphere, which manifests the greatest divergence in political, economic and social development. It includes not only the wealthy countries of the north, but also the predominantly impoverished states of the Caribbean and Central and Latin America. The northern states, the USA and Canada, are characterized by the longevity and stability of their democratic political structures and their fundamentally sound domestic systems of human rights protection, while certain states lying to the south have been wracked by frequent violent changes in totalitarian forms of government, the fragility of their economic and social systems and their abject failure in protecting human rights. Indeed, the names of certain of these states have become bywords for some of the worst human rights abuses in recent years. Chile, Argentina, Uruguay, Guatemala and El Salvador are countries in which some of the worst excesses of the last decade have been perpetrated by governments against their own civilian populations using military units and 'private' death squads. Disappearances, torture, arbitrary detention and extra-judicial executions have been the hallmarks of certain American regimes. It is also ironic to note that, in most of these states, apart from periodic declarations of states of emergency, siege or exception, to use the various terminology, sophisticated constitutional mechanisms for human rights protection were in place and technically capable of full utilization by individuals. Yet the remedies of habeas corpus and *amparo* (a remedy guaranteeing protection of constitutional rights) proved to be entirely illusory, demonstrating the truism that human rights instruments and legal remedies are of little immediate utility in the absence of appropriate political and social conditions for securing their observance. None the less, as a period of democracy emerges in a number – but by no means all – Central and Latin American states, the debt owed to human rights ideology and activism becomes apparent. The strengthening of democratic institutions based on respect for human rights and the rule of law has become a priority of newly elected regimes as a means of reinforcing their democratic base. It is the purpose of this chapter to examine the structure and processes of the inter-American human rights system in order to assess how it helps to underpin this process.

THE INTER-AMERICAN SYSTEM

The inter-American system for the protection of human rights has evolved within the framework of the Organization of American States (OAS). This is an inter-governmental organization that was founded in 1948 and which is defined as a 'regional agency' within the meaning of Article 52 of the UN Charter. In most respects, the objectives and the institutional structure of the OAS mirror those of the global UN organization. Thus, the OAS Charter is concerned with establishing systems for the peaceful settlement of disputes among its members and undertaking regional enforcement action where this is necessary. It is also concerned with the promotion of social and economic development and the promotion and protection of human rights. The work of the OAS is carried out through a number of institutions which, again, mirror those of the UN. The General Assembly is the plenary organ having general competence to oversee the totality of the organization's activities, while the Permanent Council is the analogue to the UN Security Council and serves as the executive organ of the OAS in permanent session having competence to deal with matters of peace and security. There is also an Inter-American Commission on Human Rights, which, as we shall see, has a dual status and general competence in the field of human rights under both the Charter and the American Convention on Human Rights (ACHR).

The inter-American human rights system is distinctive as it has its origins in two separate but substantially interrelated legal instruments. First, part of the system has developed within the context of the Charter itself. All member states have assumed human rights obligations under the Charter simply by becoming members of the Organization. Second, some states have also voluntarily assumed human rights obligations under the ACHR and its

Additional Protocol by becoming parties to those instruments. The two parts of the system, however, share a common institution in the Inter-American Commission on Human Rights, although it operates under different procedures depending upon whether it is acting as a Charter or ACHR institution. The Inter-American Court of Human Rights, which was created by the Convention, also has certain advisory competences relating to the human rights provisions of the Charter. Furthermore, the normative standards developed under the Charter system and those of the ACHR are capable of overlapping with, and influencing the development of, each other. Clearly, this does not make the process of explication easy, and perhaps the best way of analysing the system is by examining the two strands of human rights protection separately and noting, where appropriate, their points of convergence and interaction.

THE CHARTER SYSTEM

The regime for the protection of human rights under the OAS Charter has undergone a number of important changes since its entry into force in 1951.[1] The historical evolution of these changes will be considered in this section.

Under the original Charter Article 3(j), now Article 5(j), the member states proclaimed 'the fundamental rights of the individual without distinction as to race, nationality, creed or sex'. Article 13, now Article 16, further provided that each state in exercising its right to develop its cultural, political and economic life was obliged to 'respect the rights of the individual and the principles of universal morality'. Nowhere, however, did the Charter define or elaborate what was meant by the 'fundamental rights of the individual.' This omission was partially remedied at the same Bogota Conference at which the Charter was adopted by the passing of a resolution entitled the American Declaration of the Rights and Duties of Man.[2] The Declaration contains a list of civil and political, and economic and social, rights. It also contains a number of duties setting out an individual's obligations to the society in which he or she lives.[3] Like its UN counterpart, which it pre-dated and to which it is similar in many respects, the American Declaration was a simple conference resolution of the organization and was not intended to be legally binding *per se* nor by incorporation into the Charter system. This, however, is no longer the case. The American Declaration has acquired the status of an authoritative interpretation of the references to human rights within the Charter. How it has assumed this status can only be understood by reference to the institutional development of the Inter-American Commission on Human Rights under the Charter.

The Inter-American Commission on Human Rights

At the Fifth Meeting of Consultation of Ministers of Foreign Affairs of the OAS in Santiago, Chile in 1959, a resolution was adopted by which the Permanent Council was required to establish an Inter-American Commission on Human Rights charged with the mandate of promoting respect for human rights.[4] The Statute of the seven-person Commission, which was adopted by the Permanent Council in 1960, described it as an 'autonomous entity' of the OAS. This appeared to mean that, being a creature of a resolution, the Commission had no precise legal status as an institution under the Charter. In fulfilling its obligations to promote human rights, Article 2 of the Commission's Statute declared: 'For the purposes of the present Statute, human rights are understood to be the rights set forth in the American Declaration of the Rights and Duties of Man.'

Although under Article 9 of its Statute the Commission was limited to advisory and recommendatory functions, nevertheless it decided, through a process of auto-interpretation of its constituent instrument, that it had power to make specific recommendations on human rights violations to member states and to undertake studies and make reports on human rights situations in states where large-scale violations were alleged to have taken place.[5] Despite the receipt of a large number of individual communications from persons alleging violations of human rights, the Commission decided that it had no competence to take cognisance of, nor act upon, such information.[6] This lack of competence was, however, remedied at a Second Special Inter-American Conference at Rio de Janeiro in Brazil in 1965,[7] when a resolution added Article 9 (*bis*) to the Commission's Statute. This new provision empowered it to receive communications from individuals alleging violation of certain specified rights, to seek information on the individual communications and to make recommendations to states in respect of them. The rights of which the Commission was mandated to take particular note in receiving such communications were Articles I (right to life, liberty and security of the person), II (right to equality before the law), III (right to religious freedom and worship), IV (right to freedom of investigation, opinion, expression and dissemination of opinions), XVIII (right to a fair trial), XXV (right to protection from arbitrary arrest) and XXVI (right to due process of law).

Despite its weak constitutional foundations, the Commission was able to fashion a remarkably effective system of protection on the basis of its Statute. As well as dealing with a large number of individual communications and making recommendations to concerned member states thereon, it performed a large number of country studies to investigate allegations of widespread human rights abuses. In making its country studies, the Commission established the practice of requesting permission from the state involved to conduct on-site investigations, to review documentation, to visit government institutions such as prisons and to interview authors of communications and government personnel. This was often facilitated by conducting meetings of the full Commission in the territories of the states where widespread violations had been alleged.

In 1970, following an amendment to the Charter by the Protocol of Buenos Aires, the Commission was transformed by Article 51(e) into an organ of the OAS. A new Article 112 clearly stated the Commission's functions under the Charter. These were 'to promote the observance and protection of human rights and to serve as a consultative organ of the Organization in these matters'. Article 112 also provided, however, that the structure, competence and procedure of the Commission would be determined by, as at that time, a non-existent American convention on human rights. Until such a convention entered into force, Article 150 provided that the 'present Inter-American Commission on Human Rights shall keep vigilance over the observance of human rights'. This led some commentators to speculate that there might be two Commissions when the ACHR came into being – a Commission for the Charter and a Commission for the Convention. The Commission's new Statute, which was adopted in 1979 when the ACHR entered into force, made it clear, however, that there would be a single Commission with separate procedures under the Charter and the Convention. Article 1(2) of the Commission's Statute therefore provided:

> For the purposes of the present Statute, human rights are understood to be:
> a) The rights set forth in the American Convention on Human Rights in relation to the States Parties thereto;
> b) The rights set forth in the American Declaration of the Rights and Duties of Man.

Thus all member states of the OAS who were not parties to the ACHR continued to be bound by the human rights standards established by the Charter. Furthermore, the mechanisms established by the Commission as a Charter institution were specifically preserved. The overall effects of the amendments to the Charter in 1970 were to institutionalize not only the Commission's procedures under Article 9 and 9(*bis*) but also to confer through the process of incorporation a normative status upon the hitherto non-binding Declaration. What, however, is the status of the Declaration under the Charter? This question has been addressed on two occasion: first, by the Commission itself and, second by the Inter-American Court in an advisory opinion.

The Commission in the '*Baby Boy*' case[8] was called upon by a United States NGO, Catholics for Christian Political Action (CCPA), to rule that the abortion of a male foetus by a doctor in Massachusetts violated the right to life of the 'baby boy' which was protected by Article I of the Declaration. The abortion had taken place following liberalizing decisions of the American Supreme Court in *Roe v Wade*[9] and *Doe v Bolton*[10] and was not therefore an offence in the USA. Before the Commission could consider the merits of the application, it had to determine whether the case was admissible. This in turn depended upon whether or not the USA was bound by any human rights obligations under the Charter. The Commission held that the USA was so bound. Its reasoning was that as a consequence of Articles 3(j) and 16, which obligate member states to respect human rights, and the incorporation of the Commission and its Statute into the Charter system, the American Declaration had acquired 'binding force'. This seems to suggest that the Declaration had taken on a treaty-like quality and provided legally binding obligations for all OAS member states to adhere to the standards established by the Declaration. This view, however, was not espoused by the Court in a request by Colombia for an advisory opinion upon whether the Declaration was a 'treaty concerning the protection of human rights in the American States' within the meaning of Article 64(1) of the American Convention.[11] Here, the Court ruled that while the Declaration was not a treaty within the meaning of Article 2(1)(a) of the Vienna Convention on the Law of Treaties,[12] none the less it constituted an authoritative interpretation of the human rights provisions of the Charter. The Court said:

> . . . it may be said that by means of an authoritative interpretation, the members states of the Organization have signaled their agreement that the Declaration contains and defines the fundamental human rights referred to in the Charter. Thus the Charter of the Organization cannot be interpreted and applied as far as human rights are concerned without relating its norms, consistent with the practice of the organs of the OAS, to the corresponding provisions of the Declaration (para. 44).

The Court further observed that Articles 1(2)(b) and 20 (which replaced Article 9 and 9(*bis*)) of the Commission's Statute made it clear that the Declaration was a 'source of international obligation related to the Charter of the Organization'. While this language is not particularly clear, it would nevertheless seem to indicate that the Declaration, as an authoritative interpretation of the Charter, creates a legally binding standard for all member states of the OAS. Article 29(d) of the ACHR also supports the view that the Declaration is intended to have legal effects since this provides:

No provision of this Convention shall be interpreted as:

e) excluding or limiting the effect that the American Declaration . . . and other international acts of the same nature may have.

It would therefore seem that the American Declaration has since its adoption in 1948 acquired a potent status within the Charter system. It is now without doubt that nearly every state in the Western Hemisphere is legally bound to adhere to the human rights standards established by the Declaration. In its submissions to the Court in the *Interpretation of the American Declaration Case*, the USA argued that it was undesirable to translate the Declaration into a legally binding obligation since this not only jeopardized a fundamental aspect of treaty law, namely that states can only be bound by their consent, but also because it would be impossible to determine the precise content of the exiguously stated rights in the Declaration. This objection is not, however, insuperable simply because both the Commission and the Court, exercising its advisory jurisdiction with respect to the Charter, are competent to interpret the extent of the rights in question. This point should not be lost on the USA, whose own Bill of Rights is composed of bare declarations of rights which must be interpreted by its own competent institution, the Supreme Court.

The Commission under the Charter

As we saw above, the Commission fulfils a number of functions under the Charter. These might be classified as promotional, advisory, consultative and protective. The Commission serves as the organ of consultation in the field of human rights for the General Assembly of the OAS, it has drafted a number of human rights instruments, including the American Convention and its Protocol of San Salvador, and it has been employed by the OAS to mediate in a number of situations, perhaps the most notorious being when armed conflict broke out between Honduras and El Salvador following a highly charged international soccer match. It is, however, in the performance of its protective function that the Commission might be observed operating most effectively under the Charter. Here, a distinction may be made between the Commission's country studies and on-site investigation procedures on the one hand and its individual petition system on the other. These will be examined in turn.

Country studies and on-site investigations

Like the UN Commission on Human Rights,[13] the Inter-American Commission, when it was first established by resolution in 1960, received a large number of individual communications claiming human rights violations by

OAS member states. Also, like the UN Commission, the Inter-American Commission had no legal competence to act on these individual applications, but could only deal with them in accordance with its general mandate under Article 9 of its Statute. It therefore utilized the individual communications as evidence in attempting to determine the state of human rights in the member states against which they were addressed. Where a large number of communications was received, the Commission would decide to initiate a country study in order to investigate fully the position in the state in question. Where possible, the Commission undertook the investigation in the territory of the state concerned. This it was empowered to do by its Statute, but since the sovereignty of the state under investigation was at issue, the Commission could only convene in the territory of the state with its consent.

The Commission's first country studies dealing with Cuba, Haiti and the Dominican Republic were prepared in the early 1960s. While Cuba and Haiti were not prepared to allow the Commission to enter their territory, the Dominican Republic granted it permission to carry out its work on-site. These first three studies enabled the Commission to establish its *modus operandi*. It heard witnesses, interviewed government officials and, in the case of the Dominican Republic, visited official institutions and interviewed opposition and community leaders. The practices employed in the Dominican Republic on-site investigation have been followed in subsequent country studies in Argentina, Nicaragua, Guatemala, El Salvador and Surinam.

Once a state has agreed to allow the Commission to conduct an on-site investigation, its obligations are set out in detail in Articles 55–59 of the Commission's Regulations. It is required to place all the facilities necessary for the execution of the Commission's task at its disposal. The members of the Commission are to be allowed to travel freely throughout the state's territory, and the state must ensure the safety of Commission members during their stay and their travels in the country. The state is also obliged to allow the Commission to interview any person requested, and must undertake not to retaliate against individuals who supply information to it. Such on-site investigations are undertaken by a Special Commission convened in accordance with Article 56 of the Commission's Regulations, which precludes nationals or residents of the state under investigation from serving with the Commission in order to prevent a conflict of interests.

On-site investigations have been a particularly useful device. They not only allow the Commission to obtain fuller information about the state of affairs in the country being studied, but they also allow it to corroborate by direct observation allegations made by individuals. Two of the most graphic accounts of the latter are to be found in the El Salvador and Argentina reports.[14] In the former report, the Commission was able to verify the existence of torture chambers used by the armed forces, and in the latter the Special Commission actually discovered the existence of a number of *desaparecedos* in a jail in the northern Argentinian city of Cordoba. Furthermore, as Buergenthal points out,[15] the very presence of the Commission in a state may ameliorate the human rights situation there. Here, he cites the example of the Dominican Republic's civil war in 1965 when the Commission was able to save hundreds of lives and secured the release from prison of large numbers of political detainees.

In preparing country reports, the Commission adopts a three-stage procedure. First, it produces a draft report based on all the evidence it has assembled. Second, the draft report is then submitted to the government of the state concerned for its comments. If the government's comments are considered well-founded by the Commission, it will amend the report to take account of them. Third, the Commission must take a decision whether or not to publish the report. Article 62 of the Commission's Regulations requires it to publish the report if a state has not responded to the request for observations on the draft, but more recently the Commission has decided to publish reports together with the government's observations in full. The Commission may also transmit the report to the OAS General Assembly for consideration. Originally, the General Assembly simply noted receipt of the country reports, but in 1975 it changed its practice by debating fully the report of the Commission on the situation of human rights in Pinochet's Chile and adopting a resolution on the issue calling on Chile to comply with its obligations. Since then, the General Assembly has debated to a greater or lesser degree a number of country reports and the Commission's annual reports. The publicity which attends the Commission's publication of its reports and the debates upon them in the General Assembly is one of the more potent 'sanctions' available within the inter-American system. Governments, for the most part, dislike being castigated as delinquents and, furthermore, an adverse human rights record may affect other aspects of international relations such as defence, trade or foreign aid. The US Senate, for example, is obliged by law to withhold military and economic aid from a state which attracts an adverse report on human rights from the State Department.[16] Of course, when one reaches the realms of political sanctions, such as a condemnatory resolution of the OAS General Assembly, the weightiness of the response is likely to depend on the political complexion of the body itself. During Latin America's 'totalitarian phase' of the 1970s, condemnation of certain events was difficult to achieve. It is easier to attract such condemnation in the region's current 'democratic phase'.

Individual petitions under the Charter

As we saw above, the Commission, following amendment of its Statute at

Rio de Janeiro in 1965, was entitled to receive and act upon individual communications under Article 9(*bis*). When, however, the ACHR entered into force in 1979, control of this function was transferred to Article 20 of the Commission's new Statute. Although Article 20 reiterates the list of Declaration rights to which the Commission is obliged to pay particular attention, its Regulations none the less make it clear that it is able to deal with the violation of any rights contained in that instrument, including the economic and social rights.[17]

The procedure of the Commission concerning the admissibility of communications under the Charter is the same as that for admissibility under the Convention. The difference in treatment of the two types of communication lies at the post-admissibility stage, and this will be the main focus here. The requirements for admissibility will be dealt with in detail in the section on the procedures under the ACHR. Suffice it to say at this point that applicants must have exhausted all local remedies and that their applications must be timely and well-founded. Once admitted, the Commission investigates the communication by utilizing all information at its disposal, including the observations of the state which is invited to comment on the allegations. Having completed the investigatory stage of its proceedings, the Commission then compiles a final decision which comprises a statement of facts, the Commission's findings or conclusions and, where appropriate, recommendations to the state concerned.[18] Again, the 'sanction' on a state which fails to implement the Commission's recommendation is that of publicity, since the Commission is at liberty to publish the final decision in its annual report to the OAS General Assembly.[19] Unlike the case of country reports, however, the General Assembly has generally not shown itself to be particularly concerned with the question of individual communications. Cynics might argue that this is because there is little political mileage to be made out of isolated cases of human rights abuse.

Clearly, while the possibility of individual communication under the Charter represents an important step forward in terms of international and regional human rights protection, the system is none the less defective in a number of ways. First, there is no possibility – as there is under the Convention – of the Commission securing a friendly settlement between the state and the aggrieved individual. Second, the 'final decisions' of the Commission are not legally binding, although of course the 'sanction' of publicity may have some deterrent force or corrective utility where serious human rights violations are concerned. Third, the Court has no role to play within the individual application procedure under the Charter system, and therefore there is no possibility of legally binding judicial determination of the issues. Finally, there is no provision for the award of monetary compensation for individual victims.

THE AMERICAN CONVENTION ON HUMAN RIGHTS

The American Convention on Human Rights, also known as the Pact of San José, and its Protocol of San Salvador on Economic, Social and Cultural Rights comprise the second part of the inter-American human rights system. The ACHR was adopted at a special inter-governmental conference at San José, Costa Rica in 1969 and entered into force in July 1978.[20] The more recent Protocol was approved by the states parties to the ACHR on 14 November 1988 and was subsequently confirmed by the General Assembly of the OAS at its eighteenth regular session in San Salvador, El Salvador.[21] The Protocol is not yet in force.[22]

The format of the ACHR and its institutional structure is similar to that of the European Convention on Human Rights and Fundamental Freedoms of 1950, but it is apparent that the drafters of the American Convention drew on the accumulated experience under the European Convention and thereby managed to avoid some of its defects. The European Convention was not, however, the only source of inspiration for the drafters of the American Convention, who also drew on the ICCPR and, more particularly, the American Declaration. Similarly, the Protocol to the ACHR draws upon both the American Declaration and the ICESCR, but has novel elements both in the rights protected[23] and in the mechanisms for enforcement of those rights.[24]

Both the ACHR and its Protocol contain the traditional range of civil and political, and economic and social, rights, although it is clear that a number of the rights in both the Convention and Protocol are drafted in much broader terms than those in analogous instruments. As in other international human rights treaties, the dichotomy between the two broad groups of rights is identifiable. The civil and political rights are expressed in absolute and immediate terms, whereas the economic and social rights are framed in exhortatory terms and are to be implemented progressively. Article 1(1) of the ACHR requires states parties to 'respect the rights and freedoms recognized' and to 'ensure to all persons subject to their jurisdiction the free and full exercise of those rights and freedoms . . .', while Article 1 of the Protocol simply demands that states parties take appropriate measures 'for the purpose of achieving *progressively* . . . the full observance of the rights recognized in the Protocol'.[25]

Article 27(1) of the Convention permits states to take measures derogating from their obligations 'in time of war, public danger, or other emergency that threatens the independence or security of a state party . . . to the extent and period of time strictly required by the exigencies of the situation . . .'. Such measures must not, however, be discriminatory, and certain rights are classified as non-derogable in any circumstances.[26] The ACHR further states that the judicial remedies essential for the protection of the non-derogable rights may not be suspended. The Court in an advisory opinion given at the request of the Commission,[27] declared that this meant that the remedies of habeas corpus and *amparo* could never be suspended where they related to such non-derogable rights. Under Article 27(3), all derogations, the reasons for which they were taken and the period for which they are adopted must be communicated to the other member states of the OAS by informing the Secretary-General.

The institutional structure of the American Convention

Like the ECHR, the American Convention establishes two organs to supervise the implementation and enforcement of the rights contained within it: the Commission and the Court.

The Commission

Under Article 34 of the ACHR, as under the Charter, the Commission is composed of seven members who are required to be nationals of an OAS member state and persons of 'high moral character and competence in the field of human rights'. The Commission members serve for a period of four years in an independent capacity.[28] As a Convention institution, the Commission's many roles are defined by Article 41. Briefly stated they are educational, investigative, advisory, administrative and supervisory. These tasks are complementary and mutually supporting, and permit the Commission to oversee the totality of human rights activities in the states parties to the ACHR.

The Court

The Court is also composed of seven members who are required to be nationals of an OAS member state. They are elected in an individual capacity for a period of six years from among 'jurists of the highest moral authority and of recognized competence in the field of human rights, who possess the qualifications required for the exercise of the highest judicial functions . . .'.[29] The Court has two forms of jurisdiction: contentious and advisory. Under Article 62, states must accept the Court's contentious jurisdiction either unconditionally, conditionally or in specific cases. The Court's advisory jurisdiction, as we shall see below, may be used by any member state of the OAS without prior acceptance.

The Complaint Machinery

There are two categories of complaints which may be made under the Convention. The first is complaints by persons denouncing violations of the Convention by a state party under Article 44 of the ACHR. The second is complaints by states parties that another state party has violated the human rights protected by the Convention under Article 45. In analysing Article 44, two important points should be noted. First, all states which become party to the ACHR automatically recognize the competence of the Commission to receive complaints from persons alleging violation of their rights. This differs from Article 25 of the ECHR, which, as we have already seen, requires a declaration by a state party that it recognizes the competence of the European Commission to receive communications.[30] Indeed, the Court itself in *Viviana Gallardo*[31] described the American Convention as 'unique' among human rights instruments in making the right of private petition applicable against states parties as soon as they ratify the Convention. Second, while under article 25 of ECHR only 'victims' may author communications, under Article 44 of the ACHR:

> Any person or group of persons, or any non-governmental entity legally recognized in one or more member states of the Organization, may lodge petitions with the Commission containing denunciations or complaints of violation of this Convention by a State Party.

This is clearly drafted in wide terms and avoids the problems encountered by the European Commission in determining whether petitions may be received from persons who are themselves not victims, but who are petitioning on behalf of alleged victims. Thus, it is clear that unlike the European Convention which does not permit an *actio popularis*, the American Convention does.

In considering the second, inter-state system of complaints, it is clear that while Article 24 of the ECHR makes inter-state complaints mandatory for states parties, the ACHR requires states wishing to allow such complaints to make a declaration to that effect under Article 45. Even then, complaints may only be instituted on a reciprocal basis. The reason for making inter-state complaints subject to an optional declaration under the ACHR probably derives from the political sensitivity which would inevitably accompany such action in a hemisphere with widely differing political systems. An inter-state petition system can, as the ECHR system demonstrates, be abused by states wishing to make political capital out of disputes over alleged human rights violations.

The procedure for the admissibility of an individual communication under Article 44 or an inter-state communication under Article 45 is contained in Articles 46 and 47 of the ACHR. Article 46 establishes four conditions which must be met for admissibility. These are:

1 It must be demonstrated that all remedies under domestic law have been exhausted in accordance with the generally recognized principles of international law (Article 46(1)(a)).
2 The petition or communication has been lodged within six months from the date on which the party alleging violation of the rights was notified of the final judgment (Article 46(1)(b)).
3 The subject of the petition or communication must not be pending before another international proceeding for settlement. In the case of individual petitions, this effectively means the subject of the petition must not be under consideration by the HRC under the Optional Protocol to the ICCPR (Article 46(1)(c)).
4 In the case of individual petitions, the petition must not be anonymous and must contain details of the nationality, profession, domicile and signature of the person or the legal representative of the person lodging the petition (Article 46(1)(d)).

It should be noted, however, that the first two conditions are not applicable if the domestic legislation of the state complained of does not afford due process for the protection of the allegedly violated rights[32] or if the party alleging violation of the rights has been denied access to the remedies under domestic law or has been prevented from exhausting them.[33] In the latter context, the Court has held that where an individual has been unable to secure legal representation because of a generalized fear in the legal community that representing certain clients will lead to state retribution, it is unnecessary to exhaust local remedies.[34] This is a very real issue in a number of Central and Latin American states where lawyers may be unwilling or afraid to take on criminal defence cases because they are tainted with a 'political' element and may result in threats, maiming or death to them and their families. The Court also held in the same case that where indigence may prevent an individual from securing legal representation in circumstances where an absence of representation might affect the right to a fair trial, the individual is not under an obligation to exhaust local remedies. Furthermore, under Article 46(2), if remedies are shown to be either inadequate or ineffective, individuals are not required to exhaust them. In addition, unwarranted tardiness by a local court in giving final judgment in cases where effective local remedies are available will also obviate the need to exhaust domestic remedies. If a state alleges that a complainant has not exhausted local remedies, the burden of proof is upon the state to demonstrate this.

When the Commission is satisfied that the conditions in Article 46 have been fulfilled, it then proceeds to consider whether any of the factors which are contained in Article 47 exist and thereby render a petition or communication inadmissible. Once again, Article 47 contains four grounds occasioning inadmissibility:

1 That any of the requirements in Article 46 have not, in fact, been met (Article 47(1)(a)).
2 That the petition or communication does not state facts which tend to establish a violation of the rights guaranteed by the Convention (Article 47(1)(b)).
3 That the statements of the petitioner or of the state indicate that the petition or communication is manifestly groundless or obviously out of order (Article 47(1)(c)).
4 That the petition or communication is substantially the same as one previously 'studied' by the Commission or other international organization (Article 47(1)(d)).

Once a petition or communication has been declared prima facie admissible, the Commission then proceeds to its second stage. Here the Commission performs a number of parallel tasks under Article 48 of the ACHR. Its primary function is to obtain all the necessary evidence from the parties both in writing and during the course of oral proceedings. When it considers it 'necessary and advisable', the Commission may carry out an on-site investigation so as to verify the facts disclosed in a communication.[35] Such an investigation depends, of course, on the consent of the state party in question. If, during the course of its proceedings in the second stage, the Commission becomes aware of facts which indicate that the petition or communication ought not to have been admitted in the first place, it may still declare them inadmissible. The procedure contained in Article 48 may, however, be expedited in serious and urgent cases. Here, only the formal requirements of admissibility, that is those contained in Articles 46 and 47, are required before the Commission is empowered to conduct an on-site investigation with the prior consent of the state in whose territory the alleged violation has been committed.

During the investigative process contained in Article 48, the Commission is also required to perform a conciliatory function. Article 48(1)(f) provides:

> The Commission shall place itself at the disposal of the parties concerned with the view to reaching a friendly settlement of the matter on the basis of respect for the human rights recognized in this Convention.

If a friendly settlement is reached in accordance with this procedure, the Commission must draw up and transmit a report containing a brief statement of the facts and the solution reached to the Secretary-General of the OAS for publication.[36] Where a friendly settlement is not achieved, the Commission must draw up a report under Article 50 stating the facts and its conclusions and transmit it to the state party concerned within 180 days.

The Commission may make any proposal or recommendation which it sees fit to the state party, which is not at liberty to publish the report.[37]

After transmission of the report to the state concerned, a period of three months begins to run during which time the case may either be settled by the parties or submitted to the Court either by the Commission or the concerned state.[38] If neither of these occur within the time limit, the Commission may set forth its opinion and conclusions on the issue,[39] together with recommendations concerning the remedial measures which the state must take and the time limit within which they must be effected.[40] After this time limit has expired, the Commission must decide by a majority of its members whether the delinquent state has taken adequate measures to remedy the breach, and also whether or not to publish its report.[41]

From the foregoing it can be seen that the Commission has a broad discretion to decide whether or not to deal with an issue itself or to transmit it to the Court if, of course, the state concerned has accepted the Court's jurisdiction. There is no guidance in the ACHR or the Commission's Statute, Regulations or Rules of Procedure about when a contentious case should be disposed of by remitting it to the Court rather than by the other methods envisaged by Article 51. In its advisory opinion in *Compulsory Membership*,[42] the Court gave an indication of which cases ought to be submitted to the Court's contentious jurisdiction. Here, the Court was requested by Costa Rica to give an advisory opinion on whether a Costa Rican law requiring those who wished to practise the profession of journalism to be members of an organization prescribed by law, conflicted with Articles 13 and 29 of the ACHR. Although submitted as a request for an advisory opinion, the case had its origins in an individual petition presented to the Commission by a US citizen, Stephen Schmidt, who had practised journalism without being a member of the specified organization and who had consequently been convicted and sentenced to three months imprisonment under Costa Rican law.[43] Costa Rica won the case before the Commission, but neither the Commission nor Costa Rica decided at that stage to submit the case to the Court's contentious jurisdiction. The Court nevertheless considered that the Commission should have done so because the case raised controversial legal issues on which neither the domestic courts nor the Commission had been able to agree. Furthermore, the issue was of considerable importance to other states of the hemisphere since it had not been considered by the Court in the past.

While this decision is specific to the *Compulsory Membership* case, it seems that cases bearing these characteristics should be referred to the Court as a matter of course. It is also interesting to note that the state which is the object of a communication may also send the case to the Court within the three-month period. This is clearly a safeguard for any state that may wish to contest the validity of a decision reached by the Commission in its case. Like the European Convention, which as yet remains unamended by Protocol No. 9,[44] individuals have no competence to seise the Court of a case.

Although proceedings before the Commission appear to be cumbersome and lengthy, it should be noted that the main objective of the procedure, like that of the European Commission, is the friendly settlement of the dispute between the complainant and the respondent state. There are two opportunities for this: first, during the Commission's investigatory procedure under Article 48 where it exercises its conciliatory function and, second, at the stage of its first report under Article 51 where the state party may simply comply with the recommendations made by the Commission.

Contentious proceedings before the Court

As indicated above, under Article 62 contentious proceedings can only be initiated before the Court if the state party or states parties concerned have accepted its jurisdiction in such matters. Furthermore, proceedings cannot be initiated either by the Commission or a state party unless the procedures before the Commission have been fully completed. A state may not waive the Commission's procedures and take the matter directly to the Court. In *Viviana Gallardo*,[45] Gallardo, a suspected terrorist, was murdered in her prison cell by a member of the Costa Rican National Guard who had been instructed to guard her. Costa Rica attempted to bypass the Commission's procedures by waiving them and taking the substantive issues directly to the Court for determination. The Court held, however, that it lacked jurisdiction to hear the case in such circumstances, because first, on a literal interpretation of the relevant Convention provisions, it was clear that completion of the Commission's procedures were mandatory and not optional and, second, as a matter of policy, the Commission's procedures had not been created solely for the benefit of states, but in order to allow victims to protect their rights. The main concern of the Court here was that if a state were permitted to take a case directly to the Court, this would circumvent the Commission's important conciliatory function and would thus distort the integrity of the Convention's structure. None the less, the Court left open the question of whether certain categories of proceedings, particularly inter-state applications, might not be taken directly to the Court. Here, the issue of individual rights protection might not be so acute and might not therefore affect the integrity of the Convention's structure.

Once a case has been properly referred to the Court, it has the competence to review the Commission's findings of fact and law *de novo*. Thus, the Court can determine whether or not an individual has properly complied with the procedural requirements, particularly the exhaustion of domestic remedies, before the Commission. In reviewing questions of fact, the Court may also have regard to whether or not the burden of proof has been adequately discharged. This issue has been dealt with by the Court in three cases against Honduras involving the enforced disappearance of a number of individuals.[46] While the Court adopts the general principle of 'equality of arms' in international judicial proceedings, that is both parties start on an equal footing, and that it is the responsibility of the party adducing a particular fact to prove that fact, it has also made a number of modifications in order to take account of the specific human rights context. In particular, it has noted that the standards of proof in such proceedings are far less formalistic and rigid than in domestic proceedings, and that in cases where states are uncooperative or have actively participated in the suppression of evidence about certain practices, substantial recourse may be had to circumstantial evidence and matters of inference. The Court has also made it abundantly clear that it does not see human rights proceedings as the international analogue of domestic criminal proceedings, since the main objective of such proceedings is to secure state compliance with its obligations and redress for any violations which may have occurred; it is not to punish the state.[47]

In determining questions of evidence and proof, the Court may not only have regard to documentary evidence, but may also hear witnesses in person. States are under an obligation to facilitate the Court's access to such witnesses and are required not to take measures of reprisal against individuals who testify. While proceedings before the Court are normally held in public, it is possible for the Court to sit in closed session where the evidence of certain witnesses may touch upon matters of national security or be otherwise sensitive to the government in question. In fact, this occurred in *Velasquez Rodriguez*, where the head of Honduran national security was permitted to give evidence *in camera*.

A contentious case normally terminates with a judgment by the Court that there has or has not been a violation of one or more of the rights in the ACHR. The Court, however, enjoys a discretion to keep a case open in order to ensure effective supervision and enforcement of its judgment. Although a judgment of the Court is final and cannot be the subject of an appeal, it may, at the request of any of the parties, within ninety days of the communication of the judgment to them, be the subject of a request for interpretation.[48] This has already occurred in *Interpretation of Compensatory Damages*,[49] where the Court was requested to rule whether an award of damages made by it to the victim's next of kin in the *Velasquez Rodriguez* case inferred any obligation on the part of Honduras to index link the award to ensure that its value was maintained over a long period of time.

If a breach of the Convention is found, the delinquent state is under an obligation to ensure that the injured party enjoys the rights affected, and, where appropriate, the circumstances which gave rise to the breach be remedied and fair compensation paid.[50] States parties to the ACHR undertake to comply with the judgment of the Court in cases to which they are party, and therefore decisions of the Court are binding upon them.[51] While the Court has not yet had an opportunity to rule on the question of positive measures to be taken in the event of a violation, it has been able to rule on the issue of compensatory damages.

In *Velasquez Rodriguez – Compensatory Damages,*[52] the Court was required to determine the amount of damages which should be awarded to the next of kin of Velasquez who had been disappeared by agents of the Honduran government. The Court took the view here that the objective of the damages was to remedy in full the damage caused by the state's delinquency. Honduras was required, as far as was possible, to put Velasquez's next of kin in the position which they would have enjoyed had it not been for the breach of the Convention. Thus the next of kin were indemnified for Velasquez's loss of earnings throughout the remainder of his life, based on an assessment of his career prospects as a teacher and on actuarial principles. The Court also found in this case, however, that the state should compensate for the emotional and moral harm done to Velasquez's wife and children as a consequence of his disappearance and murder. This approach is different to the European Court, which has been reluctant to accept that emotional and moral damage can be quantified in any meaningful way.

In its judgment, the Court also determined how the damages were to be paid to the next of kin. A quarter of the sum was to be paid directly to Velasquez's wife, and the remainder was to be placed in trust for his children. It was this part of the judgment which prompted the Commission to request an interpretation of the judgment under Article 67 of the ACHR. Here, the Commission was concerned about the possible erosion of the children's damages by inflation unless the Court insisted that the award be index-linked. The Court, however, pointed out in *Interpretation of Compensatory Damages*[53] that by placing a substantial portion of the damages in a trust fund – which was to be managed 'under the most favorable conditions' – implied that an element of indexing was already inherent to the award.

If the Court awards damages against a state, under Article 68(2) the state may, at its option, give effect to the judgment 'in accordance with the domestic procedure governing the execution of judgments against the state'. Although Costa Rica in its headquarters' agreement with the Court has provided that judgments of the Court will be enforced in that state as if they were judgments of local courts, this approach does not appear to be mandatory. The absence of a mandatory enforcement mechanism would seem to be a major gap in the Convention's protective system.

As far as execution of other parts of the Court's judgments is concerned, there is, similarly, no provision which deals with this matter directly. Article

65, however, provides that the Court, when making its annual report to the regular session of the OAS General Assembly, must specify cases in which a state has not complied with its ruling. The issue of noncompliance, therefore, is to be resolved essentially by political processes. Once again, therefore, we see that the primary 'sanction' in this realm is that of political pressure and adverse publicity.

The judgments of the Court in contentious cases are in effect declaratory, since technically they are only binding upon the parties to the case in question. Nevertheless, it is clear that the Court's interpretation of the ACHR and the rights protected by it is authoritative and therefore its judgments have a greater practical significance than their formal status would appear to imply. While states which are not party to proceedings are obviously under no obligation to comply with the judgment, a prudent state will recognize the authority of the Court's rulings and seek to bring its own laws into line with them. Furthermore, it is evident from the practice of the Court to date that it will, like the European Court, develop a *jurisprudence constante* or a practice of referring back to its own judgments in which it considers it has made a particularly important ruling on some legal principle arising from the Convention. In the absence of any system of precedent, this lends a degree of continuity and predictability to the Court's judgments.

Provisional measures

One vitally important power of the Court which requires some comment is its ability to order provisional measures in order to deal with urgent situations. Article 63(2) provides:

> In cases of extreme gravity and urgency, and where necessary to avoid irreparable damage to persons, the Court shall adopt such provisional measures as it deems pertinent in matters it has under consideration. With respect to a case not yet submitted to the Court, it may act at the request of the Commission.

The operation of this provision was vividly demonstrated in the Honduran disappearance cases. Here, a number of witnesses who had either testified or were about to testify before the Court were assassinated. A number of other potential witnesses had also had their lives and property threatened. The Court therefore ordered two sets of provisional measures: one requiring Honduras to take measures to protect the witnesses and the second requiring the state to investigate the assassinations and to bring the perpetrators to justice.[54]

Advisory opinions

The advisory jurisdiction of the Inter-American Court is broader in scope than that of any other international tribunal yet in existence, and compares favourably to the exceptionally narrow and technical advisory competence of the European Court of Human Rights under ECHR Protocol 2.[55] Article 64 of the ACHR provides:

> 1. The member states of the [OAS] may consult the Court regarding the interpretation of the Convention or of any other treaties concerning the protection of human rights in the American states. Within their spheres of competence, the organs listed in Chapter X of the Charter of the [OAS], as amended by the Protocol of Buenos Aires, may in like manner consult the Court.

> 2. The Court, at the request of a member state of the [OAS], may provide that state with opinions regarding the compatibility of any of its domestic laws with the aforesaid international instruments.

While there are a number of points to note about Article 64, perhaps the most salient is that it is not only the parties to the ACHR which have the power to request an opinion from the Court, but also any member state of the OAS whether they are parties to the Convention or not. Furthermore, these states are not only competent to request an interpretation of the instruments referred to in Article 64, but are entitled to ask the Court whether their domestic laws are compatible with such instruments. This gives the Court a jurisdiction reasonably similar to that of the Court of Justice of the EC under Article 177 of the EEC Treaty, and enhances the integrationist potential in this field. Such a conclusion may be further supported by reference to the fact that the Court may also render advisory opinions at the request of a wide variety of OAS organs. The only requirements which an OAS organ need show in order to seek an advisory opinion are that the issue falls within its sphere of competence and that it has a 'legitimate institutional interest' in so doing.[56] As the Court pointed out in *Effect of Reservations*, the Commission will, as a matter of principle, always be able to satisfy these requirements and will therefore always be competent to seek a ruling. By extension, it would seem that the OAS General Assembly will always fall into this category.

Since most of the Court's jurisprudence has been developed through the medium of its advisory jurisdiction, it has had considerable opportunity to interpret Article 64 and to define the limits of its application. Thus the Court has declared that it has a broad discretion under Article 64 in deciding whether or not to offer an opinion in any given case.[57] This enables it to deal with circumstances in which a request for an advisory opinion might be seen as an abuse of process. Such a potential abuse might occur, for example, where a request for an advisory opinion is, in reality, a disguised contentious case, since it deals with matters which are the subject of an actual dispute.[58] However, even where a request for an advisory opinion deals with an ongoing dispute between identifiable parties, the Court will not necessarily refuse to exercise its jurisdiction if it considers that the opinion might achieve some useful purpose, such as assisting one of the OAS organs to fulfil its role under the Convention. Furthermore, the Court has interpreted a request to rule on the compatibility of a state's domestic law with its international human rights obligations, as including competence to rule on the compatibility of draft domestic laws.[59] In seeking an advisory opinion on all these matters, the request must come from a competent governmental representative. The Court's view here seems to imply that it must be a member of the state's executive; a request from a state's legislature has been found to be inadequate.[60]

Another question arising in the context of Article 64(1) has been the meaning of 'other treaties concerning the protection of human rights in the American states'.[61] Here, the Court interpreted the phrase broadly to mean any treaty to which an OAS member state was party which affected the protection of human rights in that state. The Court made it clear that the phrase was not restricted to human rights treaties concluded within the inter-American system. The Court thus empowered itself to interpret any other human rights treaty, such as the ICCPR, if it affected any OAS member. The objection that this might lead to differing interpretations of the same instrument by different human rights institutions, was discounted by the Court, which observed that the possibility of conflicting interpretation existed in all legal systems that were not hierarchically integrated. None the less, it is apparent that the Court will take into account authoritative interpretations of other instruments by the competent institutions, such as the Human Rights Committee, under those instruments.

Since these opinions of the Court are, by definition, advisory, technically they have no legal binding force. Nevertheless, if one examines the competence of the Court, which is to ensure the fulfilment of the commitments undertaken by the states parties and to interpret and apply the ACHR, it is apparent that the force of the Court's opinion's derive from its inherent authority. Clearly, if a state were to act in a manner contrary to one of the Court's advisory opinions, it would be difficult to avoid the conclusion that it had, in effect, breached its obligations, as interpreted by the Court, under the Convention.

The Court's techniques of interpretation

The Court has begun to develop a significant jurisprudence under both its contentious and, to a greater extent, its advisory jurisdiction. This has not only involved the interpretation of a number of substantive rights, but the Court has also made the most of its opportunities to develop certain principles of international human rights law which are applicable to the field in general. Before briefly examining some of the advances made by the Court in this area, it is appropriate to analyse its techniques of interpretation. In nearly all its judgments, the Court has declared that the laws appropriate for treaty interpretation are the rules contained in Articles 31 and 32 of the Vienna Convention on the Law of Treaties.[62] Like its European counterpart, however, the Inter-American Court has not been constrained by narrow rules of textuality, but has, to a limited degree – given the relative paucity of decided cases – employed the principles of effectiveness and teleology. In a general sense, however, the Court has been guided by the proposition that the primary object and purpose of the ACHR is to guarantee and protect the rights of individuals. Its approach, therefore, has been to interpret the rights and guarantees in favour of individuals.

This view has also been reflected in the Court's approach to questions of general international human rights law. In particular, it has taken the view that modern human rights treaties are not simply multilateral treaties of the traditional type concluded to accomplish reciprocal exchanges of rights and obligations between the contracting parties, but that they are more in the nature of unilateral commitments made by states in order to ensure the protection of individuals' rights.[63] The practical consequences of such a view are that reservations to the ACHR cannot be interpreted in such a way as to limit the enjoyment of individual rights, nor may they be entered against a non-derogable right.[64] This particular line of argument has also brought the Court close to, but not actually to the point of, declaring that some of the rights in the ACHR and in the American Declaration are representative of *ius cogens*.

In the Honduran disappearance cases, the Court was required to deal with a phenomenon which was not referred to specifically in the ACHR. None the less, it was able to reduce the practice of disappearances to its central components. Thus, the Court found that disappearances violate the right to life (Article 4), the right to humane treatment (Article 5) and the right to personal liberty (Article 7). It was a feature of the Court's judgment in these cases, however, that it did not attempt to elaborate in detail the precise content of these rights. This was perhaps inevitable, since most of the cases were concerned with procedural issues and the proof of evidence. Once the Court had the evidence before it demonstrating that Honduras was responsible for the practice, it apparently felt that it needed to go no further in order to establish state liability.

In its advisory opinions, the Court has dealt with issues concerning the freedom of thought and expression in a case involving the compulsory licensing of journalists and the guaranteed right of reply to published injurious statements;[65] the right to nationality;[66] and a number of cases involving derogations from, and limitations to, the rights protected by the Convention.[67] Each of these cases is characterized by extremely careful, well-elaborated judgments of the highest quality which all bear careful scrutiny. Although the Court is, in institutional terms, only in its infancy, it has already begun to make its mark as a human rights organ of considerable importance.

A final question which needs to be considered, however, is why there has not been greater use of the Court's contentious procedure in the last ten years. There is a stark incongruity between the level of human rights violations in the Western Hemisphere and the degree of the Court's utilization in individual cases. There are perhaps a number of reasons for this. The first is that the Court's contentious procedure suffers from the same drawbacks as other human rights institutions and procedures. The primary obstacle here is that of state sovereignty. States are notoriously unwilling to submit to international adjudication of any form, preferring instead to operate through the medium of diplomatic and political fora. Within the inter-American context, there could, until recently, be seen to be a general reluctance on the part of states to accept the compulsory jurisdiction of the Court. State resistance to compulsory jurisdiction in the current democratic phase seems to be lessening.

A second major obstacle to the Court's use is that the socio-economic climate in the Western Hemisphere has not generally been conducive to human rights protection. High levels of poverty and lack of education coupled with widespread fear of challenging the state have made human right petitioning under an individual system neither easy nor an attractive proposition if one valued longevity. An associated major factor, as one of the Court's advisory opinions disclosed, is both the availability of affordable legal services in many American states, and, perhaps more pertinently, the willingness of lawyers to offer their services in cases where the victim appears to be politically 'tainted'.

Finally, the structure of the ACHR itself is a hindrance to its effective operation. Individuals, as we have seen, have no direct access to the Court, but must wait for the Commission's procedures to be completed. These procedures can be extremely lengthy and their focus is not on seeking redress for individuals but upon reaching a friendly accommodation between the allegedly delinquent state and the complainant. In the inter-American context, the opportunity for state interference with this process is self-evident. As Judge Piza Escalante observed in a separate opinion in *Viviana Gallardo*,[68] the Commission's procedures are 'a veritable obstacle course that is almost insurmountable'. He further observed that there was nothing that the Commission could do which could not be done as effectively by the

Court. In addition to these criticisms is the fact that the Commission enjoys a discretion in determining whether to refer a case to the Court. While the Court has been able to offer some guidance to the Commission on when a case should be referred in *Compulsory Membership*,[69] it is ironic that the Commission had refused to refer that case to the Court and that it had been left to the goodwill of Costa Rica to do so, when it clearly had nothing tangible to gain from the reference.

With increasing democratization in a number of Latin American states, it is probable that the contentious jurisdiction of the Court will be put to greater use. Certainly, the prospects are for a less despairing statement from a retiring judge than that of Judge Maximo Cisneros who said in *Compulsory Membership*:

> Now, whereas in signing this Advisory Opinion I am performing my last act as a judge of the Inter-American Court of Human Rights, I wish to say that the "love" that we have put into our work has not been sufficient to avoid the sense of frustration that I feel in leaving the Court before it has had the opportunity to hear a single case of a violation of human rights, in spite of the sad reality of America in this field.

FURTHER READING

Buergenthal, T., 'The American Convention on Human Rights: Illusions and Hopes', (1971) 21 *Buffalo Law Review* 121–36.

Buergenthal, T., 'The Revised OAS Charter and the Protection of Human Rights', (1975) 69 *AJIL* 828-36.

Buergenthal, T., 'The Inter-American Court of Human Rights', (1982) 76 *AJIL* 231–45.

Buergenthal, T., 'The Advisory Practice of the Inter-American Court of Human Rights', (1985) 79 *AJIL* 1–27.

Buergenthal, T., 'The Inter-American Court of Human Rights and the OAS', (1986) 7 *HRLJ* 157–64.

Buergenthal, T., 'The Inter-American System for the Protection of Human Rights', in *Meron*, pp. 439–93.

Buergenthal, T., Norris, R. and Shelton, D., *Protecting Human Rights in the Americas* (Kehl-am-Rhein: Engel, 3rd edn, 1990).

Camargo, P.P., 'The American Convention on Human Rights', (1970) 3 *Human Rights Journal* 333–56.

Davidson, S., *The Inter-American Court of Human Rights* (Aldershot: Dartmouth, 1992).

Fenwick, C.G., *The Organization of American States* (Washington, DC, 1963).

Gros Espiell, H., 'The Organization of American States (OAS)', in *Vasak*, Vol. 2, pp. 543–74.

LeBlanc, L.J., *The OAS and the Promotion and Protection of Human Rights* (The Hague: Martinus Nijhoff, 1977).

Nikken, P., 'The Impact of the World Crisis on Human Rights', in Silva-Michelana, J. (ed.), *Latin America: Peace, Democratization and Economic Crisis* (Tokyo: UN University/London and New York: Zed Books, 1988), pp. 187–201.

Norris, R.E., 'The New Statute of the Inter-American Commission on Human Rights', (1980) 1 *HRLJ* 379–87.

Norris, R.E., 'The Individual Petition Procedure of the Inter-American System for the Protection of Human Rights', in Hannum, H. (ed.), *Guide to International Human Rights Practice* (Philadelphia: University of Pennsylvania Press, 1984), pp. 108–14.

Robertson, A.H. and Merrills, J.G., *Human Rights in the World* (Manchester: Manchester University Press, 1989), ch. 5.

THE AFRICAN SYSTEM FOR PROTECTING HUMAN AND PEOPLES' RIGHTS

INTRODUCTION

While the last three chapters of this book have dealt with human rights instruments and institutions which have been in place and functioning for some time, it is the purpose of this chapter to examine a system of more recent origin.

THE AFRICAN CHARTER ON HUMAN AND PEOPLES' RIGHTS

The African Charter, sometimes known as the Banjul Charter after the capital of the Gambia where it was drafted, is the most recent of the regional human rights instruments to come into force. It was adopted at the Eighteenth Assembly of Heads of State and Government of the Organization of African Unity (OAU) in Nairobi, Kenya in June 1981 and entered into force on 21 October 1986.[1] As we shall see, the Charter differs considerably from its other regional counterparts, both in the catalogue of rights protected and in the means of implementation and protection. This is not surprising, since it was drafted to take account of African culture and legal philosophy, and is specifically directed towards African needs. Indeed, the Preamble to the Charter speaks of 'the virtue of the [member states'] historical tradition and the values of African civilization which should inspire and characterize their reflection on the concept of human and peoples' rights'.

It might also be argued that of all the regional instruments, the African Charter faces the most acute challenges. Many African states are recently decolonized and are struggling with the legacies of economic underdevelopment, lack of education and inter-communal strife resulting from the colonial imposition of artificial boundaries. Furthermore, many of the political systems in a number of African states are not conducive to the proper functioning of democratic institutions – whether one uses the term democratic in a Western or an African sense – underpinned by the rule of law. None the less, the OAU Charter – which was adopted in 1963 – committed the member states 'to promote international cooperation, having due regard to the Charter of the United Nations and the Universal Declaration of Human Rights'. The African Charter may be seen as the fruit of this commitment.

The rights protected

This is the first area in which the African Charter differs considerably from its other regional analogues. Not only does the Charter seek to protect individual civil and political rights, it also seeks to promote, within the single instrument, economic and social rights and the controversial category of third-generation rights. It also spells out clearly the *duties* owed by individuals to family, society and the state. This holistic approach to human rights is prefaced by the Preamble to the Charter, which states:

> . . . that it is henceforth essential to pay particular attention to the right to development and that civil and political rights cannot be dissociated from economic, social and cultural rights in their conception as well as universality and that the satisfaction of economic, social and cultural rights is a guarantee for the enjoyment of civil and political rights.

The civil and political rights, which are protected by Articles 2–13, comprise the traditional range of rights that are included in the ICCPR and the other regional instruments. One particular freedom that represents a particular African concern is Article 12, which prohibits the mass expulsion of non-nationals and is aimed at national, racial, ethnic or religious groups. There have on occasion been mass expulsions of non-nationals from states, for example the Nigerian expulsion of all Ghanaians from its territory in 1983, and it is this form of action at which Article 12 is directed. All the substantive rights in the Charter are to be accorded to individuals without discrimination on any ground. It is interesting to note that this includes the injunction that there should be no discrimination on the grounds of a person's 'fortune', which implies African recognition that the enforcement of rights may depend upon a person's general circumstances or status in society.

The economic and social rights contained in the Charter also largely reflect the range of such rights in other international instruments. However, there are a number of additions which are worthy of note. The right to education, for example, in Article 17, is supplemented by a duty upon the state whose obligation it is to promote and protect the 'morals and traditional values recognized by the community'. Article 18 reflects similar African concerns and provides:

1. The family shall be the natural unit and basis of society. It shall be protected by the State which shall take care of its physical and moral health.

2. The State shall have the duty to assist the family which is the custodian of morals and traditional values recognized by the community.

Article 18(3) also contains one of the most comprehensive clauses concerning the prohibition of discrimination against women by providing that 'the state shall ensure the elimination of every discrimination against women and also ensure the protection of the rights of the woman and the child as stipulated in international declarations and conventions'. This extremely broad incorporation of other international instruments clearly makes no distinction as to whether or not they are in force for states parties to the Charter: those states will automatically be bound by the standards established by the relevant instruments on becoming party to the Charter.

The African Charter is the only regional human rights instrument to incorporate third-generation rights. In protecting the right to self-determination, the Charter not only traverses the familiar ground of the UN Covenants, but it also includes rather more controversial rights such as the right to economic, social and cultural development 'with due regard to their freedom and identity and in equal enjoyment of the common heritage of mankind'.[2] Article 24 of the Charter also includes the right of peoples to peace and security and to a 'general satisfactory environment favourable to their development'. Clearly, these rights impose obligations on states not only to order their internal affairs in such a way as to preserve or improve environmental factors, but they also require that they pursue particular forms of foreign policy calculated to achieve such an end.

Although the American Declaration deals with the question of duties as well as rights, it is only in the African Charter that duties are imposed on individuals as a matter of international legal obligation. Again, the reason for this is that the African sense of family and community places great emphasis upon the individual's responsibility to both groups. Many of the rights contained in the Charter thus have a correlative duty attached to them. Broad concepts of duty to the family, society and the state are established by Articles 27 and 28 of the Charter, while Article 29 lists the specific duties which are imposed upon the individual. Some of these duties have a particularly nebulous quality, and in many cases it is difficult to see where their limits might lie.[3]

Another area in which the African Charter differs from other human rights instruments is the absence of a provision permitting derogation from the rights protected in particular circumstances. While the rights concerning the physical integrity of the person appear to be absolute, many of the individual rights which deal with matters such as freedom of expression and association are formulated in a manner which implies the possibility of derogations.

Articles 8–13 all provide for the enjoyment of rights within certain limitations. Article 8 provides for freedom of conscience and religion and declares that 'no one may, *subject to law and order*, be submitted to measures restricting the exercise of these freedoms'. Article 9(2) provides that 'every individual shall have the right to express and disseminate his opinions *within the law*'. Article 10(1) states that 'every individual shall have the right *to free association provided that he abides by the law*'. Articles 11–13 continue in similar vein. It may be argued, however, that far from implying a right of derogation, these formulations simply indicate that the limits to these rights are prescribed by law in accordance with the concept of democratic legitimacy. This conclusion can, however, only be tentative, because unlike the preambles to the European and American Conventions, the African Charter nowhere refers to the fundamental importance of democracy and democratic institutions. None the less, since the Charter is a human rights instrument, it must be assumed that its provisions must be construed in favour of the primacy of rights and against state interference, even if it is justified by formally adopted legal measures. Here again, the notion of constitutional legitimacy may be implied. It is arguable, however, that the formulation of the individual civil and political rights in the Charter is weaker and more susceptible to being undercut by 'legal' measures than those in its European and American counterparts.

Supervision under the Charter

Article 1 of the Charter requires states to recognize the rights, duties and freedoms enshrined in it and to undertake to adopt legislative or other measures to give effect to them. The Charter also imposes two further classes of obligation upon states parties. First, under Article 25, they are 'to promote and ensure through teaching, education and publication the respect of the rights and freedoms contained in the . . . Charter and to see to it that these freedoms and rights as well as corresponding obligations and duties are understood'. Second, by Article 26, parties are under a duty to guarantee the independence of the courts and 'shall allow the establishment and improvement of appropriate national institutions entrusted with the promotion and protection of the rights and freedoms guaranteed by the present Charter'.

The major perceptible difference between the institutional structure of the Charter and that of other regional human rights instruments is the absence of any court to settle disputes between states or to rule on individual grievances. The reason for this, according to one African jurist,[4] is that Africans tend to focus on reconciliation and consensus as a means of settling disputes, rather than upon contentious procedures. Article 30 of the Charter simply provides for the establishment of a Commission 'established within the framework of the [OAU] to promote human and peoples' rights and ensure their protection in Africa'. The Commission is composed of eleven members elected by the Assembly of Heads of State and Government of the OAU 'from amongst African personalities of the highest reputation, known for their high morality, integrity, impartiality and competence in matters of human and peoples' rights' for a period of six years.[5] The African Commission, therefore, unlike its other regional analogues, is drawn from all members of its sponsoring regional organization, rather than parties to the Charter. The probable reason for this is that in the absence of any court, the Commission must exercise quasi-judicial functions and needs therefore to reflect the wider African community. The members of the Commission, however, serve in their individual capacities and not as government representatives.[6]

The African Commission's mandate

The Commission enjoys a broad and multifaceted role under Article 45 of the Charter. It operates under four main heads: promotional, protective, interpretative and consultative. Its promotional role entails the totality of activities commonly associated with this field. It is required, *inter alia*, to undertake 'studies and researches [*sic*]' on African human and peoples' rights problems, to organize seminars, symposia and conferences and so on. More importantly, however, it is also mandated 'should the case arise' to give its views or to make recommendations to governments. This language is reminiscent of the OAS Charter in so far as it relates to the competences of the Inter-American Commission. We have already seen how creative that institution has been in developing its country studies and on-site investigation procedures, but it will be interesting to see if the African Commission can similarly develop its competences.

Within the context of the Commission's promotional activities, it is also possible to discern a standard-setting role. Article 45(1)(b) requires the Commission to 'formulate and lay down, principles and rules aimed at solving legal problems relating to human and peoples' rights . . . upon which African Governments may base their legislation'. This implies a proactive and quasi-legislative role for the Commission which, on the basis of this provision, may undertake drafting programmes of its own motion.

The protective function of the Commission comprises two aspects: an inter-state and an individual communication procedure. As we have already seen, these are common to the other regional human rights instruments, save that in the case of the African system, the procedures begin and end with the Commission since there is no court. These procedures will be examined in detail later.

The Commission's interpretative task once again assumes substantial significance in the absence of a court which is competent to offer authoritative interpretations of the Charter. Under Article 45(3) of the Charter, the Commission is mandated to 'interpret all the provisions of the present Charter at the request of a State party, an institution of the OAU or an African Organization recognized by the OAU'. This gives the Commission a role similar to that of the Inter-American Court of Human Rights under Article 64 of the American Convention. Whether the Commission will utilize this competence as creatively as the Inter-American Court remains to be seen. It should be noted that in addition to this formal quasi-judicial power of the Commission under Article 45, it will also be required to exercise its interpretative competences under the communications procedures under Chapter III of the Charter.

Before leaving these general matters concerned with the Commission's mandate, some mention should be made of Articles 60 and 61. These are omnibus provisions which have the effect of integrating regional African human rights standards and practices with those of the universal and other regional systems. Article 60 provides that the Commission 'shall draw inspiration from international law on human and peoples' rights'. It then lists, by way of example, a large number of universal instruments, both actual and potential, including the UN Charter, the Universal Declaration and all the human rights instruments made or to be made under the auspices of the UN. The effect of this provision is to create a deep reservoir of principles and rules from which the African Commission can draw. The depth of the reservoir is further increased by Article 61, which provides that the Commission 'shall also take into consideration, *as subsidiary measures to determine the principles of law*', other international instruments, which would seem to mean in this context the other regional human rights instruments, and 'African practices consistent with international norms on human and peoples' rights, customs generally accepted as law, general principles of law recognized by African states as well as legal precedents and doctrine'. The net effect of Articles 60 and 61 is to provide the Commission with the means by which to ensure the adequate integration of the African regional system into the mainstream of human rights law. In this respect, it is more adequately equipped than its American counterpart, which in turn occupies a better position than the European Commission.

The Commission's procedures

Before examining the Commission's inter-state and individual communications procedures, it is appropriate to note that the Charter provides an extremely wide competence to that institution in carrying out its functions. Article 46 states: 'The Commission may resort to any appropriate method of investigation; it may hear from The Secretary-General of the [OAU] or any other person capable of enlightening it.'

Inter-state complaints

There are two forms of inter-state complaint mechanism contained in the Charter. The first, under Article 47, permits a state party which believes another to have violated its obligations under the Convention to address a communication directly to the delinquent state. The communication must also be copied to the Secretary-General of the OAU and to the Chairman of the Commission. Within three months, the state to which the communication is addressed must respond fully, indicating the redress already given or the courses of action available to remedy the violation. If within three months the issue is not settled to the satisfaction of the two states through bilateral negotiations or through other mechanisms of peaceful dispute settlement, then either party may refer the matter to the Commission. This procedure does not differ from other forms of international dispute resolution, save in the fact that the Commission's jurisdiction is mandatory for parties to the Charter if either of the parties should choose to submit the matter of the dispute to the Commission. If neither of the parties wishes to submit the dispute to the Commission, then there is no time limit to the proceedings. Should the dispute be submitted to the Commission, the procedures for dealing with it are exactly the same as those where a dispute is brought before the Commission under Article 49.

The alternative procedure is initiated under Article 49 by a state complaining directly to the Commission that another state party has violated the provisions of the Charter. Before the Commission can deal with a complaint under Articles 47 or 49, however, it must satisfy itself that 'all local remedies, if they exist, have been exhausted'. There is no need to exhaust local remedies where the procedure for obtaining them is unreasonably prolonged. The inclusion of this particular provision in an inter-state procedure seems to be superfluous. If there is a breach of the Charter by a state, whether it relates to a substantive right or some other matter, under the general principles of international law, that will automatically give rise to a direct international wrong. Here, there is no requirement – indeed, there is no possibility – for another state to exhaust local remedies, since a state is unlikely to have the necessary legal standing before an appropriate domestic tribunal. Similarly, if the breach relates to the ill-treatment of an individual which the complaining state is seeking to espouse, it is the individual who must exhaust the local remedies within the respondent state, before the complaining state can take up the individual's cause. If the individual has not exhausted available local remedies, there can, by definition, be no breach of the Charter.

Once the Commission has satisfied itself, however, that local remedies have been exhausted, it then may ask the states concerned to present to it all relevant information. There is no indication of who is to determine what is or is not relevant information, but presumably this lies within the province of the Commission. Furthermore, the Commission when considering the matter, may ask the states involved to submit written or oral representations to it. This should also be read in the light of Article 46 which, it will be recalled, allows the Commission to hear 'from any other person capable of enlightening it'. It would seem, therefore, that the Commission has a very wide power to call witnesses, including the alleged victim if there be one. If, after following this procedure, no 'amicable solution based on the respect of Human and Peoples' Rights' has been achieved by the Commission, it must draw up a report which is to be sent to the OAU Heads of State and Government. The report must not only contain the facts and findings of the Commission, but it may also contain such recommendations as the Commission 'deems useful'. Two points may be noted about this procedure. First, the reference to an 'amicable solution' in Article 52 suggests that the primary concern of the Commission is to achieve a friendly settlement. This is nowhere explicitly stated, but such an approach would seem consistent both with African legal philosophy and the techniques of other human rights institutions. Second, the final destination of the Commission's reports is clearly the dominant political organ of the OAU. This implies that any final decision on the reports is likely to be based on political rather than legal considerations. This conclusion is further reinforced when it is recalled that these are inter-state disputes under the Charter, which are hardly likely to be conducive to good relations between the parties. This may very well translate itself into political alliances in the meeting of the Heads of State and Government.

Individual communications

It is perhaps a misnomer to refer to individual communications under the Charter, since the heading of the appropriate part refers to '*other* communications'. A quick perusal of the procedure to be applied in such cases also indicates that it is unlike that utilized in the two other regional conventions, but appears to be a fusion of ECOSOC and the regional conventions' procedures.

Article 55 requires the Secretary of the Commission to draw up separate lists of inter-state and other communications under the Charter and to transmit them to the Commission. It would seem that the use of the term 'other communications' together with the admissibility requirements in Article 56 implies that the drafters of the Charter envisaged such communications would be most likely to originate from individuals, but the absence of exclusive language in Article 55 suggests that communications may also be received from NGOs and other bodies. What is clear, however, is that the African Charter does not require, like Article 45 of the American Convention, that the complainant be a victim of a violation. This means that not only can a person, group of persons or NGO submit a communication on behalf of another individual or individuals, but that the Charter also recognizes class actions.

The admissibility requirements in Article 56 are similar to those of other human rights instruments. Thus, communications must not be anonymous (although anonymity can be requested by the author) and they must not be written in disparaging or insulting language. Local remedies must also have been exhausted, although there is no stipulation that this must have been done in accordance with the general principles of international law. It must be assumed, however, that the Commission would be willing to imply such a requirement, especially since Article 56(5) states that such remedies must not be unduly tardy. Once local remedies have been exhausted, communications must be submitted 'within a reasonable time'. One admissibility requirement peculiar to the African Charter is that communications must not be 'based exclusively on news disseminated through the mass media'. Perhaps it would have been easier here for the drafters simply to refer to the requirement that the communication be well-founded, since this would not only allow the Commission to dispose of communications relying exclusively on media coverage, but would also allow it to deal with other cognate matters casting doubt upon the legitimacy of a communication's admissibility.

The main feature of the Charter's individual petition system which distinguishes it from the other regional systems and the Optional Protocol to the ICCPR is that it deals not with individual violations of human rights, but only with 'special cases which reveal the existence of a series of serious or massive violations of human and peoples' rights'. In this respect, the Charter's individual communication procedure has more in common with the Commission on Human Rights' procedures under ECOSOC Resolutions 1235 and 1503. Thus, if an individual communication does not reveal a series of serious or massive violations of human rights, the Commission will not take any notice of it. The Commission must therefore wait until an accumulation of individual petitions discloses such a state of affairs. It can hardly be said that this assists the Commission to carry out its preventive function, and indeed, it may be asserted that the mechanism is highly unsatisfactory. However, the right of individual communication was clearly excluded for particular reasons. The recent history of human and peoples' rights in Africa has been one which has involved particularly widespread and brutal violations, largely based on inter-communal disputes. It may be said that these gross violations are of greater concern to Africans than the more 'peripheral' violations which occur within the European context. It may also be argued that the African concern for community above the individual, makes these matters of greater import within the African context.

If the Commission decides that a complaint or series of complaints discloses the series of serious or massive widespread violations required by Article 51, it must then be referred to the OAU's Assembly of Heads of State and Government. The Assembly must than decide whether or not to request the Commission to undertake 'an in-depth study' of the cases and to make a factual report and recommendations on its findings. In cases of emergency duly notified to the Commission, the Chairman of the Assembly is mandated to take this decision on behalf of the plenary body. Whether the Commission undertakes an 'in-depth study' depends upon the determination of the OAU's political organ. Under Article 10 of the Charter of the OAU, all such decisions must be taken by a two-thirds majority of states present and voting.

Any in-depth study which is authorized by the Assembly remains confidential until such time as it decides that it might be made public. Similarly, the annual report of the Commission's activities may not be published until it has been considered by the Assembly. Both these provisions seem to suggest that, in the absence of the appropriate two-thirds majority, both the studies and reports may remain confidential. This deprives the system of one of the most valuable sanctions available in the human rights field – the sanction of adverse publicity. It is, perhaps, a mark of the lack of effectiveness of this system, that after four years in existence, the Assembly has not yet taken any decisions on reports or individual communications.

FURTHER READING

Bello, E.G., 'The African Charter on Human and Peoples' Rights', (1985–6) 194 *Hague Recueil* 13–268.
Gittleman, R., 'The African Charter on Human and Peoples' Rights: A Legal Analysis', (1982) 22 *Virginia Journal of International Law* 667–714.
Gittleman, R., 'The African Commission on Human and Peoples' Rights: Prospects and Procedures', in Hannum, H. (ed.), *Guide to International Human Rights Practice* (Philadelphia: University of Pennsylvania Press, 1984), pp. 153–85.
International Commission of Jurists, *Human and Peoples' Rights in Africa and the African Charter* (Geneva: International Commission of Jurists, 1985).
Kiwanuka, R.N. 'The Meaning of People in the African Charter on Human and Peoples' Rights', (1988) 80 *AJIL* 80–101.
M'Baye, K. and Ndiaye, B., 'The Organisation of African Unity', in *Vasak*, Vol. 2, pp. 583–650.
Okere, B.O., 'The Protection of Human Rights in Africa and the African Charter on Human and Peoples' Rights: A Comparative Analysis with the European and American Systems', (1984) 6 *HRQ* 141–79.
Umozurike, U.O., 'The African Charter on Human and Peoples' Rights', (1983) 77 *AJIL* 902–12.
van Boven, T., 'The Relations between Peoples' Rights and Human Rights in the African Charter', (1986) 7 *HRLJ* 183–94.

8

CONCLUDING OBSERVATIONS

INTRODUCTION

Human rights are part of contemporary political and legal discourse at both national and international level. Individuals claim that their human rights have been violated by this or that government action or inaction; allegations of human rights violations are made in diplomatic exchanges between governments, and some governments, such as the Carter administration in the USA (1975–79), have even made respect for human rights a central element of their foreign policy. Few areas of national or international life now remain untouched by the influence of human rights. This stands in stark contrast to the pre-1939 era when the systematic and large-scale violation of human rights by governments went unacknowledged and unaddressed by other members of the international system. The fact that human rights are part of the domestic and international political agenda must reflect, at minimum, a realization by governments that behaviour in this field is crucial to their reputation in world affairs, and that it may even affect in a concrete fashion the way they are treated in their dealings with other states and in international fora in general. It may also be evidence of the fact that larger numbers of individuals are now aware of the rights which they possess and of their potential potency when deployed against a delinquent state. Central to all this are two major factors: education and publicity. Individuals and groups have been able to exploit the leverage which human rights give them in domestic or international affairs because they are aware of those rights and how they may be used, either through formal international mechanisms and institutions or simply through exposure of violations or potential violations to public gaze. The second element of publicity is, perhaps, even more crucial, since, as we have seen in earlier chapters, it is very often the threat of exposure of wrongdoing which compels states to comply with their international obligations.

Casual perusal of any number of UN and NGO reports on action in the field of human rights none the less bear testimony to the fact that, despite the exponential growth in human rights instruments and institutions since the end of the Second World War, there are still widespread violations of human rights in many parts of the world. However, the fact that these violations are themselves of international concern signifies, as previously indicated, a major achievement. How, then, do we attempt to measure what has happened in the international law of human rights since 1945? Is it, in fact, possible to make any kind of meaningful measurement? What, in any case, do we measure? The diminution of reported human rights violations? The decrease in gross violations? Or is there some other way to gauge what has been happening in the field?

Comment on this aspect of human rights tends usually to be impressionistic and, sometimes, intuitive – it is felt or assumed that the human rights situation in the world has improved quite simply because there are a large number of institutions with relatively sophisticated implementation mechanisms. Any view of the effectiveness or otherwise of human rights law and institutions also tends to be coloured by the subjective vantage point of the observer, and may even be subject to the distortions of relativism – a decrease, for example, in the number of enforced disappearances in state X might be taken as an indicator that the human rights situation has improved. To be sure, a decrease in the number of enforced disappearances is a desirable consequence of the application of human rights standards by human rights institutions, but would not the absence of all disappearances and all other human rights violations in state X be the objectively desirable outcome? Might not, in fact, the removal of the clearly undemocratic government of state X and its obviously corrupt security forces not be the most desirable result as far as the future protection of human rights in state X is concerned?

This leads to another issue which must be addressed when considering the broad field of human rights: the interaction of law and politics. As well as being legal, philosophical and historical concepts, human rights are also an intensely political phenomena. It is arguable that civil and political rights reflect, for the most part, the traditions of Western liberal thought. Such rights are predominantly individualistic in nature and, as we have seen from Dworkin's theory of rights,[1] can be used to 'trump' forms of government action which are harmful to protected individual preferences. This view of rights not only reflects a particular view of the individual in society, but also implies a particular form of political organization, for it is primarily within states possessing forms of liberal democratic organization that any value is attached to individualistic rights of this kind. In totalitarian states, whether of the left or right, individual rights do not count on the scale of the state's preferences. Indeed, when one examines the human rights records of totalitarian states of recent memory such as Chile, Argentina and the USSR, one finds that the denial of human rights stands in direct proportion to the denial of democratic participation in government. The same can be said for modern totalitarian states such as Burma and China. This is not to exercise a value-judgment which argues that liberal-democracy is a better form of political organization, rather it is to suggest that the chances for protection of individual rights – civil and political rights – seems better assured in states organized along such lines. Support for this view can be found explicitly in the European and American Conventions, where the precepts of democratic participation, the rule of law and the protection of human rights are tightly interwoven. As the Inter-American Court said in *Habeas Corpus in Emergency Situations*:[2]

> The concept of rights and freedoms as well as that of their guarantees cannot be divorced from the system of values and principles that inspire it. In a democratic society, the rights and freedoms inherent to the human person, the guarantees applicable to them and the rule of law form a triad. Each component thereof defines itself, complements and depends on the others for its meaning.

To focus this discussion entirely upon largely individualistic civil and political rights would, however, be to give a misleading impression, for, as we have seen, economic, social and cultural rights have played a dominant role not only in placing a protective barrier between 'victim citizens' and the state, but also in transforming the state into an active participant in rights implementation. This too, however, has its political dimensions. In the past, economic, social and cultural rights have been seen largely as one of the primary manifestations of the socialist state and have suffered condemnation from Western governments as a result. From a political stance which is right of centre, economic, social and cultural rights, which smack of a kind of Rawlsian distributive justice, are seen as removing freedom of choice by emphasizing the dominance of social welfare programmes. Clearly, in a Nozickian theoretical setting, such rights would not be worthy of the name, since they violate the principles of morality which lie at the foundation of the minimal state.[3] At a practical level, the different categories of rights have often been used as devices for political sparring. When US President Ronald Reagan criticized Soviet President Mikhail Gorbachev at the

Reykjavik Summit in 1986 for the denial of civil and political rights to some groups in the USSR, thereby implicitly asserting the primacy of such rights, Mr Gorbachev reminded Mr Reagan of the poor economic and social rights record of the USA as reflected in large-scale unemployment. Similarly, the cliché 'what use is freedom of speech to a starving peasant' has often been heard, as if denial of freedom of speech would somehow help to fill the peasant's belly. Indeed, the converse could be argued that from such freedom of speech might come ideas that would help overcome poverty and malnutrition. Such partisan use of human rights in political debate, however, has done little to enhance their status and may even be said to have been counter-productive. When the divisibility and relativity of human rights categories is accentuated, the worth of the rights *qua* rights is devalued.

How, then, are we to look at human rights law as the twentieth century draws to a close? Is it to be viewed as an international success story, or is it simply a fanciful illusion created by the juridical equivalent of mirrors and lights? Perhaps these two starkly juxtaposed positions miss the point. Perhaps international human rights law is, like the international system itself, part of an continuing dynamic which simply reflects changes in the wider system. None the less, it is possible to make some observations on the progress made in international human rights law, by examining two broad areas. The first of these is the institutional structure of international human rights law, and the second is the changing environment of international human rights law.

THE INSTITUTIONAL STRUCTURE OF INTERNATIONAL HUMAN RIGHTS LAW

When discussing the institutional structure of international human rights law there is little doubt that 1945 – the end of the Second World War – was a remarkable watershed. If the position of individuals in the international legal system in the pre-1945 world is compared with their post-1945 position, there would be few who would not admit that there had been a sea-change. From a status of near rightlessness within the system, the position of the individual had been transformed into one of the system's focal points. To what can this change be attributed? There is no doubt that the horrors of the Nazi holocaust made a decisive impact on world opinion, but so too did the oppressive behaviour of the other Axis states who, through aggressive war, invasion and terror, had reduced many of their neighbours to alien domination. The terms of the Allied Powers' Atlantic Charter made it clear that such domination through the use of force should never happen again, and that the protection of individual freedoms was one method through which safeguards might be provided.

In all this one should not forget, however, the role played by theory. The resurgence of natural law to provide an objective measure against which the positive laws of states might be judged is evident in the writings of such jurists as Sir Hersch Lauterpacht and in international instruments such as the UN Charter and the Universal Declaration of Human Rights. To a large extent, therefore, like their domestic predecessors, these instruments may be viewed as natural law documents. But they were natural law documents with a pragmatic edge. The UN Charter in particular recognized that stable world conditions might only be achieved by paying due attention to the central role of human rights and self-determination in maintaining peace between states.

Perhaps the most notable feature of post-1945 developments has been the dramatic increase in the number of international instruments for protecting human rights. Associated with this are a number of important doctrinal factors. First, states through accession to such documents have submitted themselves to a variety of international controls supervised by a number of international institutions. This has led to a weakening of the exlusivity of state sovereignty in the human rights field, and no longer can states legitimately claim that matters concerning human rights are entirely within their purview. Some states, such as Uruguay in the early days of the operation of the Human Rights Committee under the ICCPR Optional Protocol, may have underestimated the impact of human rights instruments and institutions to which they had committed themselves, but they paid the price of international notoriety for their lack of honesty of intention and absence of perspicacity. Those states which violated human rights and then wished to argue that international human rights institutions had no power to interfere in areas essentially within their domestic jurisdiction badly underestimated the tenacity of those institutions.

Corresponding to the erosion of state sovereignty over matters concerning human rights has been an increase in the status of the individual within the international legal system. While pre-1945 the individual was merely an object of the law, throughout the ensuing five decades there has been a steady development in the number of international human rights instruments which allow individuals the procedural right to petition a variety of international institutions in order to vindicate their substantive rights and to secure appropriate redress therefor. Thus, individuals have moved from a position in which they enjoyed no procedural capacity under international law to one in which the likelihood of attaining such capacity has been dramatically increased. Coupled with the increase in the individual's procedural capacity under international law has been the increase in the potential for effective adjudication in human rights matters. The Human Rights Committee, the European Court of Human Rights, the Inter-American Court of Human Rights and the African Commission all provide impartial fora for authoritative determination of human rights violations. As we have seen in the case of the Inter-American Court and, potentially, the African Commission, with the increase in the number of adjudicative bodies there has been a corresponding willingness – indeed, an obligation imposed by their founding documents – to refer to decisions and modes of reasoning of other human rights bodies. This has the effect of both co-ordinating and implementing human rights standards among the various adjudicative agencies. Decisions made by these institutions are also increasingly impacting upon the jurisprudence of domestic tribunals, further integrating human rights into the administration of justice at the national level. Admittedly, however, this trend is more apparent in some jurisdictions than others, and the UK, because of the constitutional inability of its courts to apply international human rights treaties, perhaps stands out as something of a recidivist in this area.[4]

It is also possible to perceive a change in the fabric of traditional international law itself in the area of human rights. The development of peremptory norms of international law – *ius cogens*[5] – and the acknowledgment of the existence of such norms by the ICJ and the Inter-American Court of Human Rights, as well as Article 53 of the Vienna Convention on the Law of Treaties 1969, perhaps bodes well for international human rights protection. As we have seen,[6] a strong argument can be mounted for the proposition that non-derogable norms of international human rights law, such as the prohibition of torture, are now so deeply rooted in the substructure of the international legal order that they represent a kind of international public policy upon which states, whether they are bound by specific human rights treaties or not, are forbidden from trespassing. It is also arguable that the international law of treaties has been decisively affected by the development of international human rights law. As we have seen,[7] the Inter-American Court of Human Rights and commentators such as Lillich and Buergenthal have argued forcefully that human rights treaties are not of the conventional multilateral variety producing reciprocal rights and obligations for the various parties, rather they are unilateral commitments made by states through the medium of multilateral devices. The effect of this, once again, is to reinforce the view that just as in the past certain basic principles of international law, such as state sovereignty and non-intervention, were modified to accommodate international society's concern with the protection of human rights, other basic principles are now being modified to achieve the same end.

This is not, however, to suggest that all states have abandoned claims of sovereignty and the exclusivity of jurisdiction over their citizens. Some states have consistently refused to become party to human rights treaties for the very reason that such a move would be deleterious to their sovereign independence. Others, for the same reason, have become party to such treaties but have refused to accept the optional supervisory mechanisms under them, especially in the area of individual application. Yet other states have become party to human rights treaties for purely cosmetic reasons, but have rendered themselves doubly delinquent not only by continuing to violate human rights, but also by their failure to comply with the minimum supervisory mechanisms of such instruments. A glimpse, for example, at Amnesty International's annual report for 1991 demonstrates that a number of states parties to the ICCPR have failed to submit their periodic reports to the HRC, despite repeated requests to do so.

The failure to comply with periodic reporting procedures may very well raise legitimate questions about why such states become parties to human rights conventions at all if they are aware at the outset that they are unable or unwilling to comply with the obligations established by such instruments. There may be a number of answers to this question, but two will be suggested here. First, as indicated above, states may become parties to a variety of humanitarian instruments for what may be described as cosmetic reasons. They believe that membership of such instruments alone is likely to enhance their standing in the international community. States, in general, see human rights as 'good things', the mere subscription to which, as manifested in becoming party to human rights instruments, will reinforce their reputation as a state committed to domestic justice. What such states often fail to realize is that by becoming parties to such instruments they open themselves to legitimate international investigation, supervision and, ultimately, censure and international notoriety. In the context of the First Optional Protocol to the ICCPR, it is apparent that both Uruguay and Zaire underestimated the potential impact of the HRC's procedures under the system of individual communications.[8] Second, although it is convenient to talk about 'the state' as the basic unit of international law, and although the continuity of the state is a fundamental aspect of the doctrine of international law, it is clear that the governments of states change. They may change in a constitutional manner or there may be unconstitutional changes either by a *coup d'état* or a revolution. Whatever the reasons for the cause of a change in a state's government, it is clear that some governments will be more predisposed to carrying out their inherited human rights obligations than others. A regime which takes power through a *coup d'état* is perhaps less likely to be inhibited in violating human rights protected by a treaty to which it has succeeded, than a government which assumes office through normal constitutional means. The Greek case[9] under the ECHR is probably the most obvious and effective illustration of this point. There, the Greek 'Colonels', who had taken power through a *coup d'état*, simply violated the standards established by the Convention and then denounced the Convention when it became clear that they were likely to be declared international delinquents under it. The Greek case also demonstrates another truism, namely that legal instruments alone are incapable of ensuring human rights, and that much depends upon the political and social context of the state in question. This relates to the environment of human rights, which will be discussed below.

Failure to comply with periodic reporting obligations must not, however, be seen entirely in terms of delinquent states failing to fulfil their international human rights obligations. Very often states, especially in the developing world, will have inadequate resources with which to respond to the demands of international institutions. The small island states of the Caribbean, for example, are occasionally unable to comply with their reporting obligations and demands made by international bodies for detailed information in specific cases because they do not have the staff with which to deal expeditiously with human rights questions. Very often the legal staff in foreign ministries that are required to deal with such matters are few in number and must frequently oversee a wide variety of other international legal issues and obligations. In addition to this, their legal colleagues in other ministries, particularly ministries of justice, may not always be aware of the importance of liaising with their foreign ministry colleagues and may be slow in supplying relevant information to them. Occasions may even arise when the relevance or otherwise of a particular situation may be the subject of an inter-ministry dispute. It may well be argued that small states which are unable to conform to their international obligations should not have undertaken those obligations in the first place. In the human rights field, however, perhaps the assumption of obligations ought to be encouraged with, as in fact is often the case, an intimation by the appropriate UN bodies that some flexibility in the application of time limits is available for states which are unable for genuine reasons to meet them.

Despite the recalcitrant behaviour of some states regarding their obligations under certain human rights instruments, the important fact should not be overlooked that a significantly large number of states has become party to the major treaties. The ICCPR, for example, now has 89 states parties of which 48 are parties to the First Optional Protocol. Its sister Covenant, the ICESCR, also has 95 parties. This means that well over half the members of the world community have submitted themselves to forms of international supervision over the way in which they treat individuals within their jurisdiction. It also means that a good proportion of the world community takes the view that the implementation of second-generation rights stands co-equal with the guarantee of respect for first-generation rights. As indicated above, certain states, despite their apparent commitment to the standards and mechanisms contained in the Covenants, fail to comply with their obligations. None the less, the very existence of those obligations and the very existence of mechanisms for their supervision make it more, rather than less, likely that both the action, and on occasion the inaction, of such states will be subject to international institutional control and, ultimately, the scrutiny of the international community.

Some comment should, however, be made about the efficacy of international supervisory mechanisms. Here it is impossible to make general observations, since each of the human rights regimes has its own advantages and disadvantages. It is, however, possible to divide human rights supervisory mechanisms into two broad categories: (1) reporting procedures and (2) individual applications.

Reporting procedures

From our consideration of UN mechanisms, it is apparent that the periodic reporting system is favoured in the variety of universal instruments which we have considered. From the ICCPR to the more recent UN Convention on the Rights of the Child, supervision is achieved by means of states submitting reports about their progress in giving effect to the various rights over a specified period of time. This type of supervision clearly has its advantages. States under this system are encouraged to engage in constructive dialogue with the various supervisory bodies and are not placed in the position of defendant before the world community. Discrete pressure can be put on states to comply – or to accelerate compliance – with their obligations, without them being exposed to adverse publicity. Nevertheless, within the Byzantine structure of UN agencies and committees, it is apparent that political considerations may dominate discussion and thereby devalue the process. This is especially true of ECOSOC and the CHR.

Individual applications

Individual applications, as we have seen, are a major facet of both a number of UN and regional human rights instruments. Save in the cases of the American and the African Conventions, the individual application procedures to international human rights institutions are optional. This being the case, it is arguable that it is only those states which are likely to comply substantially with their human rights obligations which are likely either to become party to such conventions or to accept the optional individual application provisions. Nevertheless, individual applications are perhaps the most effective way of ensuring that a state protects and gives full effect to human rights. An accumulation of individual applications against a particular state in certain areas is likely to be a clear indication that all is not well in that state. The vast number of communications against Uruguay before the HRC in the early years of its existence gave a clear indication that the military junta in that state was bent upon a programme of sustained and systematic denial of rights. Whether the views of the HRC in these cases had any impact upon the government of Uruguay is difficult to judge, but Uruguay's progressive compliance with the demands of that body over a period of time would seem to indicate that it found non-compliance increasingly embarrassing at the international level.

A distinction can also be drawn between the relative effectiveness of individual applications under the European and American Conventions. The European Convention, which has now been in existence for some 40 years, has, as we have seen, developed a diverse and rich jurisprudence. It has not had to deal with the kinds of widespread violation which its drafters envisaged, rather the European Court has operated as a kind of European 'Supreme Court', deciding cases which have tended to highlight deficiencies in particular areas of the Contracting Parties' domestic laws. This can be contrasted with the position under the American Convention where there has been practically no use of the Inter-American Court's contentious jurisdiction, largely because the political, economic and social environment is not conducive to such adjudication, but also because there are institutional deficiencies in the relationship between the Court and the Inter-American Commission. None the less, the Inter-American Commission has been rather more proactive than its European counterpart and has, through its reports and on-site investigation procedures, achieved much more than it would perhaps have done by way of more formalistic mechanisms.

One criticism which can be levelled at all individual application procedures, however, is the time which an applicant must wait in order to secure redress. Under the ICCPR First Optional Protocol and the ECHR, it is not uncommon for the respective institutions under those instruments to take up to five years to reach a decision. This is hardly speedy nor effective and runs counter to notions of due process which the human rights instruments that they administer demand of the states which are parties to them. This criticism must be seen in perspective, however. Both the HRC and the European Convention institutions are required to administer a system which applies to billions of individuals, and every year they screen an enormous number of applications. It would, perhaps, be both unfair and unrealistic to expect them to conform to the standards of domestic justice administration in wealthy Western states.

THE ENVIRONMENT OF HUMAN RIGHTS

It is impossible to discuss human rights as a legal category without having some regard to the environment within which they operate. The use of the word 'environment' here is not only intended to convey the idea of the political, economic and social context of human rights promotion and protection, it is also designed to correspond to the use of the term by McDougal[10] to explain the factors which determine why some governments respect human rights and others deny them. It also corresponds, in a sense, to Rawls' use of the term 'the worth of rights'[11] or why it is that some individuals are able to enjoy rights to their fullest extent and others are not.

If the concept of human rights is universal, that is, it possesses a validity which is good for all places and for all times, then it is apparent that there is a significant disparity in the way in which those rights are concretized from place to place and from time to time. While the idea of human rights may have a discernible homogeneity, perhaps derived from some kind of natural law theory or social reality, it is none the less clear that the implementation of those rights by states lacks a corresponding identity. This is not because the human rights of individuals vary from state to state, but rather because the conditions for the application of those rights vary. While the concept of human rights may have an objective quality, their implementation is, to a certain degree, dependent upon a large number of variable subjective factors. Without pretending that the following analysis is exhaustive, it may be possible to isolate two discrete factors which impact upon the worth or value of human rights within particular states – these are political and economic.

Political factors

Since human rights are political as well as legal phenomena, it is perhaps self-evident that the political milieu in which they are addressed is crucial to their worth. In the case of both first-and second generation rights, it is apparent that certain types of political organization are more likely to give effect to the maximum worth of human rights than others. The liberal-democratic state with its emphasis on the rule of law, the principle of democratic legitimacy and, to a greater or lesser degree, individual liberty, possesses both the institutions and the culture of respect which enable first-generation rights to be protected to the maximum extent. It is not by accident that both the Organization of American States and the Council of Europe and their respective human rights instruments demand respect for the fundamentals of liberal democracy. Indeed, the precepts of the liberal-democratic state and the notion of individualistic libertarian rights are mutually self-supporting. The right to due process, the right to be free from arbitrary treatment, the right to be free from *ex post facto* laws are all constitutive elements of the rule of law concept. Within a liberal-democratic framework the institutional essentials exist to ensure that, more likely than not, human rights will be protected. This means not only are there independent and impartial courts to adjudicate on an individual's rights, but that there are also the essential political controls in existence to ensure that, corresponding to Dworkin's view of rights, community goals are not allowed to override an individual's political 'trump'.

But what of second-generation rights? It has often been argued that socialist states are better equipped to provide proper implementation of such rights than capitalist liberal democracies. This assertion may be approached from two points of view. First, socialist states tend, as we have seen, to attribute priority to economic, social and cultural rights over civil and political rights. This primacy naturally ensues from Marxist doctrine which categorizes first-generation rights as bourgeois, property-based and egoistic.[12] Naturally enough, the attribution of primacy to second-generation rights means that the state will direct all its available resources (perhaps after it has deducted an appropriate proportion for foreign aid and military spending) to the satisfaction of its population's social needs such as housing, education, medical care and social security. While this undoubtedly accords with the theoretical commitment to social justice by socialist states, the allocation of scarce resources may ensure that, in a stagnant economy, the reality is that the implementation of social welfare rights may deteriorate over a period of time. The need for economic development and the full implementation of meaningful social welfare rights may, over time, as the experience of the Soviet Union demonstrates, raise tensions that become irreconcilable.

These observations should not be seen, however, as a paean to the alleged triumph of capitalism, but it does suggest that the liberal-democratic state with its capacity for flexibility and adaptability is perhaps better suited to the satisfaction of not only first-generation but also second-generation rights. The mixed economy with the potential for government intervention is perhaps better suited to the creation of conditions for the proper implementation of second-generation rights. It may also be that in such states the indivisibility of rights is more apparent. In the pluralistic liberal-democratic state, the dialectical process which leads to the identification of appropriate policies for the implementation of second-generation rights is itself underpinned by the commitment to first-generation rights which facilitate the interchange of beliefs and views. Some of the states which have been able to realize both first-and second-generation rights at a high level have been models of the liberal-democratic tradition. Among such states have been Sweden, Austria, Switzerland and the Netherlands; states in which tolerance, respect for individual rights and maximum protection of social welfare rights have, at least in the past, advanced on a broad and integrated front.

It is in totalitarian states, of whatever political complexion, that the worth of human rights undergoes substantial and, in some cases, absolute devaluation. One need not look further than the 1991 Amnesty International annual report to discover that it is in states governed by military juntas and hardline communist regimes that some of the worst of recent human rights violations have taken place. Allegations of torture, extra-judicial executions, disappearances and arbitrary detentions are the most common aspects of active disregard for human rights in such states. It is, however, not only civil and political rights that are violated by such states. Totalitarian regimes, particularly those of right-wing persuasion, also demonstrate a pronounced tendency to deny second-generation rights. The inequalities of power and wealth in, for example, many Central and Latin American states are particularly marked, and the failure of governments to redress such stark divergencies violates not only second-generation rights, but also compounds the widespread denial of first-generation rights. Once again, in such circumstances, the interdependence of different types of rights becomes particularly apparent.

A number of reasons may be adduced in order to explain why the culture of totalitarianism is antithetical to the promotion and protection of human rights. First, in totalitarian states, the individual is subordinated to the requirements of the state. Unlike the liberal-democratic model, the individual has no rights with which to 'trump' the goals of society which are set by the state. Second, the institutions of the state are designed not to protect the individual, but to further the objectives of the state. Judicial tribunals, if they exist, are servants of the state and not of individuals. Third, totalitarian regimes tend to insist on uniformity and obedience. Dissent is not tolerated, since it detracts from the onward march of the unitary state, and certain ethnic or religious groups are often seen as a challenge to the very existence of the state. These aspects of totalitarian culture are particularly marked in right-wing, military regimes, as the experience of Central and Latin America in the 1970s and 1980s demonstrates. Some of the worst human rights excesses of the post-Second World War period took place in that region during these decades. The mass disappearances in Argentina, Chile and Uruguay, together with the institutionalization of torture, became the hallmark of the regimes in these states. The excuse often adduced by the perpetrators of these gross violations was that they were a society under threat from left-wing subversion, and thus it was necessary to declare states of emergency or siege under which it was permissible to derogate from the right to due process and to take other exceptional measures. Even in states where there was no state of emergency or siege, the climate of fear was such that defence lawyers would not take 'political' cases, and available remedies were simply illusory. The work of the Inter-American Commission on Human Rights in this extremely hostile environment was substantial, and reading the reports of that body's on-site and other investigations demonstrates quite clearly its valuable role at a time of great difficulty in the Western Hemisphere.[13]

Economic factors

It is when we examine the environment and worth of human rights that the concept of the indivisibility of rights takes on clear importance. The arguments about whether rights constitute a single category or whether they can be divided into discrete categories has already been rehearsed above, but it is in the field of human rights implementation that the importance of their symbiotic relationship becomes acute.

For a very large proportion of the world's population, grinding poverty is the only reality which they are able to comprehend. Anything beyond subsistence is simply an ideal to contemplate – if the rigours of daily survival permit even this. It is not surprising, therefore, that in these circumstances developing countries have placed an emphasis on the realization of second- and third-generation rights as their priority. Thus the rights to food, water, clothing, shelter, primary health care and education tend to dominate rights thinking and rights discourse in these states. The satisfaction of civil and political rights is not seen as an immediate priority. None the less, a conscious decision to place second- and third-generation rights as a higher priority should not necessarily mean the denial of first-generation rights. As indicated in Chapter 2, certain civil and political rights, such as the right to a fair trial or due process, require considerable public spending for their implementation. One could not therefore criticize a developing state for failing to accord an individual the defence counsel of their choice, if the state were either unable to find or pay such counsel in a remote rural area. On the other hand, there are certain first-generation rights, such as freedom of expression, which require little or no implementation, and it would appear to be difficult to sustain an argument that granting priority to economic and social rights should necessarily result in a denial of such civil and political rights whose implementation is cost-free.

In discussing the worth of rights and the way in which this is affected by a state's economic environment, perhaps a distinction may be drawn between those states which by reason of a paucity of natural resources and inhospitable geographical or climatic conditions are unable to fulfil the needs of their populations, and those states which because of their governments ensure that the majority of people are condemned to live in poverty while the minority enjoy substantial affluence. While the former may naturally claim that their rights priorities are different, it is harder for the latter to sustain such an argument. In certain Central and Latin American states, such as El Salvador for example, the divergence between wealthy landowners and landless peasants is particularly marked. The right-wing Salvadoran regime has consistently refused to contemplate land tenure or agrarian reform, which has simply served to accentuate disparities in wealth and also in the worth of rights between the *campesinos* and the affluent landowners. Not only has such a situation constituted a continuing violation of economic and social rights, but as the Inter-American Commission pointed out, 'the social and economic conditions explain, to a considerable extent, the serious violations of human rights that have occurred and continue to occur in El Salvador . . . Naturally such conditions cannot in any case justify the violations of the basic political and civil rights.'[14]

It is also apparent that the worth of all human rights may be affected by economic and social conditions which prevent the full realization of the right to education. Literacy and numeracy often form not only the basic requisites for full participation in society, but they are also crucial for the enjoyment of first-and second-generation rights. Furthermore, lack of education about human rights themselves and the part which they can play in furthering the goals of society, including the objectives of economic and social development, frequently prevent individuals from making a full contribution to the life of their state. Of course, it may be in the interests of a ruling elite to keep its population in ignorance for fear that knowledge of rights, and means of rights enforcement either at the domestic or international level, may affect its position of dominance or pre-eminence.

THE PAST, PRESENT AND FUTURE OF HUMAN RIGHTS

Our survey of human rights in this book has involved consideration of many issues other than those which may be strictly classified as 'legal'. We have dealt with human rights as historical and revolutionary concepts. We have traced their development on the international plane. We have examined in substantial detail the multifarious instruments and institutions for their protection, and latterly we have examined something of the environment within which human rights function. Although it is not pretended that the treatment of human rights in this work is either exhaustive or particularly profound, it does perhaps demonstrate the important point that human rights are a dynamic phenomenon. History has demonstrated that ideas of human rights are not static, but develop in response to new modes of political thought and in response to changes in the international environment.

To undertake speculation on the future of human rights is difficult and perhaps unwise. Doubtless we will see claims to new kinds of rights, and perhaps a growing recognition of third-generation rights by First World states. However, changes in the complexion of international society – the demise of the Soviet Union and the Eastern Bloc, the continuing democratization of the Western Hemisphere, the consolidation of the world into larger and larger trading blocs – may suggest a deepening commitment to existing human rights instruments and mechanisms rather than a broadening of claims to new kinds of rights. The future may also hold the prospect of new regional human rights instruments in, for example, the Islamic world and perhaps even the South-East Asian and South Pacific areas. What one can say with some certainty, however, is that human rights will continue to be a central part of the international agenda in the Twenty First Century.

FURTHER READING

Cassesse, A., *Human Rights in a Changing World* (Philadelphia: Temple University Press, 1990), esp. Part III.

Falk, R., *Human Rights and State Sovereignty* (New York: Holmes and Meier, 1981).

Forsythe, R.P., *Human Rights and World Politics* (Lincoln: University of Nebraska Press, 1983).

Henkin, L., *The Rights of Man Today* (London: Stevens, 1979), chs 2 and 3.

Moskowitz, M., *International Concern with Human Rights* (Leyden: Sijthoff, 1974).

van Boven, T., 'The Future Codification of Human Rights. Status of Deliberations: A Critical Analysis', (1989) 10 *HRLJ* 1–11.

Vasak, K., 'Toward a Specific International Human Rights Law', in *Vasak*, Vol. 2, pp. 671–9.

Vincent, R.J. (ed.), *Foreign Policy and Human Rights* (Cambridge: Cambridge University Press, 1986).

Vincent R.J., *Human Rights and International Relations* (Cambridge: Cambridge University Press, 1986).

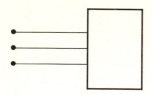

NOTES

Chapter 1

1 1 *UNTS* xvi; *UKTS* 67 (1946).
2 See, for example, the works by Weston, Henkin, Tay and Szabo cited under 'Further Reading', pp. 21–23.
3 1215, c. 29.
4 1 William and Mary, Sess. 2, c. 2.
5 K. Marx and F. Engels, *The Communist Manifesto*, ed. D. Ryazanoff (New York: Russell and Russell, 1963).
6 See, for example, G.M. Trevelyan, *The English Revolution 1688–89* (Oxford: Oxford University Press, 1965).
7 The Declaration is conveniently reproduced in *Encyclopedia Brittanica*.
8 See Chapter 2.
9 For a treatment of the various species of rights, see Chapter 2.
10 K. Vasak, 'A 30-year Struggle', *Unesco Courier*, 1977, pp. 29–32.
11 See Chapter 2.
12 I. Szabo, 'Historical Foundations of Human Rights and Subsequent Developments', in *Vasak*, Vol. 1, p. 11.
13 For a discussion of the current status of the individual in international law, see Chapter 3.
14 For further discussion of the notion of state responsibility in this field, see Chapter 3.
15 The phrase is that of Sir Hersch Lauterpacht. See Oppenheim, *International Law, Vol. 1: Peace*, edited by H. Lauterpacht (London: Longman, 8th edn, 1955), p. 312.

16 The International Court of Justice appears to have ruled out any modern claim to a right of humanitarian intervention in *Nicaragua v USA (Merits)* 1986, *ICJ Rep.* 14.

17 60 *LNTS* 253; *UKTS* 16 (1927).

18 See pp. 14–15.

19 212 *UNTS* 17; *UKTS* 24 (1956).

20 266 *UNTS* 3; *UKTS* 59 (1957).

21 *UKTS* 4 (1919); 13 *AJIL* suppl. 151; 16 *AJIL* suppl. 207.

22 *UKTS* 47 (1948); 31 *AJIL* suppl. 67 and 38 *UNTS* 3; *UKTS* 64 (1948).

23 13 *AJIL* suppl. 128, 361.

24 Ibid., Article 22.

25 See the section in this chapter entitled 'The UN and decolonization'.

26 See, for example, Article 12 of the Polish Treaty.

27 5 *UNTS* 251; *UKTS* 4 (1945); (1945) 39 *AJIL* suppl. 257.

28 On these bodies, see Chapter 4.

29 Ibid.

30 999 *UNTS* 171; *UKTS* 6 (1977); (1967) 6 *ILM* 368.

31 993 *UNTS* 3; *UKTS* 6 (1977); (1967) 6 *ILM* 360.

32 On the various UN procedures and bodies see Chapter 4.

33 Ibid.

34 Ibid.

35 (1975) 14 *ILM* 1292.

36 (1991) 30 *ILM* 193.

37 213 *UNTS* 221; *ETS* No. 5; *UKTS* 7 (1953); 45 *AJIL* suppl. 24.

38 529 *UNTS* 89; *UKTS* 38 (1965).

39 529 *UNTS* 48; 46 *AJIL* suppl. 43.

40 Resolution XXX, Final Act of the Ninth International Conference of American States, Bogota, Colombia, 30 March–2 May 1948, p. 48.

41 Advisory Opinion OC-10/89 of July 14, 1989, *Interpretation of the American Declaration of the Rights and Duties of Man Within the Framework of Article 64 of the American Convention on Human Rights*, (1990) 29 *ILM* 379; (1990) 11 *HRLJ* 118. For further consideration of this case, see Chapter 6.

42 (1970) 9 *ILM* 673; 65 *AJIL* 679; 3 *HRJ* 151.

43 (1989) 28 *ILM* 156.

44 See Chapter 6.

45 (1982) 21 *ILM* 59.

Chapter 2

1 D. Weissbrodt, 'Human Rights: An Historical Perspective', in Davies P. (ed.), *Human Rights* (London: Routledge, 1988), p. 1.

2 K. Vasak, 'Toward a Specific International Human Rights Law', in *Vasak*, Vol. 2, p. 672.

3 H. Grotius, *Of the Law of War and Peace* (1625), 1646 edition translated by F.W. Kelsey (Indianapolis: Bobbs Merrill, 1957).

4 J. Locke, *The Second Treatise of Civil Government and a Letter Concerning Toleration*, edited by J.W. Gough (Oxford: Blackwell, 1946).

5 J.-J. Rousseau, *The Social Contract and Discourses*, edited by J.H. Brummfitt and J.C. Hall (London: Dent, 1973).

6 J. Bentham, *Anarchical Fallacies* (1824).

7 D. Hume, *A Treatise of Human Nature*, edited by D.G.C. McNabb (London: Fontana Collins, 1970).

8 See J. Bentham, *An Introduction to the Principles and Morals of Legislation*, edited by J.H. Burns and H.L.A. Hart (London: The Athlone Press, 1982).

9 *The Province of Jurisprudence Determined* (London: John Murray, 1861–3).

10 W.N. Hohfeld, *Fundamental Legal Conceptions as Applied in Judicial Reasoning* (New Haven, Conn.: Yale University Press, 1932). Hohfeld's analysis is concerned solely with the explanation of legal rights and does much to clarify the various uses of the term 'rights'.

11 H.L.A. Hart, *The Concept of Law* (Oxford: Clarendon Press, 1971).

12 R. Nozick, *Anarchy, State and Utopia* (New York: Basic Books, 1974).

13 R. Dworkin, *Taking Rights Seriously* (London: Duckworth, 1971).

14 Dworkin, op.cit., note 13, p. xi.

15 Ibid., p. xv.

16 J. Rawls, *A Theory of Justice* (Oxford: Clarendon Press, 1972).

17 Ibid., p. 28.

18 *Jurisprudence* (1962).

19 *Jurisprudence* (1959).

20 J. Shestack, 'The Jurisprudence of Human Rights', in *Meron*, p. 85.

21 M.S. McDougal, H.D. Laswell and L.-C. Chen, *Human Rights and World Public Order* (West Haven, CN: Yale University Press, 1980).

22 M. Cranston, *What are Human Rights?* (London: Bodley Head, 1973).

23 G.I. Tunkin, *Theory of International Law*, translated by W.E. Butler (London: Allen and Unwin, 1974), pp. 79–83.

24 General Assembly Resolution 32/130.

25 T. van Boven, 'Distinguishing Criteria of Human Rights', in *Vasak*, Vol. 1, p. 43.

26 Ibid., p. 48 (emphasis added).

27 For a full list of rights, derogable and non-derogable, contained in the various instruments, see Appendix 1.

28 See Chapter 3 on the concept of *ius cogens*.

29 T. van Boven, op.cit., note 28, p. 48.

30 Article 2(1).

31 Ibid.

32 From a moral position, however, it is interesting to note Tom Farer's observation that 'there is neither a moral nor practical difference between a government executing innocent people or one which tolerates their death by sickness or starvation when it has the means to obtain the food or health care that could save them'. Quoted by P. Alston, 'Development and the Rule of Law: Prevention versus Cure as a Human Rights Strategy', in International Commission of Jurists, *Development and Human Rights and the Rule of Law* (Oxford: Pergamon Press, 1981), p. 52.

33 'Human Rights' (1986) 6 *HRQ* 257–82 at p. 266.

34 P. Alston, 'Conjuring up New Human Rights: A Proposal for Quality Control' (1984) 78 *AJIL* 607–21.

Chapter 3

1 On the question of international personality, see pp. 49–50.
2 I. Brownlie, *Principles of Public International Law* (Oxford: Clarendon Press, 4th edn, 1990), p. 287.
3 L. Oppenheim, *International Law*, *Vol. 1: Peace*, edited by H. Lauterpacht (London: Longman, 8th edn, 1955), p. 305.
4 General Assembly Resolution 2625(XXV) 24 October 1970.
5 *Nicaragua v USA (Merits)* 1986, *ICJ Rep.* 14 at pp. 98, 109–10.
6 Op. cit., note 5.
7 See Chapter 1.
8 This is known as 'indirect responsibility' in international law.
9 *PCIJ, Ser. B*, No. 15 (1928); 4 *ILR* 287.
10 (1974) 41 *AJIL* 172.
11 *ICJ Rep*, 1959, 6.
12 1155 *UNTS* 331; *UKTS* 58 (1980); (1969) 8 *ILM* 679.
13 On this point see, for example, the decision of the Inter-American Court of Human Rights, Advisory Opinion OC-3/83 of September 8, 1983, *Restrictions to the Death Penalty*, (1984) 23 *ILM* 320; (1983) 4 *HRLJ* 339, para. 61.
14 For a list of such rights, see Appendix 1.
15 Article 32 of the Vienna Convention on the Law of Treaties.
16 See Chapter 5.
17 6 *YB* 796.
18 Advisory Opinion OC-2/82 of September 24, 1982, *Entry into Force of the American Convention for a State Ratifying or Adhering with a Reservation*, (1983) 22 *ILM* 37; (1982) 3 *HRLJ* 153, para. 30.
19 See *Nicaragua v USA (Merits)* 1986, *ICJ Rep.* 14 at p. 109.
20 See Article 10 of the UN Charter.
21 See pp. 64–5.
22 *Reservations to the Genocide Convention Case*, *ICJ Rep.*, 1951, p. 15.
23 *Barcelona Traction Light and Power Company Limited* (Belgium v Spain), *ICJ Rep.*, 1978, p. 3.
24 See *Interpretation of the American Declaration* for the Court's strongest statement that human rights constitute a form of *erga omnes* obligation, that is, an obligation binding on all states. Advisory Opinion OC-10/89 of July 14, 1989, *Interpretation of the American Declaration of the Rights and Duties of Man Within the Framework of Article 64 of the American Convention on Human Rights*, (1990) 29 *ILM* 379; (1990) 11 *HRLJ* 118.
25 H. Waldock, 'General Course on International Law', 106 *Hague Recueil* 54.
26 630 F.2d.876. (1980).
27 See *Trendtex Trading Corporation v Central Bank of Nigeria* [1977] 2 WLR 356 per Lord Denning MR at p. 365.
28 *Maclaine Watson v Department of Trade and Industry* [1989] 3 All ER 523 per Lord Oliver at pp. 544–5 and per Lord Templeman at p. 526.
29 *Salomon v Commissioners of Customs and Excise* [1967] 2 QB 116 per Lord Diplock at p. 143. See also *Maclaine Watson v DTI*, op. cit., note 31, per Lord Oliver at p. 545.

30 *Ellerman Lines v Murray* [1931] AC 126; *IRC v Collco Dealings* [1962] AC 1.
31 See, for example, *Waddington v Miah* [1974] 1 WLR 683; *R v Chief Immigration Officer Heathrow Airport, ex parte Salaman Bibi* [1976] 1 WLR 979. Lord Denning MR in *Birdi v Secretary of State for Home Affairs* (unreported) indicated that he might hold an Act of Parliament invalid if it violated the Convention, but he later resiled from this position in *R v Secretary of State for Home Affairs, ex parte Bhajan Singh* [1976] QB 198 saying he 'went too far'.
32 *Brind and Others v Secretary of State for the Home Department* [1991] 1 All ER 720.
33 Op. cit., note 35 at pp. 734–5.
34 38 Cal.(2d) 718. (1952).

Chapter 4

1 *ICJ Rep.* 1966, p. 6.
2 General Assembly Resolution 217A (III), GAOR, 3rd Session, Part I, Resolutions, p. 71.
3 For a discussion of general principles of law, see Chapter 3.
4 For a discussion of customary international law, see Chapter 3.
5 For a discussion of *ius cogens*, see Chapter 3.
6 R.B. Lillich, 'Civil Rights', in *Meron*, pp. 116–8.
7 See Appendix 1.
8 J.P. Humphrey, 'The Magna Carta of Mankind', in P. Davies (ed.), *Human Rights* (London: Routledge, 1988), pp. 21–9.
9 These are: First Committee (Disarmament and Related Matters); Second Committee (Economic and Financial Matters); Third Committee (Humanitarian and Cultural Matters); Fourth Committee (Decolonization and Trust Territories); Fifth Committee (Administrative and Budgetary Matters); Sixth Committee (Legal Matters); and the Special Political Committee. The First, Fourth and Sixth Committees have at times dealt extensively with human rights issues.
10 Article 10 UN Charter.
11 ECOSOC Resolution E/1979/36.
12 ECOSOC Resolution 5(I) of 16 February 1946 and Resolution 5(II) of 21 June 1946.
13 ECOSOC Resolution E/1979/36.
14 General Assembly Resolution 32/130.
15 H. Saba, 'Unesco and Human Rights', in *Vasak*, Vol. 1, at p. 401.
16 Decision 104.EX/3.3.
17 Ibid., para. 14.
18 Ibid., para. 10.
19 Ibid., para. 18.
20 *ICJ Rep.* 1949, p. 4.
21 *ICJ Rep.* 1950, p. 266.
22 *South West Africa Cases (Second Phase), ICJ Rep.* 1966, p. 6; *Legal Consequences for State of the Continued Presence of South Africa in Namibia (South*

West Africa) Notwithstanding Security Council Resolution 276 (1970), ICJ Rep.
1971, p. 16.
23 *ICJ Rep.* 1951, p. 15.
24 Article 2(1) ICCPR; Article 2(2) ICESCR.
25 For a comparative table of the respective rights and freedoms, see Appendix 1.
26 These rights are: Article 6 (right to life); Article 7 (freedom from torture, inhuman and degrading treatment); Article 8(1) and (2) (freedom from slavery and servitude); Article 11 (imprisonment for failure to meet a contractual obligation); Article 15 (non-retroactivity of penal law); Article 16 (right to recognition as a person); and Article 18 (right to freedom of thought, conscience and religion).
27 R. Higgins, 'Derogations under Human Rights Treaties', (1979) 48 *BYIL* 281–320.
28 See pp. 82–3.
29 Article 37(2) ICCPR.
30 Article 28(1) ICCPR.
31 Article 28(2) ICCPR.
32 Articles 29 and 32 ICCPR.
33 Article 29(2) ICCPR.
34 Article 28(3) ICCPR.
35 M. Nowak, 'The Effectiveness of the International Covenant on Civil and Political Rights – Stocktaking After the First Eleven Sessions of the United Nations Human Rights Committee', (1980) 1 *HRLJ* 136–70 at p. 165.
36 Usually 3–5 years.
37 See (1982) 3 *HRLJ* 393–403.
38 On the exhaustion of local remedies see, pp. 50–2.
39 See, for example, *Massera v. Uruguay*, Communication No. R 1/5, (1980) 1 *HRLJ* 209; *Torres Ramirez v. Uruguay*, Communication No. R 1/4, (1980) 1 *HRLJ* 226; *Lovelace v Canada*, Communication No. 6/24, (1981) 2 *HRLJ* 158; *Luyeye Magana ex-Philibert v Zaire*, Communication No. R 22/90, (1980) 4 *HRLJ* 195; *M.A. v Italy*, Communication No. R 26/117, (1984) 5 *HRLJ* 191; *M.T. v Spain*, Communication No. 310/88, (1991) 12 *HRLJ* 299.
40 Article 4 Protocol.
41 Article 4(2) Protocol.
42 Article 5(3) Protocol provides 'The Committee shall hold closed meetings when examining communications under the present protocol.'
43 Rule 90(2)(b).
44 Op. cit., note 40.
45 As has occurred in a number of cases. A priest has also been regarded as competent to author a communication on behalf of an alleged victim: *J.M. v Jamaica*, Communication No. 165/1984, (1986) 7 *HRLJ* 271.
46 See, for example, *A Group of Associations for the Defence of the Rights of Disabled and Handicapped Persons in Italy v Italy*, Communication No. 163/1984, (1984) 5 *HRLJ* 193.
47 Communication No. R 9/35, (1981) 2 *HRLJ* 139.
48 *A.D. v Canada*, Communication No. R 19/78, (1984) 3 *HRLJ* 194; *B. Ominayak and the Lake Lubicon Band v Canada*, Communication No. 167/1984, (1990) 11

HRLJ 305; *A.B. et al. v Italy (South Tirol Case)*, Communication No. 413/1990, (1991) *HRLJ* 25.

49 *Vidal Martins v Uruguay*, Communication R 13/57, (1982) 3 *HRLJ* 165.
50 This was also the claim in *Waksman v Uruguay*, Communication No. R 7/31, (1980) 1 *HRLJ* 220. The Committee did not investigate the merits of the claim here since Uruguay granted a remedy by way of the issue of a passport to the author of the complaint. See also *Varela v Uruguay*, Communication No. R 25/108, (1983) 4 *HRLJ* 204.
51 Communication No. R 13/56, (1981) 2 *HRLJ* 145.
52 Ibid., para. 10(2). The Committee also went on to say in para. 10(3): 'it would be unconscionable to so interpret the responsibility under Article 2 of the Covenant as to permit a State party to perpetrate a violation of the Covenant on the territory of another state, which violation it could not perpetrate on its own territory'. See also *Quinteros v Uruguay*, Communication No. R 24/107, (1983) 4 *HRLJ* 195 (abduction of a Uruguayan citizen from the Venezuelan Embassy in Montevideo) where the same point was made.
53 Communication No. R 1/6, (1980) 1 *HRLJ* 231.
54 Op. cit., note 52.
55 Communication No. R 2/11, (1980) 1 *HRLJ* 237.
56 *A.M. v Denmark*, Communication No. R 26/121, (1982) 3 *HRLJ* 188; *V.M.O. v Norway*, Communication No. 168/1984, (1985) 2 *HRLJ* 268.
57 For an application of this rule, see *J.M. v Jamaica*, Communication No. 165/1984, (1986) 7 *HRLJ* 271 and *C.F. et al. v Canada*, Communication No. 113/1981, (1986) 7 *HRLJ* 300.
58 Communication No. R 2/8, (1980) 1 *HRLJ* 221.
59 Communication No. R 24/104, (1983) 4 *HRLJ* 193. On abuse of process, see *M.A. v Italy*, Communication No. R 26/117, (1984) 5 *HRLJ* 191, in which a person who was convicted and imprisoned pursuant to a law forbidding the reorganization of the dissolved fascist party was found to fall without the Covenant *ratione materiae* by virtue of Article 5. Article 5 provides: 'Nothing in the present Covenant may be interpreted as implying for any State, group or person any right to engage in any activity or perform any act aimed at the destruction of any of the rights and freedoms recognized herein . . .'.
60 Communication No. 178/1984, (1985) 6 *HRLJ* 231.
61 Communication No. 185/1984, (1986) 7 *HRLJ* 267.
62 Ibid., para. 5.2.
63 C. Tomuschat, 'Evolving Procedural Rules: The United Nations Human Rights Committee's First Two Years of Dealing with Individual Communications', (1980) 1 *HRLJ* 249–57 at p. 252. More recently, Zaire has proved to be unreliable. See *Ngalula Mpandanjila et al. v Zaire*, Communication No. 138/1983, (1986) 2 *HRLJ* 277 and *Andre Alphonse Mpaka-Nsusu v Zaire*, Communication No. 157/1983, (1986) 7 *HRLJ* 280.
64 Op.cit., note 40.
65 See, for example, *Quinteros v Uruguay*, op.cit., note 53.
66 Communication No. R 2/9, (1980) 1 *HRLJ* 216.
67 See also *Bleier v Uruguay*, Communication No. R 7/30, (1982) 3 *HRLJ* 212 and *Quinteros v Uruguay*, op.cit., note 53.

68 Para. 7 (emphasis added). Mr Tarnopolsky in an individual opinion was not so reticent and found that a violation of the Covenant had been proved. Five other Committee members agreed with Mr Tarnopolsky.
69 Communication No. R 2/11, (1980) 1 *HRLJ* 237.
70 Ibid., para. 10.
71 Ibid., para. 15. See also *Lopez Burgos v Uruguay*, Communication No. R 12/52, (1981) 2 *HRLJ* 150.
72 Op. cit., note 53.
73 Op. cit., note 65 at p. 255.
74 Ibid.
75 See pp. 78–9.
76 D. Trubek, 'Economic, Social and Cultural Rights in the Third World: Human Rights and Human Needs', in *Meron*, pp. 205–71.
77 78 *UNTS* 277.
78 B. Whitaker, 'Genocide: The Ultimate Crime', in P. Davies (ed.), *Human Rights* (London; Routledge, 1988), p. 51.
79 Article III.
80 See Chapter 3.
81 Ibid.
82 60 *UNTS* 195; *UKTS* 77 (1969); (1966) 5 *ILM* 352.
83 Op.cit., note 23.
84 Article 9.
85 Article 14.
86 1015 *UNTS* 243.
87 Article II.
88 Ibid.
89 Article III.
90 Article VII.
91 Article X.
92 *UKTS* 2 (1989); (1980) 19 *ILM* 33.
93 Article 18.
94 Article 17.
95 (1984) 23 *ILM* 1027; (1985) 24 *ILM* 535.
96 Article 7.
97 Article 11.
98 A number of individual communications have already been addressed to the Committee but they have been rejected on various grounds: *Communication Nos. 1,2 and 3/1988 O.R., M.M. and M.S. (on behalf of deceased relatives) v Turkey*, (1990) 11 *HRLJ* 134 (inadmissible *ratione temporis*); *Communication No. 4/1990, R.E. v Turkey*, (1991) 12 *HRLJ* 237 (inadmissible because of non-exhaustion of local remedies); *Communication 5/1990 W.J. v Austria*, (1991) 12 *HRLJ* 26 (submitted to another procedure of international investigation).
99 UN Doc. A/44/736 (1989); (1989) 28 *ILM* 1456.
100 Article 43.
101 Article 44.

Chapter 5

1　213 *UNTS* 221; *UKTS* 71 (1953).
2　529 *UNTS* 89; *UKTS* 38 (1965).
3　87 *UNTS* 103; *UKTS* 51 (1949).
4　K. Vasak, 'The Council of Europe', in *Vasak*, Vol. 2, pp. 457–542 at p. 457.
5　Chapter 1.
6　12 *YB* (Special Volume).
7　See Chapter 1.
8　See N. Grief, 'The Domestic Impact of the European Convention on Human Rights as Mediated through Community Law', (1991) *PL* 555–67.
9　See Appendix 1.
10　Article 20 ECHR.
11　Article 22 ECHR.
12　Article 20 ECHR.
13　Article 33 ECHR.
14　Article 38 ECHR.
15　Article 43 ECHR.
16　R. Beddard, *Human Rights and Europe* (London: Sweet and Maxwell, 2nd edn, 1980), p. 36.
17　Article 46 ECHR.
18　See Chapter 7.
19　2 *YB* 182 and 186.
20　6 *YB* 742.
21　21 *YB* 602; Eur.Ct.H.R., Series A, No. 25.
22　18 *YB* 82 and 20 *YB* 98.
23　Op. cit., note 6.
24　8 EHRR 205.
25　Eur.Ct.H.R., Series A, No. 31.
26　Eur.Ct.H.R., Series A, No. 21.
27　See *Ireland v UK*, op. cit., note 21.
28　Eur.Ct.H.R., Series A, No. 12.
29　Eur.Ct.H.R., Series A, No. 77.
30　Eur.Ct.H.R., Series A, No. 5.
31　2 *YB* 214.
32　See R. Beddard, op. cit., note 16, p. 156.
33　21 *YB* 622.
34　9 *YB* 426.
35　2 *YB* 308.
36　Op. cit., note 21.
37　Op. cit., note 34.
38　Article 33 ECHR.
39　Quoted in R. Beddard, op. cit., note 16, pp. 41–2.
40　16 *YB* 356.
41　Article 32(1) ECHR. Protocol No. 10, adopted in 1992, but not yet in force, will reduce the requisite majority from two thirds to a simple majority, (1992) 13 *HRLJ* 182–3.

42 Article 38(2) ECHR.
43 Article 32(4) ECHR.
44 Rule 40 (as amended).
45 See, for example, *Marckx*, Eur.Ct.H.R., Series A, No. 12.
46 Eur.Ct.H.R., Series A, No. 30.
47 Eur.Ct.H.R., Series A, No. 26.
48 Eur.Ct.H.R., Series A, No. 48.
49 Eur.Ct.H.R., Series A, No. 161.
50 Judgment of 20 March 1991 (46/1990/257/307).
51 Sir Ian Sinclair, *The Vienna Convention on the Law of Treaties* (Manchester: Manchester University Press, 2nd edn, 1984), p. 128.
52 In *Soering*, op. cit., note 48.
53 K. Vasak, op. cit., note 4, pp. 538–9.
54 Article 25 ESC.
55 Article 27 ESC.
56 Article 28 ESC.
57 (1988) 27 *ILM* 575.
58 Protocol Amending the European Social Charter, (1992) *ILM* 155. See also the useful introductory note by D.J. Harris, ibid.
59 (1988) 27 *ILM* 1152.
60 Articles 1–4 European Convention for the Prevention of Torture (ECPT).
61 Articles 7 and 8 ECPT.
62 Article 8 ECPT.
63 Article 9 ECPT.
64 Article 10(1) ECPT.
65 Article 10(2) ECPT.

Chapter 6

1 119 *UNTS* 48.
2 Resolution XXX, Final Act of the Ninth International Conference of American States, Bogota, Colombia, 30 March–2 May 1948, p. 48.
3 See Appendix 1.
4 Resolution VII, Fifth Meeting of Consultation of Ministers of Foreign Affairs, 12–18 August 1959, Final Act, OAS Doc. OEA/Ser.C/II.5.
5 Inter-American Commission on Human Rights, *Report on the Work Accomplished During its First Session*, 3–28 October 1960, OAS Doc. OEA/Ser.L/V/II.2, Doc. 32 at 10.
6 Ibid., at 9.
7 Resolution XXII, Second Special Inter-American Conference, 17–30 November 1965, Final Act OAS Doc. OEA/Ser.C/I.13 at 32–4.
8 Resolution No. 23/81, 6 March 1981, (1981) 2 *HRLJ* 110.
9 410 US 113 (1973).
10 410 US 179 (1973).
11 Advisory Opinion OC-10 of July 14, 1989, *Interpretation of the American Declaration of the Rights and Duties of Man Within the Framework of Article 64 of the American Convention on Human Rights (Interpretation of the American Declaration Case)*, (1990) 29 *ILM* 379; (1990) 11 *HRLJ* 118.

12 On the law of treaties, see pp. 53–6.

13 On the CHR, see Chapter 4.

14 See the extracts from these reports which are reproduced in Buergenthal, T., Norris, R. and Shelton, D., *Protecting Human Rights in the Americas* (Kehl-am-Rhein: Engel, 2nd edn, 1986), pp. 168–81.

15 T. Buergenthal, 'The Inter-American System for the Protection of Human Rights', in *Meron*, pp. 439–93 at p. 481.

16 See the US Foreign Assistance Act 1961 (as amended), 22 USC.

17 Article 26 Commission Regulations.

18 Article 53(1) Commission Regulations.

19 Articles 53(3) and (4) Commission Regulations.

20 (1970) 9 *ILM* 679.

21 (1989) 28 *ILM* 156.

22 It will enter into force when it receives eleven ratifications or accessions. Article 21(3) Protocol. Signatories to the Protocol as of 25 May 1990 were Argentina, Bolivia, Costa Rica, Dominican Republic, Ecuador, El Salvador, Guatemala, Haiti, Mexico, Nicaragua, Panama, Peru, Uruguay and Venezuela.

23 Not only are some of the rights novel, but certain categories of rights are more broadly drafted than those of analogous human rights instruments. See, for example, Article 8(3) (no-one may be compelled to join a trade union), Article 11 (right to a healthy environment), Article 16 (rights of children), Article 17 (protection of the elderly) and Article 18 (protection of the handicapped).

24 While the main mechanism for the supervision of the rights protected in the Protocol is a system of periodic reports, the full institutional system established by Articles 44–51 and Articles 61–69 ACHR comes into play if Article 8(1)(a) (right to organize and join a trade union) or Article 13 (right to education) are directly violated by a state party: Article 19 Protocol. On the mechanisms of protection, see Chapter 3.

25 Article 1, Protocol (emphasis added).

26 Article 27(2) ACHR. See Appendix 1 for a list of the non-derogable rights.

27 Advisory Opinion OC-9/87 of October 6, 1987, *Judicial Guarantees in States of Emergency*, (1988) 9 *HRLJ* 118.

28 Articles 36 and 37 ACHR.

29 Articles 52 and 54 ACHR.

30 See p. 105.

31 *Government of Costa Rica (In the Matter of Viviana Gallardo et al.)*, No. G. 101/81, Judgment of November 13, 1981, (1981) 20 *ILM* 1424; (1981) 2 *HRLJ* 328 at para. 22.

32 Article 46(2)(a) ACHR.

33 Article 46(2)(b) ACHR.

34 Advisory Opinion OC-11/90 of August 10, 1990, *Exceptions to the Exhaustion of Domestic Remedies in Articles 46(2)(a) and 46(2)(b) of the American Convention on Human Rights*, (1991) *HRLJ* 20.

35 Article 48(1)(d) ACHR. As the Court indicated in *Velasquez Rodriguez (Preliminary Objections)*, this procedure is discretionary and not mandatory.

36 Article 49 ACHR.

37 Articles 50(1) and 50(2) ACHR.

38 Article 51(1) ACHR.

39 Ibid.
40 Ibid. and Article 51(2) ACHR.
41 Article 51(3) ACHR.
42 Advisory Opinion OC-5/85 of November 13, 1985, *Compulsory Membership in an Association Prescribed by Law for the Practice of Journalism* ('*Compulsory Membership*'), (1986) 25 *ILM* 123; (1986) 7 *HRLJ* 74.
43 See Inter-American Commission on Human Rights, Resolution No. 1784, Case 9178 (Stephen Schmidt) (Costa Rica), October 3, 1984, (1985) 6 *HRLJ* 211.
44 See pp. 114–15.
45 Op. cit., note 32.
46 *Velasquez Rodriguez*, Judgment of July 29, 1988; *Godinez Cruz*, (1988); *Fairen Garbi and Solis Corrales*, (1988), (1989) 28 *ILM* 1424; (1981) 2 *HRLJ* 328.
47 *Velasquez Rodriguez*, op. cit., note 48, para. 134.
48 Article 67 ACHR.
49 *Velasquez Rodriguez – Interpretation of the Courts Judgment of July 21, 1989, Assessing Compensatory Damages against the State of Honduras*, (1991) 12 *HRLJ* 14.
50 Article 63(1) ACHR.
51 Article 68(1) ACHR.
52 Judgment of July 21, 1989, (1990) 11 *HRLJ* 127.
53 Op. cit., note 51.
54 *Order of January 15, 1988 (Order of Protection)* and *Order of 15 January, 1988 (Order of Investigation)*, (1988) 9 *HRLJ* pp. 104–5.
55 See p. 103.
56 Advisory Opinion OC-2/82 of September 24, 1982, *Entry into Force of the American Convention for a State Ratifying or Adhering with a Reservation* ('*Effect of Reservations*'), (1983) 22 *ILM* 37; (1982) 3 *HRLJ* 153.
57 Advisory Opinion OC-1/82 of September 24, 1982, *Interpretation of the Meaning of 'Other Treaties' in Article 64 of the American Convention* ('*Other Treaties*'), (1983) 22 *ILM* 51; (1982) 3 *HRLJ* 140.
58 As was claimed by Guatemala in OC-3/83 of September 8, 1983, *Restrictions to the Death Penalty*, (1984) 23 *ILM* 320; (1983) 4 *HRLJ* 339.
59 OC-4/84 of January 19, 1984, *Proposed Amendments to the Naturalization Provisions of the Political Constitution of Costa Rica* ('*Proposed Amendments*'), (1984) 5 *HRLJ* 161.
60 Ibid.
61 *Other Treaties*, op. cit., note 57.
62 *Restrictions to the Death Penalty*, op. cit., note 58, para. 48.
63 *Effect of Reservations*, op. cit., note 56, para. 29.
64 *Restrictions to the Death Penalty*, op. cit., note 58.
65 Advisory Opinion OC-5/85 of November 13, 1985, *Compulsory Membership in an Association Prescribed by Law for the Practice of Journalism* ('*Compulsory Membership*'), (1986) 25 *ILM* 123; (1986) 7 *HRLJ* 153 and Advisory Opinion OC-7/85 of August 29, 1986, *Character and Scope of the Right to Reply or Correction Recognized in the American Convention* ('*Right to Reply*'), (1986) 7 *HRLJ* 238.
66 *Proposed Amendments*, op. cit., note 61.

67 Advisory Opinion OC-6/86 of May 9, 1986, *Restrictions of the Rights and Freedoms of the American Convention – The Word 'Laws' in Article 30 ('The Word "Laws" ')*, (1986) 7 *HRLJ* 231; Advisory Opinion OC-8/87 of January 30, 1987, *Habeas Corpus in Emergency Situations*, (1988) 27 *ILM* 512; (1988) 9 *HRLJ* 204; Advisory Opinion OC-9/87 of October 6, 1987, *Judicial Guarantees in States of Emergency*, (1988) 9 *HRLJ* 118.

68 Op. cit., note 32.

69 Op. cit., note 43, *Declaration of Judge Maximo Cisneros*.

Chapter 7

1 (1982) 21 *ILM* 59.

2 Article 22 of the African Convention on Human and Peoples' Rights (ACHPR). The latter concept – the Common Heritage of Mankind – refers to the equitable distribution of the proceeds from exploitation of the resources of the deep sea-bed which, the developing states have argued, should not be reducible to private or individual state ownership.

3 Article 29 ACHPR provides:

The individual shall also have the duty:
1 To preserve the harmonious development of the family and to work for the cohesion and respect of the family; to respect his parents at all times, to maintain them in case of need;
2 To serve his national community by placing his physical and intellectual abilities at its service;
3 Not to compromise the security of the State whose national or resident he is;
4 To preserve and strengthen social and national solidarity, particularly when the latter is threatened;
5 To preserve and strengthen the national independence and the territorial integrity of his country and to contribute to its defence in accordance with the law;
6 To work to the best of his abilities and competence, and to pay taxes imposed by law in the interest of the society;
7 To preserve and strengthen positive African cultural values in his relations with other members of the society, in the spirit of tolerance, dialogue and consultation and, in general, to contribute to the promotion of the moral well being of society;
8 To contribute to the best of his abilities, at all times and at all levels, to the promotion and achievement of African unity.

4 K. M'Baye, 'Introduction to the African Charter on Human and Peoples' Rights', in International Commission of Jurists, *The African Charter on Human and Peoples' Rights: A Legal Analysis* (Geneva: International Commission of Jurists, 1985), p. 27.

5 Articles 31, 33 and 36 ACHPR.

6 Article 38 ACHPR.

Chapter 8

1 See Chapter 2.
2 See para. 26.
3 See Chapter 2.
4 See Chapter 3.
5 Ibid.
6 See Chapter 3.
7 See Chapter 7.
8 See Chapter 4.
9 See p. 17.
10 See Chapter 2.
11 Ibid.
12 Ibid.
13 See Chapter 6.
14 *Report on the Situation of Human Rights in El Salvador*, OAS Doc. Oea/
Ser.L/V.II.46, doc.23 rev.1 of 17 November 1978. Quoted in Buergenthal,
T., Norris, R. and Shelton, D., *Protecting Human Rights in the Americas*
(Kehl-am-Rhein: Engel, 2nd edn, 1986), pp. 45–8.

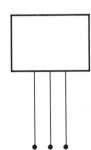

APPENDIX 1: COMPARATIVE TABLE OF RIGHTS AND FREEDOMS PROTECTED BY THE MAJOR HUMAN RIGHTS INSTRUMENTS

Right/freedom protected	UD	CPR	ESC	EC	EUSC	AD	AC	AFC
Life	3	6*		2*		1	4*	4
Liberty and security of person	3	9, 10		5		1, 25	7	6
Slavery or servitude	4	8*		4*			6*	
Compulsory or forced labour		8*		4				
Torture, cruel, inhuman and degrading treatment	5	7*		3*		25, 26	5*	5
No imprisonment for breach of civil obligations		11*		P4:1		25		
Recognition of legal personality	6	16				17	3*	5
Equality before the law	7	14, 26					24	3
Arbitrary arrest and detention	9	9		5, P4		1	7	6
Fair trial	10	14		6		18	8, 25	7
Presumption of innocence	11	14		6		26		7

Right/freedom protected	UD	CPR	ESC	EC	EUSC	AD	AC	AFC
Ex post facto penal laws	11	15*		7*		25	9*	
Privacy, family, home and correspondence	12	17		8		5, 9, 10	11	
Freedom of movement and residence	13	12		P4:2		8	22	12
Expulsion of aliens only pursuant to law		13					22	12
Freedom from mass/collective expulsion				P4:3, 4				12
Asylum	14					27	22	12
Nationality	15					19	20	
Right to petition competent authorities						24		
Marriage and founding a family	16	23		12		6	17*, P, 15	
Protection of the family			10		16	18	P, 15	
Protection of women during pregnancy and nursing								
Protection of children		24			7, 17	7	19*, P, 16	
Protection of the elderly						7	P, 17	
Protection of the handicapped							P, 18	
Name							18*	
Property	17			P1:1		23	21	14
Thought, conscience and religion	18	18*		9		3, 4	12*	8
Opinion and expression	19	19		10			13	9
Right of reply to injurious statements							14	

Peaceful assembly	20	21		11		21	15	11
Freedom of association	20	22		11		22	16	10
Participation in government and public affairs	21	25					23*	13
Access to public service	21	25						13
Democracy	21	27		P1:3		20	23*	13
Culture, religion and language	22							
Social security			9		12, 13	16	P, 9	
Social welfare services					14			
Work and choice of work	23		6		1	14	P, 6	15
Just and favourable conditions of work	23		7		2, 4	14	P, 7	15
Vocational guidance					9			
Vocational training					10			
Vocational training for the handicapped					15			
Protection of employed women					8			
Protection of migrant workers					19			
Collective bargaining					6			
Formation and membership of trade unions			8		5		P, 8	
Safe and healthy working conditions					3			
Rest, leisure and paid holidays	24							
Adequate standard of living	25		11		2	15		
Food			12				P, 12	
Health	25			P1, 2	11	12	P, 14	16
Education	26		13, 14			13	P, 13	17
Participation in cultural, scientific life	27		15				P, 13	
Protection of intellectual property rights	27					13	P, 14	
International and social order for realizing rights	28							

Right/freedom protected	UD	CPR	ESC	EC	EUSC	AD	AC	AFC
Political self-determination		1	1					20
Equality of peoples								19
Peoples' right to existence								20
Economic self-determination		1	1					21
Development								22
Peace and security								23
Satisfactory/healthy environment							11	24

Key:
UD   Universal Declaration of Human Rights
CPR   International Covenant on Civil and Political Rights
ESC   International Covenant on Economic, Social and Cultural Rights
EC   European Convention on Human Rights and Fundamental Freedoms
EUSC   European Social Charter
AD   American Declaration on the Rights and Duties of Man
AC   American Convention on Human Rights
AFR   African Charter on Human and Peoples' Rights

Numbers in the table refer to provisions in the relevant instruments by article number.
* Rights which may not be derogated from; P, Protocol.

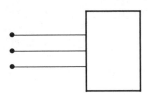

APPENDIX 2: TREATIES, STATUTES AND CASES

TREATIES

1966   International Covenant on Economic and Social Rights, 993 *UNTS* 3; *UKTS* 6 (1977); (1967) 6 *ILM* 360

1966   International Covenant on Civil and Political Rights, 999 *UNTS* 171; *UKTS* 6 (1977); (1967) 6 *ILM* 368.

1969   Vienna Convention on the Law of Treaties, 1155 *UNTS* 331; *UKTS* 58 (1980); (1969) 8 *ILM* 679

1969   American Convention on Human Rights (Pact of San Jose), (1970) 9 *ILM* 673; 65 *AJIL* 679; 3 *HRLJ* 151

1973   International Convention on the Suppression and Punishment of the Crime of Apartheid, 1015 *UNTS* 243

1979   Convention on the Elimination of All Forms of Discrimination Against Women, *UKTS* 2 (1989); (1980) 19 *ILM* 33

1981   African Charter on Human and Peoples' Rights (Banjul Charter), (1982) 21 *ILM* 59

1984   UN Convention Against Torture and Other Cruel, Inhuman or Degrading Treatment, (1984) 23 *ILM* 1027; (1985) 24 *ILM* 535

1987   The European Convention for the Prevention of Torture and Inhuman or Degrading Treatment or Punishment, (1988) 27 *ILM* 1152

1989   UN Convention on the Rights of the Child, UN Doc. A/44/736 (1989); (1989) 28 *ILM* 1456

1989   Protocol to the American Convention on Human Rights Pact of San Salvador, (1989) 28 *ILM* 156

STATUTES

United Kingdom

Magna Carta 1215, c. 29.
Bill of Rights 1 William & Mary, Sess. 2, c. 2.

United States

US Foreign Assistance Act 1961 (as amended), 22 USC

CASES

International Court of Justice

Asylum Case (Colombia v Peru), *ICJ Rep.* 1950, p. 266

Barcelona Traction Light and Power Company Limited (Belgium v Spain), *ICJ Rep.* 1978, p. 3.

Corfu Channel Case (UK v Albania) *ICJ Rep.* 1949, p. 4.

Danzig Railway Officials Case PCIJ, Ser. B, No. 15 (1928); 4 *ILR* 287.
Interhandel Case (Switzerland v US), *ICJ Rep.* 1959, p. 6.
Legal Consequences for State of the Continued Presence of South Africa in Namibia (South West Africa) Notwithstanding Security Council Resolution 276 (1970), ICJ Rep. 1971, p. 16
Nicaragua v USA (Merits) 1986, *ICJ Rep.* 14
Reservations to the Genocide Convention Case, ICJ Rep. 1951, p. 15.
South West Africa Cases (Second Phase), ICJ Rep. 1966, p. 6
South West Africa Cases, ICJ Rep. 1966, p. 6.

United Kingdom

Birdi v Secretary of State for Home Affairs (unreported)
Brind and Others v Secretary of State for the Home Department [1991] 1 All ER 720
Ellerman Lines v Murray [1931] AC 126
IRC v Collco Dealings [1962] AC 1
Maclaine Watson v Department of Trade and Industry [1989] 3 All ER 523
R v Chief Immigration Officer Heathrow Airport, ex parte Salaman Bibi [1976] 1 WLR 979
R v Secretary of State for Home Affairs, ex parte Bhajan Singh [1976] QB 198
Salomon v Commissioners of Customs and Excise [1967] 2 QB 116
Trendtex Trading Corporation v Central Bank of Nigeria [1977] 2 WLR 356
Waddington v Miah [1974] 1 WLR 683

United States

Doe v Bolton 410 US 179 (1973)
Roe v Wade 410 US 113 (1973)
Sei Fujii v California 38 Cal.(2d.) 718. (1952).

United Nations Human Rights Committee

A Group of Associations for the Defence of the Rights of Disabled and Handicapped Persons in Italy v Italy, Communication No. 163/1984, (1984) 5 *HRLJ* 193.
A.B. et al. v Italy (South Tirol Case), Communication No. 413/1990, (1991) *HRLJ* 25
A.D. v Canada, Communication No. R 19/78, (1984) 3 *HRLJ* 194
A.M. v Denmark, Communication No. R 26/121, (1982) 3 *HRLJ* 188
Andre Alphonse Mpaka-Nsusu v Zaire, Communication No. 157/1983, (1986) 7 *HRLJ* 280
B. Ominayak and the Lake Lubicon Band v Canada, Communication No. 167/1984, (1990) 11 *HRLJ* 305

Bleier v Uruguay, Communication No. R 7/30, (1982) 3 *HRLJ* 212
C.F. et al. v Canada, Communication No. 113/1981, (1986) 7 *HRLJ* 300
Celiberti v Uruguay, Communication No. R 13/56, (1981) 2 *HRLJ* 145
Grille Motta, Communication No. R 2/11, (1980) 1 *HRLJ* 237
Grille Motta v Uruguay, Communication No. R 2/11, (1980) 1 *HRLJ* 237
J.M. v Jamaica, Communication No. 165/1984, (1986) 7 *HRLJ* 271
J.D.B. v The Netherlands, Communication No. 178/1984, (1985) 6 *HRLJ* 231
J.M. v Jamaica, Communication No. 165/1984, (1986) 7 *HRLJ* 271
L.T.K. v Finland, Communication No. 185/1984, (1986) 7 *HRLJ* 267
Lanza v Uruguay, Communication No. R 2/8, (1980) 1 *HRLJ* 221
Lopez Burgos v Uruguay, Communication No. R 12/52, (1981) 2 *HRLJ* 150
Lovelace v Canada, Communication No. 6/24, (1981) 2 *HRLJ* 158
Luyeye Magana ex-Philibert v Zaire, Communication No. R 22/90, (1980) 4 *HRLJ* 195
M.A. v Italy, Communication No. R 26/117, (1984) 5 *HRLJ* 191
M.T. v Spain, Communication No. 310/88, (1991) 12 *HRLJ* 299
Massera v. Uruguay, Communication No. R 1/5, (1980) 1 *HRLJ* 209
Mauritian Women Case, Communication No. R 9/35, (1981) 2 *HRLJ* 139
Millan Sequeira v Uruguay, Communication No. R 1/6, (1980) 1 *HRLJ* 231
Ngalula Mpandanjila et al. v Zaire, Communication No. 138/1983, (1986) 2 *HRLJ* 277
Quinteros v Uruguay, Communication No. R 24/107, (1983) 4 *HRLJ* 195
Santullo, Communication No. R 2/9, (1980) 1 *HRLJ* 216
Taylor v Canada, Communication No. R 24/104, (1983) 4 *HRLJ* 193
Torres Ramirez v. Uruguay, Communication No. R 1/4, (1980) 1 *HRLJ* 226
V.M.O. v Norway, Communication No. 168/1984, (1985) 2 *HRLJ* 268
Varela v Uruguay, Communication No. R 25/108, (1983) 4 *HRLJ* 204
Vidal Martins v Uruguay, Communication No. R 13/57, (1982) 3 *HRLJ* 165
Waksman v Uruguay, Communication No. R 7/31, (1980) 1 *HRLJ* 220

European Convention on Human Rights

Amekrane 16 YB 356
Austria v Italy 6 YB 742
Campbell and Cosans Eur.Ct.H.R., Series A, No. 48
Cruz Varas v Sweden Judgment of 20 March 1991 (46/1990/257/307)
Cyprus v Turkey 18 YB 82 and 20 YB 98
De Becker 2 YB 214
De Wilde, Ooms and Versyp (Vagrancy Cases) Eur.Ct.H.R., Series A, No. 12
DeJong, Baljet and van den Brink Eur.Ct.H.R., Series A, No. 77
Denmark, Norway, Sweden and The Netherlands v Greece 12 YB (Special Volume)
Denmark, Norway, Sweden and The Netherlands v Turkey 8 EHRR 205
Greece v United Kingdom 2 YB 182 and 186
Ireland v United Kingdom 21 YB 602; Eur.Ct.H.R., Series A, No. 25
Klass 21 YB 622; Eur.Ct.H.R., Series A, No. 21

Lawless 2 YB 308
Marckx Eur.Ct.H.R., Series A, No. 31
Rafael v Austria 9 YB 426
Soering v United Kingdom Eur.Ct.H.R., Series A, No. 161
Sunday Times Case Eur.Ct.H.R., Series A, No. 30
Tyrer v United Kingdom Eur.Ct.H.R., Series A, No. 26
Van Oosterwijk Eur.Ct.H.R., Series A, No. 5

Inter-American system

Commission Resolution No. 23/81, March 6, 1981, (1981) 2 *HRLJ* 110 ('Baby Boy Case')
Commission Resolution No. 1784, Case 9178 (Stephen Schmidt) (Costa Rica), October 3, 1984, (1985) 6 *HRLJ* 211
Government of Costa Rica (In the Matter of Viviana Gallardo et al.), No. G. 101/81, Judgment of November 13, 1981, (1981) 20 *ILM* 1424; (1981) 2 *HRLJ* 328
Velasquez Rodriguez, Judgment of July 29, 1988; (1989) 28 *ILM* 1424; (1981) 2 *HRLJ* 328
Fairen Garbi and Solis Corrales, (1988)
Godinez Cruz (1988)
Velasquez Rodriguez – Interpretation of the Courts Judgment of July 21, 1989, Assessing Compensatory Damages against the State of Honduras, (1991) 12 *HRLJ* 14
Velasquez Rodriguez – Compensatory Damages Judgment of July 21, 1989, (1990) 11 *HRLJ* 127
Order of January 15, 1988 (Order of Protection) and *Order of 15 January, 1988 (Order of Investigation)*, (1988) 9 *HRLJ* 104–5
Advisory Opinion OC-1/82 of September 24, 1982, *Interpretation of the Meaning of 'Other Treaties' in Article 64 of the American Convention ('Other Treaties')*, (1983) 22 *ILM* 51; (1982) 3 *HRLJ* 140
Advisory Opinion OC-2/82 of September 24, 1982, *Entry into Force of the American Convention for a State Ratifying or Adhering with a Reservation ('Effect of Reservations')*, (1983) 22 *ILM* 37; (1982) 3 *HRLJ* 153
Advisory Opinion OC-3/83 of September 8, 1983, *Restrictions to the Death Penalty*, (1984) 23 *ILM* 320; (1983) 4 *HRLJ* 339
Advisory Opinion OC-4/84 of January 19, 1984, *Proposed Amendments to the Naturalization Provisions of the Political Constitution of Costa Rica ('Proposed Amendments')*, (1984) 5 *HRLJ* 161
Advisory Opinion OC-5/85 of November 13, 1985, *Compulsory Membership in an Association Prescribed by Law for the Practice of Journalism ('Compulsory Membership')*, (1986) 25 *ILM* 123; (1986) 7 *HRLJ* 153
Advisory Opinion OC-6/86 of May 9, 1986, *Restrictions of the Rights and Freedoms of the American Convention – The Word 'Laws' in Article 30 ('The Word "Laws"')*, (1986) 7 *HRLJ* 231
Advisory Opinion OC-7/85 of August 29, 1986, *Character and Scope of the Right*

to Reply or Correction Recognized in the American Convention ('Right to Reply'), (1986) 7 *HRLJ* 238

Advisory Opinion OC-8/87 of January 30, 1987, *Habeas Corpus in Emergency Situations,* (1988) 27 *ILM* 512; (1988) 9 *HRLJ* 204

Advisory Opinion OC-9/87 of October 6, 1987, *Judicial Guarantees in States of Emergency,* (1988) 9 *HRLJ* 118

Advisory Opinion OC-10/89 of July 14, 1989, *Interpretation of the American Declaration of the Rights and Duties of Man Within the Framework of Article 64 of the American Convention on Human Rights,* (1990) 29 *ILM* 379; (1990) 11 *HRLJ* 118.

Advisory Opinion OC-11/90 of August 10, 1990, *Exceptions to the Exhaustion of Domestic Remedies in Articles 46(2)(a) and 46(2)(b) of the American Convention on Human Rights,* (1991) *HRLJ* 20

MISCELLANEOUS

Final Act of the Conference on Security and Cooperation in Europe, (1975) 14 *ILM* 1292

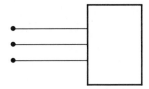

INDEX